WILLIAM
WORDSWORTH

THE P╌╌╌╌ OF GRANDEUR
╌NDERNESS

WILLIAM WORDSWORTH

THE POETRY OF GRANDEUR AND OF TENDERNESS

DAVID B. PIRIE

METHUEN
LONDON AND NEW YORK

First published in 1982 by
Methuen & Co. Ltd
11 New Fetter Lane, London EC4P 4EE
Published in the USA by
Methuen & Co.
in association with Methuen, Inc.
733 Third Avenue, New York, NY 10017

© 1982 David B. Pirie

Phototypeset in Linotron 202 Garamond by
Western Printing Services Ltd, Bristol
Printed in Great Britain at the
University Press, Cambridge

British Library Cataloguing in Publication Data

Pirie, David B.
William Wordsworth: the poetry of grandeur
and of tenderness.
1. Wordsworth, William, 1770–1850 –
Criticism and interpretation
I. Title
821'.7   PR5888
ISBN 0-416-31300-0

CONTENTS

ABBREVIATIONS

PW
: *The Poetical Works of William Wordsworth*, edited by Ernest de Selincourt, revised by Helen Darbishire, in five volumes, Oxford University Press 1949. All quotations from Wordsworth's verse, with exceptions of those from the two works specified below, use the texts of this edition. References identify first the relevant volume in roman numerals, then the page in arabic numerals and finally the lines. Thus *PW*, II.259, 1–10 refers to volume two where, on page 259, the first ten lines of *Tintern Abbey* may be found.

The Prelude
: *The Prelude, or Growth of a Poet's Mind*, edited by Ernest de Selincourt, Oxford University Press 1959. Unless otherwise stated, all quotations are from the 1805 text. References indicate first the relevant book in roman numerals and then the lines in arabic numerals. Where quotations are from manuscript fragments presented by de Selincourt in the notes at the end of his edition, I give the appropriate page number.

The Ruined Cottage
: The text edited by Jonathan Wordsworth, originally published in *The Music of Humanity*, Nelson 1969. It has since been reproduced in *The Oxford Anthology of English Literature*.

INTRODUCTION

I

Wordsworth's originality refuses to define itself as a mere inventiveness. Instead of concocting imaginary worlds for our diversion, he directs us back to the one world which is real even if its very familiarity can sometimes make it almost invisible. 'His genius', as Keats so accurately observed, 'is explorative', and Wordsworth's best poems move us to see more:

> Not in Utopia, subterraneous Fields,
> Or some secreted Island, Heaven knows where,
> But in the very world which is the world
> Of all of us, the place in which, in the end,
> We find our happiness, or not at all.
>
> (The Prelude, x. 724–8)

It is easy enough to name the fantasy lands which strike Wordsworth as so peripheral that his readers can safely ignore them. It is far harder to know how we should approach Wordsworth's definition of that 'very world' which he insists is central. He tends to explore it from two such different angles that his verse arrives at values which can sound unmanageably inconsistent. Wordsworth aims to expand our admiration for the grandeur of an impersonal universe until we learn to define ourselves as inseparable from all the myriad forms of life without which we literally would not exist. Yet he also means to concentrate our minds upon a tenderness which only human beings seem to feel, and which may sometimes compel us to ignore everything except those few people whom time, strength or skill allow us to love intensely.

'Heaven' in the lines above is no more than a casual colloquialism with which to dismiss the other, more literary, utopias as exasperatingly irrelevant. Like so much in Wordsworth's earlier verse, it implicitly denies any hope of reprieve for those who have failed to find their happiness here on earth. Yet where we now stand is often exposed by Wordsworth's greatest poems as the shifting ground of a debate about nothing less than who we are.

It is the seesaw of our own, peculiarly human, experience whose contradictions demand a disturbingly elaborate balancing act. We have leanings towards a sense of place large enough to secure people as almost mathematically pure figures within a landscape whose elegant equations embrace us as needed, if slight, additions to the sum total of its complex unity. Yet we are also propelled in the opposite direction by a passionately disproportionate homing instinct which can narrow our minds to one poignantly pointed question: how can we find a safe position for the individuality of anyone whom we would set apart as uniquely valuable when we must do so in an environment whose energy, if not actively hostile, is dynamically impartial? Our moody minds hover between the ease of the earth's joyfully all-embracing answer and the difficulty of each person's painfully specific question. Wordsworth discovers in such precarious equipoise both a touching clumsiness and an awesome dexterity. This helpless inability to make up our minds is also a triumphantly creative achievement through which the human mind *does* constantly make itself up as it goes along, building the accrued experience of its own past conflicts into a strategy with which to confront those yet to come.

II

Wordsworth's curiosity about the 'natural' and the 'human' poses questions of definition which can at first strike one as disconcertingly odd and then, on reflection, as demandingly intelligent. This book is not impertinent enough to attempt decisive solutions to problems which Wordsworth himself could never resolve. I merely hope to reveal some of the thoughtfulness with which the poetry so deftly advances its own restless enquiry. Nevertheless, much of what I have to say may seem surprising to those familiar with other published commentaries on Wordsworth's verse. To those who are not I must give due warning that my own approach, though it seems to me the only way to acknowledge the poetry's true greatness, would strike many other critics as idiosyncratic, and even perverse. What I see as the invigorating dichotomy at the heart of Wordsworth's verse has sometimes been seen as damaging, sometimes as unimportant, and sometimes (and perhaps most misleadingly) it has simply not been seen at all.

Some readings dismiss the poetry's more unsettling shifts of stance as mere blemishes whose origins are yet worth inexplicably thorough investigation. One diagnosis sees Wordsworth as feeling so betrayed in childhood by the early deaths of both his parents that, finding himself still surrounded by a landscape as evocatively permanent as the Lake District, he unconsciously invested his strongest emotional commitments in those mountainous images which had proved so much more reliable than mankind. Since his conscious mind later came to recognize the appeal to his readers and to his own rational morality of a human interest, his poetry is often to be pitied for its helpless attempts to connect his own peculiar intuitions to other people's less traumatized expectations. Alternative versions of this somewhat patronizing pathology point to the highly unlikely possibility that Wordsworth's feelings for his sister Dorothy were inhibitingly incestuous or to the proven fact that he chose to run the gauntlet of guilt by going to say a final farewell to his illegitimate daughter and her mother before turning away to marry Mary Hutchinson. Each has been argued to explain the poetry's supposed inconsistencies about human love. My own approach involves no direct rebuttal of such speculations, though I hope by detailed analyses to show that they address themselves to explaining the absence of a balance which is audibly present in the poetry. Its informed respect for the kinds of happiness which people can only find with each other seems to me profoundly moving, and its lucid investigation of the wasteful misery which only the most personal relationships can impose seems to me eminently sane. Both the sympathy and the scepticism with which Wordsworth views a single-minded commitment to tenderness are inextricably related to his own broad-minded awareness of the grandeur in the natural world – a world which, for all its apparent callousness, can no more be well lost for love than the ocean can be profitably abandoned by a pair of derangedly sentimental fish. Far from unwittingly admitting to some schizoid confusion, Wordsworth's two voices sound to me as if they are deliberately exploring a paradox which makes his work doubly important.

A second group of critics, though conceding that the poetry as a whole may tackle both issues, believe that Wordsworth does not evoke them so simultaneously within a single poem that we are forced to think about one in the light of the other. Thus a particular passage is seen as identifying wholeheartedly with the serene inclus- iveness of cosmic forces, and quite different lines are quoted to show Wordsworth's concern for the intense selectivities of human rela- tionship. My problem here is that Wordsworth, when choosing incidents to illustrate his own psychic history or the life-stories of his fictional characters, so often picks a situation whose innate duality seems bound to pull the reader's feelings in both directions at once. Moreover, he tends to describe such moments in a language designed to subvert any attempt to compartmentalize either his subject matter or the reader's responses. Sometimes he does so in a battering rhet- oric of obstrusive self-contradictions, and sometimes in a devious whisper of delicately infiltrated ambiguities, but he hardly ever allows the ear to concentrate exclusively on one trend of suggestion. So to divide the verse in hope of conquering all its obscurities may be to explain away its greatness in terms which Wordsworth has care- fully tried to avoid. In the ensuing chapters I do argue against a singularity of interpretation even at points where, as far as I know, all previous commentators have assumed that the poet has only one thing to say.

The third widely recommended approach is to claim that Words- worth achieves a fairly comfortable synthesis between our delight in the beauty of the earth and our commitment to each other. He supposedly offers a coherent philosophy, or at the very least a pattern of momentary insights, which reveals the two tendencies to be mutually supportive. My own view is that the unease of their incom- patibilities is what stirs his best verse to greatness and that, where he does try to arrange such an unlikely marriage, he usually sounds so unconvincing that the reader is simply embarrassed. The contrary view does, however, deserve serious argument. It may distract us from Wordsworth's most impressive achievements, but it does address itself to what he himself sometimes professed as his aims. My mistrust of what was on occasion the author's own approach to his work clearly needs justification.

Wordsworth lived on for nearly half a century after the composi- tion of his greatest verse. As his genius waned, his enthusiasm for revision grew, and he increasingly obscured the more probing im- plications of his earlier poems. He also diluted them by remaining enormously prolific, producing numerous feebler works which now make it harder for his readers to find the relatively few poems that matter. He published over 800 poems and yet *The Excursion* alone – which is admittedly the longest – runs to about 9000 lines, most of which have usually seemed to me almost unreadably dull. Even more damaging was the undiminished energy with which he offered to explain the meaning of his earlier works when he had apparently become unable, or unwilling, to understand what they were demonstrably saying. A shrewd sense of the specific had once given his best poems their intellectual vigour, and a firm grasp upon language's most subtle suggestiveness had provided them with their arrestingly precise voice. The older Wordsworth looked back upon them in comments which flop from one ill-defined generality to another. All too typical is the slogan which he imposed upon Book VIII of *The Prelude*: 'Love of Nature leading to Love of Man'. This subtitle still misdirects many readers in their approach to *The Prelude* as a whole and to much of Wordsworth's other poetry as well. Obediently they look out only for the verse's more facile charm, and pass obliviously by its challenge.

'Love of Nature' sounds soothingly abstract whereas the poetry itself is often defiantly concrete and insists upon the unqualified actuality of 'rocks, and stones, and trees' (*PW*, II.216, 8). Here in the last line of an elegiac 'Lucy Poem', the proximity of 'rocks, and stones' unnervingly totters on the edge of a despairing tautology where a bleakly unvarying earth may in the end bury all individuality. Yet the wish to discriminate between even such apparently simple palpabilities is innate to the deviantly human response which the poetry probes. In *Michael* the same phrase occurs, but here the distinction between 'rocks and stones' is at first explicitly one 'which you might pass by, / Might see and notice not' (*PW*, II.81, 9–17). Yet eventually the compulsion to see them as quite different lures Michael towards tragedy just as his recurring acknowledgement that ultimately they must belong together is the measure of his triumphant escape.

So the blandness suggested by 'Love of Nature' obscures the stimulating range of Wordsworth's responses to the countryside. He is remarkably successful, for instance, when he wants to sound thoroughly bored by it. *The Ruined Cottage* begins with an ill-tempered poet whose afternoon stroll has degenerated into an exhausting plod over slippery ground. Oppressed by the heat of the sun, he longs to rest his legs. But his face is besieged by buzzing flies, and in this miserably uncivilized environment even gorse bushes seem to conspire to exasperate him by adding their own 'tedious noise'. The poem's unsettling variety of tones later encompasses a poignant story about people being battered by poverty, neurosis and bereavement. A human family's gradual disintegration allows other forms of life to flourish without restraint until plants, animals, reptiles and insects have encroached deep within what had once been a cherished home. Yet this latently tragic tale is finally shown to belong with the almost comic self-portrait of Wordsworth enduring that wretched walk. Both are about people who must share their world with creatures which neither know, nor care, about human feelings.

'Nature' in *The Ruined Cottage* is further complicated by the fact that Wordsworth is told the family's story by a remarkable man who is determined to enjoy, rather than resent, the other forms of life about him. This character's resolution is so extreme that he manages to take delight even in the noise made by those initially infuriating flies. Conversely he tries to forget the existence, let alone the suffering, of the friends in whose ruined home he now stands. We are forced to respond not only to the endearing ordinariness of the poet's own impatience with the wilderness, but also to respect the extraordinary lengths to which his companion goes in trying to make the best of it. Neither can be even hinted at by phrases like 'Love of Nature'.

'Love of Man' is similarly inadequate. It cannot suggest the costly, and even bizarre, extremes which Wordsworth observes in our fondness for each other. In *The Ruined Cottage* a woman's love for her husband is so obsessive that, once he has abandoned her, she can think of nothing but the possibility of his return. Even the child whom their love had conceived and nurtured is eventually allowed to die of neglect. So the reader is presented with a daunting exposure of the self-contradictions inherent in those intensely personal relationships which our culture prizes. In *Michael*, on the other hand, it is a father's devotion to his child which explicitly threatens 'to over-set the brain, or break the heart'. Yet in the comedy of *The Idiot Boy* we are invited to laugh at a mother's anxious affection and at the wild fantasies of kidnapping and suicide which are created by her blunderingly imaginative love. In *The Prelude* and other poems, it is the poet's own tenderness which is baffled by his meetings with the apparently insensitive 'Solitaries'. He cannot see how to convince them of his compassion without reawakening them to a pained sense of their own isolation. 'Man', like 'Nature', is seldom simple in Wordsworth's verse, and hardly ever simply loved.

We must notice the peculiarities which Wordsworth uncovers in trying to relate his delight in natural scenery to his concern for people. Unless we observe the meticulousness of his enquiry, we will ignore the dichotomy which it exposes. We will go on assuming, as Douglas Bush does, that Wordsworth must be prevented from becoming 'an active force in our time' by some 'nebulous quality' which is the supposedly common ground 'of his mysticism and of his sentimental ethics' (*Wordsworth*, ed. Gilbert T. Dunklin, Princeton University Press, 1951, pp. 9, 20).

In fact it is our own twentieth-century jargons which thus gloss over emotional conflict, and they blind us to the linguistic subtlety of Wordsworth's own investigation. He speaks to the dazzlingly elaborate patterns which weave all physical things into one life. But our translation obliterates it into a mere 'ecosystem', or shuts it away in the dusty filing-cabinet of forgotten faiths under 'M' for 'Mysticism' or 'P' for 'Pantheism'. Our resistance is no less when Wordsworth contrastingly suggests that only people, and their deviant capacity to care for each other, really matter. We smother such insight under the labels of 'individualism', 'interpersonal relationships' or even 'sentimental ethics'. Such hygienic tidy-mindedness separates our love of the world and our love for each other into safely sterile compartments between which no embarrassing cross-fertilization can occur. Yet Wordsworth sees both as the incongruous origins of our experience.

His greatest verse has the courage of convictions which will not surrender to each other. On the one hand, it recovers that inclusive confidence which allows young children to feel at home nearly anywhere. It re-enacts their absorbed, or exhilarated, grasp of the grandeur in natural things. On the other hand, Wordsworth's verse embraces as an equally primal instinct that tenderness which is latently selective. We grow into choosing those whom we love, and into a sense of home which specifies one place as so significant that the rest of the world can seem relatively peripheral:

> Two feelings have we also from the first
> of grandeur and of tenderness;
> We live by admiration and by love.   (*The Prelude*, p. 571)

III

The ambivalence of those who must live by such potentially conflict-ing needs seems to me the subject of nearly all Wordsworth's greatest poems. However, I do not pretend to offer a complete survey of the verse. Closely observant readings cannot be brief and I need to be selective if the book is not to grow to unwieldy length. Each chapter is almost exclusively about only one, two or at most three poems so as to allow space for the basic task of spelling out just what each is saying and for the amount of quotation necessary to prove that even my most controversial conclusions derive from what are – however surprisingly – the words on the page.

As far as possible, I have made each chapter a self-sufficient argument with enough internal balance to stand alone as one proof of Wordsworth's own uneasy straddling between grandeur and tender-ness. The major exception is Chapter 1, which is consciously top-heavy for the sake of readers who have difficulty in giving full weight to Wordsworth's celebration of the natural world. What he means by 'grandeur' defines itself as the unity in things which do not try to divide themselves into words, so the poet's own attempt at a verbal definition is inevitably problematical. Language, unless we abuse its normal usage, may be innately repressive since its more rigid dis-criminations and exclusions can manipulate us into exile from much that in childhood we spontaneously recognized as our own. Words-worth frequently seeks to recover that inarticulate excitement with which we first discovered the world. He still sees interacting forces – for instance, in weather or in vegetation – which keep each other alive, but this endlessly regenerated 'life of things' is not easily conveyed in sentences which expire in full stops (*PW*, II. 260, 49). His voice is thus demandingly original even when it is confronting only this one side of his larger paradox. So my first chapter concentrates in the first three of its four sections on Wordsworth's response to the non-human world. Without some sense of the extraordinary claims which he makes for its most ordinary features, we cannot hope to follow his argument where these are juxtaposed with the rival claims of human affection.

The rest of my book examines specific examples of this juxtaposi-tion, and the rather different questions it raises about the adequacy of our language. We are not accustomed to a voice which insists upon two incongruous points of view, nor to a vocabulary which labels experience under contradictory headings. I have tried to give each of my chapters a title which will epitomize the verse's own refusal to oversimplify its stance by predetermining a definition of its subject. Chapter 2 considers *The Ruined Cottage* where the Pedlar at one point seeks to condemn our wasteful capacity to care for each other by calling it 'the weakness of humanity': imaginative identification with another person's grief may prevent realistic appreciation of the earth's joy. Yet the poem also suggests that the inescapably mortal weakness of men and women when confronting the power of an imperishable, and perhaps latently hostile, environment is precisely what makes their tenacity in such a hopeless cause impressive. My interpretation of *The Ruined Cottage* draws on comparison with the Matthew poems, and my evaluation of it rests on the contrasts provided by its narrator's unconvincing reappearances in both *The Pedlar* and *The Excursion*.

Chapter 3's discussion of *Michael* cannot confine its hero's 'strength of love' into some simplistic contrast with 'the weakness of humanity'. Michael's affection for his child is as strong as the love which he feels for that landscape where at best father and son can work together. As comparisons with *The Brothers* and *The Last of the Flock* suggest, a hill-farmer's unusual life-style might allow him to feel that his commitments to family and to field are wholly compatible. However, in practice the plot of *Michael* challenges the characters to choose. Its sceptical narrator anyway fears that – even if they had been able to arrive at some unified definition of love – their story might still have been so weakened by being a special case that it could hardly give strength to those who (like the poet and presumably most of his readers) must live, love and work within a far less integrated structure.

Chapter 4 relates *The Idiot Boy* to *The Immortality Ode*, wondering how far the latter's claim that a child can be an 'eye among the blind' applies to a mentally retarded lad whose wide-eyed delight in the countryside looks to the poem's anxious adults all too likely to make him stumble into a fatal accident. Both poems see ways in which either child or grown-up may see so much less than the other as to be virtually blind, and yet both poems suggest that those with the clearer vision could be putting themselves at a disadvantage.

Chapter 5 begins a two-part account of Wordsworth's Solitaries,

figures whose identification with the physical world may be so extreme that their vision has joined 'the eye of nature' and they can no
longer recognize either their own individuality or that of other
people. Whether such insight into the nature of things represents
human nature at its most enviably expansive or at its most pitiably
diminished is further investigated in Chapter 6. Here the poet of
Resolution and Independence and *The Prelude* is as curious about
what is happening in his own 'mind's eye' when he is faced by the
Leech-gatherer or the blind London Beggar as he is about what may
or may not be visible to their apparently dwindling thought-
processes.

Chapter 7 considers some of Wordsworth's explicitly autobiographical verse and his strenuous attempts to bring within 'the reach
of words' his own most ambivalent moments. In the 'Spots of Time'
an intense response to the silent grammar which structures all things
sometimes leads Wordsworth to wrench human language into a
double-jointed denial of its own tendencies. Yet 'the reach of words'
also acknowledges that even in the most solitary 'spots' those linguistic patterns which evoke our need of other people stretch out to
accompany our wanderings and remind us that we are still creatures
'of time'. So words which celebrate the security of being 'alone' and
those which mourn the vulnerability of feeling 'lonely' must reach
out to nudge each other into complexity.

Chapter 8 looks at some of the less well-known passages of *Tintern
Abbey* and at two short personal poems where Wordsworth tries to
allow both his different values to weigh upon us with an equally
impressive pressure. 'The burthen of the mystery' is not just some
passing irrelevance before those light-headed moments when we feel
that even our weightiest thoughts are no longer distinct from the
majestic mindlessness of all that surrounds us. At times we feel
inescapably burdened with an estranging compulsion to distinguish
even the members of our own species into precious friends and
irrelevant strangers. So the overall 'burthen' which is Wordsworth's
recurrent refrain is the conundrum of how one voice can relate itself
to two such different states of mind which at their most enigmatic
syncopate into a single statement.

IV

Wordsworth thus strains language beyond its normal limits. Under such tension, even the works written in his prime sometimes buckle into clumsiness. At points they even collapse into admitted defeat: then Wordsworth chooses to rail at the 'sad incompetence of human speech' rather than conspire with it and allow words to say less than he feels (*The Prelude* (1850), VI. 593). Yet these moments of frankly confessed helplessness can help: their inept honesty encourages trust in the more fluent movements which they interrupt. Moreover, the occasions when the verse can only make 'Breathings for incommunicable powers', though highly significant, are rare (*The Prelude*, IX. 188).

The poet's customary stance acknowledges difficulty but asserts resolution:

> I would give,
> While yet we may, as far as words can give,
> A substance and a life to what I feel:
> (*The Prelude*, XI. 339–41)

The pronouns here move with characteristic precision from 'I' to 'we' and back again to that singular person who has no doubt about either his wish to communicate ('I would give') or the actuality of his own emotions ('I feel'). The doubt is only how far language can be made to carry author and reader beyond its own finite boundaries so that 'we may' arrive at a shared sense where even the most elusive feelings can come vividly to life as substantiated truth. Yet there is confidence as well as doubt in that plural pronoun. It assumes that, even if the project may not be wholly successful, its pointfulness will seem to us so obvious that we will become the author's partners, building with our own creatively alert reading upon the foundations of his poetic craftsmanship. With such team-work, the verse's 'words/Which speak of nothing more than what we are' can have power to 'arouse' us from a 'sleep of Death' and reawaken us to the intriguing, and strangely moving, paradoxes by which we actually live (*PW*, v. 5, 58–61).

Wordsworth may sometimes 'deconstruct' lazily conventional patterns of language, but he never fosters the delusion that people and the world which they must inhabit are mere pawns in some wittily meaningless game where language is playing only with itself.

The wit of his own best work takes human experience seriously enough to insist that we should know what we are talking about. He expands our vocabulary, not because it has any innate importance, but because its trembling equivocations can touch 'the utmost that we know,/Both of ourselves and of the universe' (*The Prelude*, VII.618–19).

THE TYPES AND SYMBOLS
OF ETERNITY

'CROSSING THE ALPS', 'THE PRELUDE': (1805)
VI.488–572 AND (1850) VI.557–640

I

Grandeur, for Wordsworth, is anything but predictable and *The Prelude* can be a confusingly uneven poem. Its greatest moments often emerge from trivia and then subside into bathos. Conversely such bathos can itself bounce the poetry back into renewed power. Sometimes this seems to be simple incompetence and the reader may justifiably feel irritated. However, there are sequences where such unexpected transitions form the very basis of Wordsworth's meaning and forcefully signal insights which could not be conveyed in verse which was more concerned with superficial coherence and consistency. Towards the end of Book VI, the innocent reader eagerly approaches the sequence which critics have tended to call 'Crossing the Alps'. This label may not seem the most helpful introduction to lines where the poet himself admits to having no conscious knowledge of doing any such thing. Yet Wordsworth's own title for Book VI seems to be a deliberate tease. It announces not only 'Cambridge' but also 'the Alps' and we might expect some grandiose descriptions of those spectacular mountains. Certainly Wordsworth misled his readers when he published the book's climax as a self-contained poem under the heading of 'The Simplon Pass'. Back in context, the extract turns out crucially not to be about that route at its highest and most famous point but about a lower, and far less renowned, stretch of countryside which lies near a tiny Italian village called Gondo.

However, all three titles can be usefully misleading since Wordsworth's subject here is the folly, and even the destructiveness, of trying to map out a path to peak experiences. The Alps, in his day, were after all the high spot of the Grand Tour's flirtation with nature. Any young gentleman who claimed an ounce of sensitivity could look forward to profound emotion as he crossed them and an admiring audience back home whenever he chose to recall the grandeur of such a moment. These expectations are defeated for the poet and for the reader in one of *The Prelude*'s most appropriately fumbling passages.

Wordsworth and his friend, Robert Jones, make a nonsense of it all. They plan to cross the Alps with other travellers who have all stopped to have lunch at an inn before the final ascent, but the two men take longer than the rest over their meal. The main party leaves without them. Hurrying off to catch up, Wordsworth and Jones 'climb'd with eagerness' to reach the tourist's dream, but they never do catch up. Worried that they may be going the wrong way, they ask a local peasant for directions and are given shattering information. Without even noticing it, let alone enjoying suitably passionate sensations, they have already crossed the Alps.

However, out of this moment of dreary disappointment and undignified absurdity, there grows for Wordsworth the traveller – and for the apparently cheated reader – one of the finest experiences of *The Prelude*:

> The dull and heavy slackening that ensued
> Upon those tidings by the Peasant given
> Was soon dislodg'd; downwards we hurried fast,
> And enter'd with the road which we had miss'd
> Into a narrow chasm; the brook and road
> Were fellow-travellers in this gloomy Pass,
> And with them did we journey several hours
> At a slow step. The immeasurable height
> Of woods decaying, never to be decay'd,
> The stationary blasts of water-falls,
> And every where along the hollow rent
> Winds thwarting winds, bewilder'd and forlorn,
> The torrents shooting from the clear blue sky,
> The rocks that mutter'd close upon our ears,
> Black drizzling crags that spake by the way-side
> As if a voice were in them, the sick sight
> And giddy prospect of the raving stream,
> The unfetter'd clouds, and region of the Heavens,
> Tumult and peace, the darkness and the light
> Were all like workings of one mind, the features

Of the same face, blossoms upon one tree
Characters of the great Apocalypse,
The types and symbols of Eternity,
Of first and last, and midst, and without end.

(The Prelude, VI. 549–72)

It is all happening after all. What could not even be noticed by
Wordsworth when he was self-consciously seeking it, what could
not be conveyed to the reader who was attentively listening for it,
emerges for both when they least expect it.

Verse is an essentially chronological medium, and Wordsworth's
skilfully gradual movement here from the concrete and the specific to
the abstract and the generalized is all too easily obscured by commentary. Critical prose may already be preaching where the poetry is
at first merely looking. The sequence does not bully the sceptical by
leaping to its grandiloquent conclusion. Initially it gently begs a
question which seems grounded in the simple facts of wood and
waterfall and rock: do the terms of so-called 'common sense' adequately describe even such common things as these? Or is the poet
compelled by their real oddity to wrench language into self-
contradiction? The challenge of Wordsworth's verse, as Coleridge
noted, often derives from 'something corporeal, a matter-of-factness,
a clinging to the palpable';[1] and it is through a series of palpabilities –
however paradoxical as a matter of fact they have to be – that the
'immeasurable' life of the Alpine scenery is evoked.

The passage begins lamely enough. Wordsworth and his travelling
companion are stranded by 'The dull and heavy slackening' of their
tense excitement in a dreary world which merely reflects their own
disappointment:

> the brook and road
> Were fellow-travellers in this gloomy Pass,
> And with them did we journey several hours
> At a slow step.

Then the simple facts of the scene begin to be noticed by minds which
do not know that they notice: 'The immeasurable height/Of woods
decaying, never to be decay'd.' There is no fanciful poeticizing here.
The paradox is a truth by which every forester earns his living.
Woods seldom die. Each constituent tree, at one stage in its pattern of
shifting appearances, will fall or be felled, releasing light and soil for

younger trees. The wood itself lives on, flourishing upon the decay which it contains, and *The Prelude* elsewhere celebrates that strange permanence which as a species, if not as individuals, we can share:

> These forests unapproachable by death
> That shall endure as long as man endures,
>
> . . .
>
> To look with bodily eyes.   (1850. VI. 466–71)

When, by contrast, Tithonus is made by Tenyson to say that 'The woods decay, the woods decay and fall',[2] he is not being more bluntly realistic than Wordsworth; he is being less accurate. His inability to see the woods for the trees is a strange blindness since the two are indeed mutually defining. The intellect which accuses Wordsworth of failing to distinguish between them is itself suspect. To tell things apart may be to tell ourselves lies about a life which actually defines itself as an intricate unity:

> Our meddling intellect
> Mis-shapes the beauteous forms of things: –
> We murder to dissect. (*The Tables Turned*, 26–8; *PW*, IV. 57)

Carving experience into verbal categories can turn fluid energies into fixed nouns and

>   substitute a universe of death
> For that which moves with light and life informed,
> Actual, divine, and true. (*The Prelude* (1850), XIV. 157–62)

In the real world, Wordsworth argues, nothing is 'defined into absolute independent singleness', but in the work of a hack poet 'it is exactly the reverse; everything . . . is in this manner defined, insulated, dislocated, deadened'.[3]

Even conventional language admits that a waterfall cannot be 'defined into absolute independent singleness'. Only a doubling together of two nouns seems adequate. A dissection which tried to separate 'water' from 'fall' would obviously destroy what it sought to describe. A waterfall is an extreme example of 'something far more deeply interfused' (*Tintern Abbey*, 96; *PW*, II. 262).
It typifies a universe which can give us:

> Authentic tidings of invisible things;
> Of ebb and flow, and ever-during power;

And central peace, subsisting at the heart
Of endless agitation.

(*The Excursion*, IV. 1144–7; *PW*, v. 145)

So 'Crossing the Alps' follows its paradoxical woods with another of those great Wordsworthian phrases which revealingly confuse the issue: 'The stationary blasts of water-falls'. A waterfall cannot answer language's falsely precise questions. It has to express both stability and movement. It cannot be a testament of one or the other, or even of one more than the other. The poet is appropriately uncertain about his own responses: he *sees* it as 'stationary', yet he *hears* it as a 'blast'.

So Wordsworth has to struggle with his verbal medium if he is to avoid telling lies about woods and waterfalls and indeed winds: 'And every where along the hollow rent / Winds thwarting winds, bewilder'd and forlorn.' The language here is almost as meaningfully confused as the winds themselves. A reader who wishes to remain detached, and to insist on the judicious use of appropriate terms, will at first have difficulties. It is not easy to sort out noun and adjective in 'hollow rent' or to decide whether 'rent' is a verb whose subject is the ensuing winds. The attempt risks as false a separation as that involved in trying to consider one of the winds in isolation from the others. A wind on its own is unthinkable: bent grass may make it visible; tree-branches sometimes make it audible; skin can make it felt. Its essence is relationship. Meeting something else, even another wind as a cross-current, it lurches into action, finds its voice, is given – and gives – life. The winds' contrary movements are literally creative. 'Without contraries', said Blake, 'is no progression. Attraction and repulsion, reason and energy, love and hate, are necessary to human existence.'4 Wordsworth – and with him, the reader – is gradually being led towards an even more inclusive generalization, but the route is still concrete and specific.

Wordsworth's next line may however seem more vulnerably fanciful: 'The torrents shooting from the clear blue sky'. This perhaps is going too far for a reader who insists on what he calls the 'facts' of a 'material' universe. The poet is arguably passing off as observation what he knows to be a mere optical illusion. The mountain streams do not in fact flow from the sky; they merely *seem* to as they appear over the horizon. Wordsworth knows perfectly well, the sensible reader insists, that somewhere on the mountain-tops is the real source of those streams. But is it? Would not a scientist point out the absurd oversimplification of such a statement? Would he not stress numerous factors that determine the nature of streams, and would he not give a central role to those meteorological forces which – from Wordsworth's point of view looking up the mountain-side – can fairly, if very roughly, be summed up as 'sky'? It is from there that the water comes down.

Schoolchildren, of course, are taught that before the moisture falls down as rain it rose up from the earth, that the rain-cycle *is* a cycle. But *that* complication – if it does occur to a reader – helps rather than hinders Wordsworth's evocation. The water in the torrents has been – and will again be – the water in the sky, just as the woods are and are not decaying. The fact that Wordsworth sees a 'clear blue sky' rather than one darkly burdened with the water of future streams clearly reinforces, rather than undercuts, the suggestion of endless inter-action. It is the warmth of just such skies that makes sea-water rise again. *Lines Composed at Grasmere* notice that the roar of past storms and distant seas can still be audibly present within an inland valley:

> Loud is the Vale! the Voice is up
> With which she speaks when storms are gone,
> A mighty unison of streams!
> Of all her Voices, One!
> Loud is the Vale; – this inland Depth
> In peace is roaring like the Sea;   (*PW*, IV. 266, 1–6)

Faced by a river's fluid permanence, its forceful evocation at any point of its impelling past and its summoning future, Wordsworth's language sometimes asks questions which no language can answer:

> the River that flows on
> Perpetually, whence comes it, whither tends,
> Going and never gone;   (*The Prelude*, p. 572, 44–7)

The lines which reunite the tumult of the 'torrents shooting' with the peace of 'the clear blue sky' do not so much impose an optical illusion as challenge a verbal one. The conventional lucidity which thinks it sees clearly because it distinguishes may see only a dead, isolated thing and so be blind to all that exists in a world of dynamic inter-dependence.

An extreme case of things turning out to be alive is the idea that stones can speak, not as a lazy metaphor ('sermons in stones') but as an energetic fact. That idea is the next that confronts the reader and the gradually awakening tourist:

> The rocks that mutter'd close upon our ears,
> Black drizzling crags that spake by the way-side
> As if a voice were in them,

That defensive 'As if' shows that Wordsworth is well aware of the oddity of what he is saying, and the tautology (the muttering rocks and the speaking crags are presumably identical) shows an impatience with the limits of language. The poet knows that the reader is all too likely to regard 'The rocks that mutter'd close upon our ears' as nonsense, but he does not delete it as he supplies, in the following line and a half, a more acceptable verbalization. Once we know that the rocks were in fact '*drizzling* crags', the claim sounds less eccentric. At first indeed it seems dismissable as a mere poeticism, a pretence that the sounds made by water running over stone were made by the stone rather than the water. However, it then becomes obvious that our language-obsessed need to be told accurately which made the sound really demands an inaccurate answer. The shape of the rock, the volume of water, the force of gravity, the angle at which the meeting of water and stone occurs, all these make the sound, are one voice.

Of course Wordsworth, in suggesting that the voice not only 'mutter'd' but 'spake', implies a larger claim: that the noise is meaningful, that it has as much potential ability to articulate significance as can be claimed for human speech. For Wordsworth, who recognized the 'sad incompetence of human speech' (*The Prelude* (1850), VI. 593), it is not a grandiose assertion. 'The ghostly language of the ancient earth' (*The Prelude*, II. 328) is acknowledged by a writer who had remarkably little faith in the powers of human language. Roger Sharrock has remarked on Wordsworth's 'radical pessimism about poetry's capacity for recording experience',[5] and John Jones has observed that 'no poet has ever complained so much about the medium of his art'.[6] *The Prelude*'s respect for 'quiet sympathies with things that hold an inarticulate language' (MS of *Excursion; PW*, V. 400) and for 'the language of the sense' (*Tintern Abbey* 108; *PW*, II. 262), the claims that in childhood 'the earth / And common face of Nature spake . . . Rememberable things' (*The Prelude*,

I.614–16) and that the visible world 'spake perpetual logic' (*The Prelude*, III.165), these have to be seen as rivalry to a very feeble competitor. The 'drizzling crags that spake' may be as competently expressive as words, but words are arguably 'secondary work of mimic skill/Transcripts that do but mock their archetypes' (*The Prelude*, p. 576, 185). The writer, according to the Preface to the *Lyrical Ballads*, only 'describes and imitates' so 'his situation is altogether slavish and mechanical compared with the freedom and power of real and substantial action'.[7] Yet Wordsworth was committed to 'making Verse/Deal boldly with substantial things' (*The Prelude*, XII.233–4), to forcing words to evoke the 'real and substantial action' in things like water and stone, to recognizing the voice of the drizzling crags.

For the voice to function, there must be an ear to listen. Wordsworth struggles against a vocabulary which not only tends to separate water and stone but also to distinguish between sight and sound. So, as his attention moves back from the drizzling crags to the shooting torrents, he describes the turbulence of a mountain river as a wildness equally in the 'raving stream' and in his own whirling senses. Ear and eye are dizzyingly merged to face a world whose pulsing tumult makes peace as audible as its flickering light makes darkness visible:

> the sick sight
> And giddy prospect of the raving stream,
> The unfetter'd clouds, and region of the Heavens,
> Tumult and peace, the darkness and the light
> Were all like workings of one mind, . . .

The quickening pace of these lines reflects Wordsworth's excitement at discovering and revealing the falsehood of separation. The specific gives way to the generalized without the reader insisting on language's arbitrary distinctions. At first one may take 'The unfetter'd clouds' and the 'region of the Heavens' to be distinct before grasping Wordsworth's point, which is precisely that they are identical. The concrete, specified clouds – with their evocative epithet – and the abstract, almost metaphorical region of the Heavens – complete with a capital 'H' – are one. Mundane clouds are no less than the Heavens of human imagination. The Heavens are no more fanciful than the clouds of the visible world.

Wordsworth, like the hero of another *Prelude* passage, is now

> not like a man who sees in the heavens
> A blue vault merely and a glittering cloud,
> One old familiar likeness over all,
> A superficial pageant, known too well
> To be regarded; he looks nearer
>
>   . . .
>
> The converse which he holds is limitless.
>
>   (*The Prelude*, p. 575, 140–55)

Exposed to such a contention without preparation, the reader with a blind faith in the sanity of language and its distinctions would doubtless rebel. Lured towards it by the permanent and changing woods, through the static haste of the waterfall, the dialogue of moisture and rock, the giddiness of eye on river and river on eye, most readers will, however momentarily, be awake to the possibility of a world magnificently and inseparably alive.

The verse which had tightened itself for this revelation can now flow on in serenely expansive confidence:

> workings of one mind, the features
> Of the same face, blossoms upon one tree,
> Characters of the great Apocalypse,
> The types and symbols of Eternity,
> Of first and last, and midst, and without end.

The seventeen-line sentence does pause after the most inclusive line of English poetry: 'Of first, and last, and midst, and without end.' It will not, however, surrender to the falsifying tyranny of a full stop on any other terms than the 'without end' which denies it.

There is but one verb to express the activity of all the landscape's elements, of all Wordsworth's responses, the simple yet unreservedly profound verb 'to be'. 'These things *were* these things' is the sentence's grammatical skeleton. It is an inclusive verb and the ultimately intransitive one. Transitive verbs encourage the idea of one separate thing acting upon (often against) another with no chance of the victim retaliating in the same clause. Actions in Wordsworth's living universe are all expressions of a shared existence, a continuing cycle. The decaying of the woods is self-cancelling. The wild energies of the waterfall and the raving stream have all the stasis of permanence. The passage is alive with verbs as eternally present

participles, 'decaying', 'thwarting', 'shooting', 'drizzling', 'raving'.
The world that is doing all this 'mutter'd' and 'spake', but its
statement is no more and no less than these things 'were' one. To
be precise, Wordsworth's defensiveness is not even this dogmatic.
They 'Were all *like* workings of one mind', just as the crags spoke
'*As if* a voice were in them', but however considerately tentative
these phrases may be, the message of the verbs is clear. It is a world
of action, but intransitive action, expressing not the competition of
separate units but the existence of mutually defining parts.

The 'Characters of the great Apocalypse' embrace the largest permanence and yet do so by means as visibly transient as the decaying
woods. The apocalypse itself suggests the Flood, which was still in
Wordsworth's day thought to have shaped the larger features of
existing geography. Yet the rock-faces whose shapes were carved so
many centuries ago still achieve the fluent effect of handwriting. At a
literal level the idea presumably derives from a phenomenon visible
to this day: the light-grey cliffs north of Gondo curiously combine
the horizontal lines of geological strata with the dark vertical stains
made by streams which once coursed down their surfaces but now
have ceased to do so. Each winter has deposited its varying weights
and shapes of snow; each spring has melted them into making their
own individual marks. The now discarded routes of thousands of
previous streams can clearly be seen as dark streaks alongside the few
active water-courses of any given year. So the ancient unchanging
strata would be as blank as lined paper if the inky strokes of an annual
pen had not gradually transformed them into gigantic lettering. The
writing is an ongoing process revised by annual additions, and presumably by deletions as time eventually effaces the signatures of the
oldest water-courses where no subsequent thaw has found its way to
reinforcing their routes. The cycle which releases each frozen winter
into flowing spring is, of course, as unalterable as the natural law
which makes trees both grow and die. Like the strata of the rock, it is
a basic drawing-board which can 'never be decayed'. On the other
hand, its legible meaning is dependent on the essentially transient
patterns of decaying snows and streams.

Wordsworth, of course, does not require his readers to have
travelled to the sights which stimulated the imagery, and 'Characters'
in fact convey just the same implications if they are taken to refer to
the one visual experience which all his readers, by definition, have in
common, namely the recognition of the printer's lettering. The

alphabet of the letterpress is a primal given like the geological hori-
zontals, and yet its function is the essential flexibility with which it
can be constantly rearranged. The rigid heritage of the letterpress is a
meaningful survival only because of the endlessly altered relationships it offers. The 'Characters' and 'The types' are at once the
unchanging message of the earth and the essentially mobile voice of
the printed poet who leads us through it from an almost comic
self-characterization to the revelation of a mind wholly identified
with the 'symbols of eternity'. At his side, we begin with a merely
topographical approach in a language which aims at no more than
high-spots and low-spots ('we had crossed the Alps'; 'brook and
road / Were fellow-travellers in this gloomy Pass'); yet we arrive at a
typographical triumph where the world is allowed to imprint its own
symbolism on the mind.

These closing suggestions, though openly extreme in their grandiloquent inclusiveness, seem to be an organic growth from the specifics established earlier. Struggling against language's innate tendency
to polarization, to a world of mutually exclusive opposites, Wordsworth cites 'Tumult and peace, the darkness and the light'. We
remember the tumult of the waterfall's 'blast' whose impact is so
inseparable from its 'stationary' peace, the tumultuous torrents
shooting from the peacefully clear blue sky, perhaps even those
energies of growth and decay which maintain the peaceful permanence of the woods. There are quite palpable senses in which 'the
darkness and the light' of the sky, for instance, constitute an alternat-
ing pattern recognized by 'the workings of one mind'. There are fairly
precise analogies between the relationship of blossoms growing upon
one tree and that of trees growing in one wood. The torrents, with
their waterfalls, act as a concrete anchor to the final bold yoking of
'first and last, and midst, and without end', since the question of
where a river begins or ends has already been revealed as senseless. A
river is a first and a last at all points, and its current – even in the midst
of a turbulent waterfall – is 'without end'. Similarly 'the features / Of
the same face' have been prepared for by Wordsworth's own face,
inseparably composed of ears to hear and eyes to see, confronting
'the rocks that mutter'd close upon our ears' or the 'giddy prospect of
the raving stream'. The archetypal image of 'the features / Of the same
face' has already been given the humanity of a man whose face fell
with a 'dull and heavy slackening' at the news that he had passed the
most famous tourist's treat without registering it. The bathos of the

introduction – like the trivia to which this climax gives way – is part
of a total vision, aspects 'Of first and last, and midst, and without
end', a darkness without which the light of revelation would not be
its dazzling self, a dozy peace without which the tumult of an
emotional awakening could not be felt. They are in the most literal as
well as the most profound sense 'workings of one mind'.

II

The 'one mind' is at once Wordsworth's and the world's. Without his
landscape the poet here would be literally empty-headed. Without its
human eye-witness that landscape would lose a crucial way of proving the identity of its complex relationships. 'Landscape', however, is
an innately misleading term. The word serves for a painted canvas
which can offer no more than a two-dimensional and static miniatur-
ization of the world glimpsed from a single point of view, closed in a
frame and hung upon a wall. Yet 'landscape' also purports to describe
the endlessly changing appearance of the life about us, of water and
earth and air by which we – quite literally – survive. It might be more
appropriate to say, for instance, that we use our lungs to keep us alive
to the earth, and that the earth uses our lungs to preserve its witnesses. This might still suggest more consciousness than either party
to the process feels, but it would at least avoid the suggestion that we
live as chattering voyeurs on a visit to some ultimately superfluous
picture gallery. 'Landscape' is not one of Wordsworth's favourite
terms. 'Breath' is. The significance of that choice for 'Crossing the
Alps' will become clearer if we first look at Wordsworth's frequent
attempts elsewhere to find a language in which the earth can be
evoked.

The natural world, according to The Prelude, does have the power
to 'breathe / Grandeur upon the very humblest face / Of human life',
but only 'if we have eyes to see' (XII. 283–6), and looking at pictures
can be bad for the eyes. Wordsworth does admittedly give the title of
Descriptive Sketches to an earlier poem about his trip through the
Alps, but he takes trouble to spell out in a note that the poem is not
meant to be 'Picturesque'. On the contrary:

> the Alps are insulted in applying to them that term. Whoever in
> attempting to describe their sublime features, should confine him-
> self to the cold rules of painting would give his reader but a very

imperfect idea of those emotions which they have the irresistible power of communicating.

What had struck Wordsworth at this point in these 'images which disdain the pencil' was his own intense response to a temporary and localized effect, a grandiose trick of the light:

> The ideas excited by the stormy sunset I am here describing owed their sublimity to that deluge of light, or rather of fire, in which nature had wrapped the immense forms around me; any intrusion of shade, by destroying the unit of the impression, had necessarily diminish'd its grandeur.[8]

Wordsworth's is an audibly provisional vision of a developing experience: 'that deluge of light, or rather of fire'. His instinctively cumulative language defines 'grandeur' as an impressive unity which encloses, not only the various features of the visible world, but also a sequence of 'ideas excited' in the human eye.

Yet at least one modern critic can praise a dynamic sequence of Wordsworth's poetry for the very result it seeks to avoid: 'Like the more famous pictures of the *Prelude* exhibition, it is a finished composition hanging framed upon the wall.'[9] *The Prelude* was in fact composed as an overture to a significantly *un*finished work. Its title suggests that anticipation of future movements which the gradually developing line of music or verse can evoke so much more easily than the completed stroke of the artist's pencil. As the flexibly circling structure of sentence or verse paragraph leads us through each movement of its chronological experience, it can still echo a fading past and hint a looming future. Both may be excluded from a painting's more rigidly rectangular frame of reference which concentrates so much on what is present that it may confine itself to an exaggerated stability.

Draughtsmanship may trace what Book VII of *The Prelude* calls 'the mountain's outline' and 'the forms / Perennial of the ancient hills' but it can hardly speak to 'The changeful language of their countenances' which here explicitly matters as much to Wordsworth as their 'steady form'. The expressive mobility of such mountain-faces ensures that they too are communicators offering the poet a fluent dialogue with which the portrait painter's frozen moment cannot hope to keep pace. Variable weather, or advancing time of day, or the more gradual movement of the seasons, or even a shift in one's own angle of vision are all answered by unceasing alterations of texture

and tint even though our inadequate vocabulary may still suggest that
they are the same hills. What *The Prelude* prefers at this point to call
their 'pure grandeur' is not just a fact of permanence; it is a question of change, and indeed of dynamic interchange (*The Prelude*,
VII. 721–9).

To separate things for closer examination may thus be to dismantle
the shared context which gives them significance. *The Pedlar* asks
what meaning can survive if we 'Break down all grandeur' by peering
at pretty details until the earth seems flat and vision has dwindled to
no more than 'a barren picture on the mind':

> For was it meant
> That we should pore, and dwindle as we pore,
> For ever dimly pore on things minute,
> On solitary objects, still beheld
> In disconnection dead and spiritless,
> And still dividing and dividing still,
> Break down all grandeur, still unsatisfied
> With our unnatural toil, while littleness
> May yet become more little, waging thus
> An impious warfare with the very life
> Of our own souls? Or was it ever meant
> That this majestic imagery, the clouds,
> The ocean and the firmament of heaven
> Should lie a barren picture on the mind?
>
> (*PW*, V. 402, 58–71)

The picturesque approach either presses our noses so close to aesthetic minutiae that we can see nothing but our own belittling analysis, or it forces us so far back from the fertile relationships of the
physical world that they seem to blur into one frigidly inert idea.

Either position seems 'dead' and 'barren' to Wordsworth because
it disconnects us and the things which we see from a universal
life-support system. The detachment which allows the world to
appear 'spiritless' is precisely 'unnatural' because to deny our own
breath is suicidal. The breath which inspires life is, in Wordsworth's
radical cosmology, not the creative act by which an external God
initiated the human race, but the continuously articulate energy of
the earth itself. Milton's Raphael, even when talking to the very first
generation of mankind, had been able to describe creative breath as
an already past event:

he formed thee, Adam, thee O man
Dust of the ground, and in thy nostrils breathed
The breath of life;   (*Paradise Lost*, VII. 524–6)

Unsurprisingly Adam feels that even the sun must 'Acknowledge' such a creator as 'greater' than itself. For Milton's man, earthly things do not unite to celebrate the equally balanced relationships which ensure the survival of all; instead they are joined by their common obligation to acknowledge the absolute supremacy of one God:

On earth join all ye creatures to extol
Him first, him last, him midst, and without end.
                            (*Paradise Lost*, V. 164–5)

'Crossing the Alps' audibly echoes this last line, but Wordsworth presumably meant its subtle alteration to be noticed. He omits Milton's repeated pronoun which might personalize the 'unfetter'd Heavens' into a deity distinct from his creation. He thus leaves the Alpine scenery free to express nothing but the breath of its own self-generating life.

Successful alliance with such inspiration sustains, in the most palpable sense, 'the very life / Of our own souls'. Those finer distinctions into which we destructively toil to 'Break down' our experience are baffled by the elusive fluidity of breath which stays neither within us nor without us, but expresses itself as a constantly reciprocal movement. It thus provides Wordsworth with a remarkably apt image of what he elsewhere calls the 'ennobling interchange / Of action from within and from without' which unites 'the object seen, and eye that sees'. Wordsworth hopes that this primal 'balance' from which 'our dignity originates' can 'be transmitted and made visible / To other eyes' through his poetry (*The Prelude*, XII. 370–9). *Tintern Abbey* celebrates the equipoise:

of all that we behold
From this green earth; of all the mighty world
Of eye, and ear, – both what they half create,
And what perceive;   (*PW*, II. 262, 104–7)

The provisional meanings which are offered here by the ending of one line are crucially corrected at the beginning of the next so that what 'we behold' is then seen to derive 'From this green earth' and conversely the 'world' itself is then defined as one 'Of eye and ear'.

The prejudice which approaches the earth as separate from our bodies is thus lured out of hiding only to be discredited. The 'object seen, and eye that sees' prove to be essentially of 'one mind'.

The vision which seems so 'mighty' to Wordsworth is importantly not the privilege of the professional artist or author, nor even of those who appreciate their work. The senses of anyone who is able to see and hear are themselves intuitively creative, energizing the environment which they enjoy. In fact the mind of the consciously creative intellectual may contribute less as it busily searches for some crystallized image of beauty or truth. To seek is to look for the specific and the separable, and that is arguably a wild-goose chase:

> Think you, 'mid all this mighty sum
> Of things for ever speaking,
> That nothing of itself will come,
> But we must still be seeking?
>
> (*Expostulation and Reply*, 25–8; *PW*, IV. 56)

In this dialogue poem Wordsworth is replying to his friend Matthew's complaint that he should be reading books instead of dreaming his time away sitting outside and alone; but Wordsworth had not been feeling that he was alone. Indeed, to pay deliberate attention now to the words of either Matthew or of some book might cut the poet off from things whose company he is thoroughly enjoying. Listening to a single human voice requires a focus which not only concentrates but also excludes. It extracts from the 'mighty sum / Of things for ever speaking' one note whose role may be only to contribute to an overall harmony.

In Wordsworth's defiantly earthly paradise, the well-meaning Matthew may represent a seriously destructive temptation. He may lure our senses into the wastefulness of trying to distinguish the sound of the stone's shape from the noise of the water's pressure. He may encourage the language-based illusion of the controlling intellect, the fantasy that each person has a separate control box in his skull by which he can manipulate how much life he contributes and how much he notices and receives. In fact, Wordsworth tells him:

> The eye – it cannot choose but see;
> We cannot bid the ear be still;
> Our bodies feel, wheree'er they be,
> Against or with our will.   (17–20)

Matthew's desire to seize and encapsulate bits of the world in books denies those realities which seem to Wordsworth literally self-evident since life is composed of 'Powers / Which of themselves our minds impress'. So the poet argues: 'That we can feed this mind of ours / In a wise passiveness' (21–4). Grammar here speaks to a unity which confuses its own over-tidy rules and scorns the decisive lucidities of those rejected books. The singular 'mind' is shared by a plural 'we', and the intransitive passiveness is dependent on our transitively active feeding.

Matthew may choose not to notice his own contribution, but he cannot prevent his senses making it. In a companion poem, *The Tables Turned*, he is told that literature is innately divisive. It provokes ' dull and endless strife' in which the reader who tries to understand his own experience by reading about someone else's may 'grow double'. By contrast a single-mindedly direct response to the natural world admits us to a truly shared sanity: 'Spontaneous wisdom breathed by health,/Truth breathed by cheerfulness' (*PW*, IV. 57, 2–20). That liberating verb does bear repetition. In breathing our mouths are repeatedly successful at keeping in touch with a world which they so unreliably try to capture with acts of speech. We do 'half create' what we perceive, but only as one side of a give and take which is as automatic as breathing out and breathing in.

Of course the stance of these poems where the reader is invited to agree that Matthew should be harangued for reading is explicitly self-contradictory. Wordsworth knows that some of the concepts whose value he most wants to define, such as Silence or Solitude or Breath itself, are peculiarly difficult to validate in the implicitly sociable and sophisticated medium of literature. He presumably expects us to be disconcerted when, for instance, he announces in *Michael* that his hero's discovery of 'The pleasure which there is in life itself' was dependent on the mundane fact that 'he had breathed / The common air' (*PW*, II. 82, 65–77). Here Wordsworth's use of the line-ending provides an opposite kind of trap for the over-sophisticated reader who is rebuked at the beginning of the next line for expecting Wordsworth to add something more interesting than that the object of Michael's breathing was 'The common air'. It is a phrase which insists that the fact that Michael 'had breathed' is an adequately thought-provoking truth. It defies those linguistic habits which translate the earthly into the tediously mundane and dismiss all that we have in common as almost boringly familiar.

Less well-educated people seem to Wordsworth at some advantage here since their more limited vocabulary does not tempt them to verbalize away so much of their experience. He sees those who are 'unpractis'd in the strife of phrase' as putting words in their proper place and sensibly choosing to breathe elsewhere:

> Theirs is the language of the heavens.
>
>   . . .
>
> Words are but under-agents in their souls;
> When they are grasping with their greatest strength
> They do not breathe among them:
>
> (*The Prelude*, xii. 266–74)

Wordsworth is thus often in the difficult position of wanting to speak up for characters whose wisdom may lie in not speaking for themselves. He has to resort time and again to the imagery of breath whose literal power so usefully restrains the verse from becoming merely metaphorical. He pleads that the Old Cumberland Beggar should be allowed to 'breathe the freshness of the valleys' in 'the natural silence of old age' (*PW*, iv. 239, 179–82). One of the Lucy poems prays for its heroine that:

> hers shall be the breathing balm,
> And hers the silence and the calm
> Of mute insensate things.
>
> (*Three Years She Grew*; *PW*, ii. 215, 16–18)

At first this may sound like a bizarrely inhuman destiny but the unspoken and unnoticed satisfaction of our lungs does bring all of us who enjoy good health close to the experience of apparently 'mute insensate things'. So when *Lines Written in Early Spring* voice the complementary proposition 'that every flower/Enjoys the air it breathes', what could have sounded outrageously fanciful can seem like a mere truism (*PW*, iv. 58, 11–12).

Even though the more literate poet and his readers may now talk too much for their own good, they can at least remember what it was like to be less distracted by verbal language while they were still children. Then they too had a better grasp of that 'breath/And everlasting motion' which *The Prelude* hears giving serene energy 'to forms and images' in the 'first dawn/Of Childhood' (i. 430–3). Wordsworth remembers listening as a boy to the 'ceaseless music' of the River Derwent and gaining 'a knowledge, a dim earnest of the calm / That Nature breathes' (*The Prelude*, I. 279–85).

He fears, however, that in learning the language of grown-ups we may have taught ourselves to grow away from all knowledge which 'lies far hidden from the reach of words'. We may talk ourselves into gasping for breath as we struggle to communicate with other people whom our vocabulary has turned into strangers:

> Points have we all within our souls
> Where all stand single; this I feel, and make
> Breathings for incommunicable powers.
>
> (*The Prelude*, III. 185–8)

The helpless panting of a poet who tries to make words deny their own tendency can often sound banal; 'I breathe again' (*The Prelude*, I. 18). It can even sound melodramatic:

> and, when the deed was done
> I heard among the solitary hills
> Low breathings coming after me, sounds
> Of undistinguishable motion, steps
> Almost as silent as the turf they trod.
>
> (*The Prelude*, I. 328–32)

If this fleeing child is in fact hearing echoes of his own excited 'breathings', is he simply deluded in allocating them to the landscape? Or is he momentarily listening to a usually inaudible truth?

We do not in fact hold our breath within the frail compass of our own small bodies; we bounce it against what *The Prelude* elsewhere calls the 'Immense . . . Recess' of 'the circumambient world' by which all are 'embraced' (VIII. 46–8). Of course the guilty boy whose gasps seem to resound 'among the solitary hills' may be fantasizing the world into a far smaller echo-chamber which can record nothing but his own sense of isolation. So the 'Low breathings' by which he feels pursued inevitably belittle that lofty atmosphere which he and the hills actually share. Yet his ears still catch a version, however faint, of what is a truly 'undistinguishable motion', even if we are usually listening so much to our own discriminating voices that we can no longer hear it. Certainly he is right to understand the sound of his own feet as dependent on the noises from 'the turf they trod'. The inseparability of our movements and the earth through which we pass is undeniable, although our divisive language must often remain almost 'silent' on the issue.

The customary patterns of 'form and image' have to be discarded when Wordsworth remembers what it was like 'To breathe' when he could listen to the earth's own, unspeakably potent, voice. Then he could hear

> whate'er there is of power in sound
> To breathe an elevated mood, by form
> Or image unprofaned; and I would stand,
> Beneath some rock, listening to sounds that are
> The ghostly language of the ancient earth,
> Or make their dim abode in distant winds.
>
> (*The Prelude*, II. 324–9)

The poetry here wrestles to overcome the intractability of words by forcing prosaic syntax into less falsifying shapes of line-length. For instance, as Christopher Ricks points out:

> It is not just that the sounds are the ghostly language of the ancient earth, though that is pregnantly mysterious enough; the basic mystery is that they exist at all, that they are:
>
> Beneath some rock, listening to sounds that are –
>
> no other poet performs such miracles with the verb to be.[10]

Yet it seems to me that, as the passage continues, it extracts an even more elusive paradox from another verb, to remember. The memory which retains ways of feeling can reveal that the potential of human consciousness is limitless; yet the revelation may depend upon forgetting specific emotive events:

> the soul,
> Remembering how she felt, but what she felt
> Remembering not, retains an obscure sense
> Of possible sublimity, to which
> With growing faculties she doth aspire,
> With faculties still growing, feeling still
> That whatsoever point they gain, they still
> Have something to pursue.   (*The Prelude*, II. 334–41)

Our most fertile memories re-echo to a way of feeling – a 'how'. We are diminished by trying to preserve an amputated experience as a relic of something dead and separate from our present selves – a 'what'. Wordsworth can hardly be lucid here if he is to be loyal to his explicitly 'obscure sense'. Even the rules of grammar forbid his statement: a sentence, by definition, must end. Yet, for as long as we do 'breathe . . . the language of the ancient earth', our endlessly interacting capabilities accept 'That whatsoever point they gain, they still/Have something to pursue.' In giving way to that full stop, Wordsworth is arguably compelled to support a libellous insult to his own experience.

Wordsworth's largest paradox about what lazier minds call 'landscape' is the extraordinary self-confidence gained by admitting that he is absolutely dependent on other things. That egocentricity which we may mistake for self-confidence is by contrast only a belittling separation. The *Lines Left Upon a Seat in a Yew-Tree* insist that

> pride,
> Howe'er disguised in its own majesty,
> Is littleness; that he who feels contempt
> For any living thing, hath faculties
> Which he has never used; that thought with him
> Is in its infancy.   (*PW*, 1.93, 50–5)

If we are not trapped in such retarded egotism but keep our 'faculties still growing', the world will reliably return the compliment and ensure that 'they still/Have something to pursue'. Such a faith allows man to combine the unceasing energy of desire with the unqualified serenity of fulfilment:

> He feels that, be his mind however great
> In aspiration, the universe in which
> He lives is equal to his mind, that each
> Is worthy of the other; if the one
> Be insatiate, the other is inexhaustible.
>   (*The Prelude*, p. 576, 171–6)

It is perhaps in the light of such lines that we should read *Tintern Abbey*'s rather baldly phrased guarantee that 'Nature never did betray/The heart that loved her' (*PW*, 11.262, 122–3).

The 'ghostly' pre-verbal 'language of the ancient earth' does not reduce man to a helpless cog in some vast machine. It exalts him. Like the baby of *The Prelude* he is empowered

> to combine
> In one appearance all the elements
> And parts of the same object, else detach'd
>   . . .
>
> No outcast he, bewilder'd and depress'd;
> Along his infant veins are interfus'd
> The gravitation and the filial bond
> Of nature, that connect him with the world.   (II. 247–64)

He is not a vulnerable intruder importing his fragile oxygen tanks into the atmosphere of an alien planet. He is not trying to colonize dead rock in some hopeless attempt to conquer a nature which includes himself. He is not an orphan on the earth to which he was born. He is at home amongst infinite forces as partner and witness of their secure relationship, belonging with their multifarious parenthood as a matter of both scientific fact and intuitive love, of 'gravitation' and 'filial bond'. Moreover such forces can find their own most natural place in the topography of human consciousness so that 'things that are without/Live in our minds as in their native home' (MS fragment, PW, v. 343; iii). This rhetoric of assertion sometimes allows Wordsworth himself to relax like someone who has safely returned from a long journey and come back into his own.

However, Wordsworth's verse more often arrives at its positive values by a negative route. He leads us to the 'symbols of Eternity' by recalling what a fool he made of himself in his own approach to the Alps, and the extent to which we should treat our surroundings as home and family is frequently pointed by confessions of the poet's own insensitive moments of treating them like strangers. In *Nutting*, to take an extreme case, he describes his own savaging of a tree in terms not just of wasteful vandalism but of criminal rape. He recalls as a boy finding a grove of hazel trees, 'a virgin scene' of harmony in which he at first was willing to relish his own calm part: 'Breathing with such suppression of the heart/As joy delights in' (PW, II. 211, 21–3). But the temptation to be self-assertive, to try to conquer a nature which can thus be thought of as separate, grows. The language begins to patronize the world as a series of dead, 'indifferent things', to see the shared breath of life as something external: mere 'vacant air' distinct from the heart that enjoys it:

> I heard the murmur and the murmuring sound,
> In that sweet mood when pleasure loves to pay

Tribute to ease; and, of its joy secure,
The heart luxuriates with indifferent things,
Wasting its kindliness on stocks and stones,
And on the vacant air. Then up I rose,
And dragged to earth both branch and bough, with crash
And merciless ravage: and the shady nook
Of hazels, and the green and mossy bower,
Deformed and sullied, patiently gave up
Their quiet being: and, unless I now
Confound my present feelings with the past,
Ere from the mutilated bower I turned
Exulting, rich beyond the wealth of kings,
I felt a sense of pain when I beheld
The silent trees, and saw the intruding sky.   (38–53)

Dissection and rape deprive the hazel trees of their reality and Wordsworth of his relationship with them. 'Exulting' in his own power over the world, Wordsworth merely condemns himself to being an orphan, and his world to being dead and alien. The mighty sum of things for ever speaking has been 'mutilated' into a few 'silent trees'. The sky, far from finding its own 'native home' in Wordsworth's mind, seems to intrude like a stranger. The rape has 'Deformed and sullied', has 'mutilated' the poet's mood just as much as it has 'the virgin scene'. Grabbing at the world in hopes of feeling 'rich beyond the wealth of kings', he in fact deprives himself of everything except 'a sense of pain'. To have been told in time that he was about to cross the Alps would presumably have made him no richer. The seeking tourist only takes home a fading, silent blossom.

The boy rapist who goes nutting is in a sense enacting a role given him by language. He has been taught to use personal pronouns and to regard the most significant of these as 'the first person singular', the 'I', an identity to be meaningfully distinguished from the 'vacant air' and 'silent trees'. Pronouns and transitive verbs force many descriptions of relationship towards rape. They tend to involve the notion of a someone doing something to a someone else who is likely grammatically to end up as a mere object. The syntax of sexual language seldom evokes a shared consummation 'like workings of one mind'. Even in an area as palpably interdependent as the genitals, language insists on our separation. It seeks to answer meaningless questions: 'is this movement selfish or generous, for my pleasure or yours?'

'who did what to whom and with what?' Only failed sexuality can be described in words that force one person to do something to another. Loneliness can send out verbal appeals for help. Shared consummation makes its own statement.

Yet Wordsworth must try to drag through the medium of words a message which words tend to obscure. If our usual response to our world amounts to rape, then a better approach might be analogous to the one life experienced by two people living fully together, influencing each other, sharing a development which makes any attempt to comprehend the identity of one without reference to the other folly. Inevitably Wordsworth deploys the imagery of marriage. According to the Preface to the 1814 edition of *The Excursion*, 'the discerning intellect of Man' is 'wedded to this goodly universe'. 'The spousal verse / Of this great consummation' is intended to arouse us from the 'sleep of Death' by using 'words / Which speak of nothing more than what we are'. Its subject is to be:

> How exquisitely the individual Mind
> (And the progressive powers perhaps no less
> Of the whole species) to the external World
> Is fitted: – and how exquisitely, too –
> Theme this but little heard of among men –
> The external World is fitted to the Mind;
> And the creation (by no lower name
> Can it be called) which they with blended might
> Accomplish.   (*PW*, v. 4–5, 57–71)

The 'progressive powers', the growing faculties of mind and world, can only be truly expressed together. They exist for each other as surely as the genitals of the two sexes. They create one life as surely as does a successful marriage. Wordsworth carefully avoids indicating whether 'the individual Mind' is bride or bridegroom, whether the 'external World' is the impregnating man or the fertile woman. He uses 'Man' to mean 'the whole species' in which to distinguish men from women would be an irrelevance. He does his best to present the 'great consummation' as an act so wholly shared that the partners have no distinguishable roles. Pleasure is given and taken simultaneously by two beings so 'exquisitely . . . fitted' that neither is anything less than the interaction of both. The 'creation', the lovemaking, is accomplished not by the plural of two people but by a single, totally 'blended might'.

However, the English language's conception of 'marriage' or 'love' or 'sex' is somewhat biased in favour of what Wordsworth sees in *Nutting* as 'merciless ravage'. It allocates distinct roles to participants who are not expected to become a single activity. It suggests transitive and transitory actions perpetrated by one person upon another. Wordsworth's own conception is one of shared and continuing growth, a union of 'progressive powers', an unqualified compatibility endlessly present: '*is* fitted'. The result of all this is that Wordsworth's 'spousal verse' for *The Excursion* employs a metaphor that resists its meaning. Either the reader forgets the image of marriage and Wordsworth's revelation floats away into abstract obscurity no longer anchored to a concrete example, or the reader *does* think of marriage and is thus confused by associations wholly contrary to Wordsworth's intention. In trying to evoke a kind of marriage that language largely annuls, Wordsworth sounds at best pompous, at worst incomprehensible. If only in his role as a professional writer he did indeed have 'reason to lament/What man has made of man' (*Lines Written in Early Spring*, 23–4; *PW*, IV. 58). His 350 uses of the words 'silent' and 'silence' are eloquent proof that the struggle with language often seemed hopeless.

In woods and waterfalls he found images less hostile than the metaphor of marriage. Descending the Alps he rediscovers 'the ghostly language of the ancient earth' in which 'the darkness and the light' have suffered no divorce, in which the 'tumult and the peace' still accomplish the 'great consummation', in which water and stone remain one voice of 'blended might', in which no linguistic rape has distorted 'the features of the same face' into separate beings or mutilated the blossoms of the one tree into a verbal dissection. It should now be possible to return to Book VI of *The Prelude* and read with less risk of misunderstanding a passage where Wordsworth offers direct commentary upon his own description of the descent from the Alps. These lines are literally self-satisfied and yet explicitly self-forgetful. They celebrate the poet's homecoming to an earth which the dazzling glare of language so often renders invisible:

> Imagination! lifting up itself
> Before the eye and progress of my Song
> Like an unfather'd vapour; here that Power,
> In all the might of its endowments, came
> Athwart me; I was lost as in a cloud,

Halted, without a struggle to break through.
And now recovering, to my Soul I say
I recognise thy glory; in such strength
Of usurpation, in such visitings
Of awful promise, when the light of sense
Goes out in flashes that have shewn to us
The invisible world, doth Greatness make abode.
There harbours whether we be young or old.
Our destiny, our nature, and our home
Is with infinitude, and only there;
With hope it is, hope that can never die,
Effort, and expectation, and desire,
And something evermore about to be.
The mind beneath such banners militant
Thinks not of spoils or trophies, nor of aught
That may attest its prowess, blest in thoughts
That are their own perfection and reward,
Strong in itself, and in the access of joy
Which hides it like the overflowing Nile.

In *The Prelude* this passage is inserted immediately *before* the description of the descent from the Simplon. It seems intended as a kind
of preface, but like many prefaces its helpfulness can perhaps be best
appreciated retrospectively by a reader familiar with the material it
introduces. Beginning with an attempt to label innately plural abili-
ties as a single noun – 'Imagination' – Wordsworth has incited critics
to supply their own disconcerting abstracts as barriers between the
reader and the ensuing poetry. For Hartman it suggests 'consciousness of self raised to apocalyptic pitch',[11] and for Mary Moorman
'the visionary suprarational faculty';[12] but William Empson is surely
right to see Wordsworth as insisting that the world revealed by
'Imagination' to be apocalyptic is also essentially the normal world,
that this visionary light of sense is also a quite literally common
sense:

> *The light goes out* can mean 'light proceeds from the source' as well
> as 'the source fails'. By combining the two, Wordsworth induces
> his baffling *sense* to become a lighthouse occasionally flashing not
> on any spiritual world but on the dangerous and actual sea, which
> at other times is invisible merely because the captain is in
> darkness. . . . The ecstasy both destroys normal *sense* and fulfils it,

and the world thus shown is both the same as and wholly different from the common one.[13]

Wordsworth exploits this ambiguity for the same reason as he again resists a full stop, this time firmly preceding it with the cancelling phrase 'evermore about to be '. He is trying to neutralize language's capacity for partial statements.

The self-generating, 'unfather'd vapour' of the Alps is a cloud which makes the world's all-embracing atmosphere more visible. Wordsworth does not concoct it out of some pettily artistic fancy, but equally his willingness to participate in the world's literally creative 'Imagination' makes the revelation possible. Accepting that his individualistic sense of direction has become 'lost as in a cloud', he finds himself safely breathing in that normally 'invisible world' of air which is inescapably 'Our destiny, our nature, and our home'. Any 'struggle to break through' to a more clearly defined position might be as falsifying as an attempt to draw the line between the air which ebbs and flows inside our lungs and the air whose tides control the supposedly outside world and colour all we see. To respond fully to the pulsing life about us is to turn a blind eye to all such misleading lines and enjoy what *An Evening Walk* calls

> A heart that vibrates evermore, awake
> To feeling for all forms that Life can take,
> That wider still its sympathy extends
> And sees not any line where being ends;
> *(An Evening Walk*, MS 85ff; *PW*, I. 10)

In *The Pedlar's* terms, to self-assertively 'break through' would only be to self-destructively 'break down all grandeur'.

The 'Soul' whose 'glory' Wordsworth recognizes is his own, but he argues elsewhere that no one is incapable of this glory:

> there's not a man
> That lives who hath not had his god-like hours,
> And knows not what majestic sway we have,
> As natural beings in the strength of nature.
> *(The Prelude*, III. 191–4)

This is no personal vanity: the self-assertive, separated ego, the man who distinguishes between himself and the world on which he must make some individualistic mark has abdicated. The 'Soul' whose 'strength of usurpation' has dethroned it is partly what *Tintern Abbey* calls 'the mind of man', but it is essentially not the detached brain of William Wordsworth. Any attempt to prove oneself clever as an individual merely denies the larger pattern in which man can find his true glory. When Wordsworth's mind mistakenly thought of itself as separate and consciously tried to extract an impressive experience from an external landscape, it became so dull that he did not even notice that he *had* crossed the Alps.

However, although the poet's earnest efforts to have an experience may at first make it impossible, their failure does ensure a richer experience later. Here is a further complexity for Wordsworth to try to catch in ambiguous language. The 'Effort, and expectation and desire' and the sense of 'something evermore about to be' are not only the cyclical energy of the world whose life is eventually recognized. They also point to the tourists' original feelings of anticipation, those clumsy intentions which are necessary before they can be thwarted and transformed into revelation.

Words have to function retrospectively and prematurely. 'The dull and heavy slackening' of one kind of effort being frustrated may allow relaxed ears to catch the mutually creative efforts of 'winds thwarting winds'. Wordsworth says that man's mind belongs with cheery expectation: 'With hope it is, hope that can never die', and the repetition encourages a balanced reading. The petty hopes of the man who wished to be told in time that he was about to cross the Alps can in defeat achieve that humbled sensitivity to 'the hope that can never die' of a universe in which he feels at home. The tourist and the soul are no more separate than the placid blue sky and the torrents which flow so tumultuously with the water of past and future storms. The mind reacts to the present with comparisons and contrasts drawn from a bewilderingly different past. The paradox is considered in *The Prelude*, 1.355–61:

> Ah me! that all
> The terrors, all the early miseries
> Regrets, vexations, lassitudes, that all
> The thoughts and feelings which have been infus'd
> Into my mind, should ever have made up
> The calm existence that is mine when I
> Am worthy of myself!

In the Alps, Wordsworth's 'Regrets, vexations, lassitudes' as he discovers the folly of false expectations do play their paradoxical part in creating a more worthwhile 'calm existence', a mind no longer abusing the world by which it was made.

This relaxed and responsive mind sets its sights on no desired conclusion. It acknowledges no full stop between itself and the world it experiences; both are

> something evermore about to be.
> The mind beneath such banners militant
> Thinks not of spoils or trophies, nor of aught
> That may attest its prowess, blest in thoughts
> That are their own perfection and reward,

Wordsworth – and thanks to the title of Book VI, the reader – had wished to cross the Alps for spoils. Like the greedy child of *Nutting*, he was seeking a separable chunk of experience. He was hoping to extract from an endlessly mobile and unified world something static and verbalizable, something to be carried home like a trophy, to be hoarded in the memory and packaged in words for other people, something to attest the prowess of his own rare sensibility. He was trying too hard.

The experience is clearly akin to that of the boy busily attempting a dialogue with hooting owls in *The Prelude*. He too in apparent defeat discovers the living forces of the world about him. Only when a 'pause of silence' has 'baffled his best skill' is 'the visible scene' able to

> enter unawares into his mind,
> With all its solemn imagery, its rocks,
> Its woods, and that uncertain heaven, received
> Into the bosom of the steady lake.
>
> *(The Prelude* (1850), v. 384–8)

Wordsworth's own comment in the 1815 Preface is that at first the boy is too attentive to one particular element, straining his ears for the owl's reply, 'listening with something of a feverish and restless anxiety'. Only when he finds even his 'best skill' foiled, when 'the intenseness of his mind is beginning to remit', is he 'surprised into a perception of the solemn and tranquillising images'.[14] It is at the moment of apparent failure that 'a gentle shock of mild surprise' carries 'far into his heart the voice / Of mountain-torrents' (382–4). So abandoning any attempt to bully the multifarious world into revealing some singular beauty can be a creative surrender. To give up the earnest journey may be to accidentally arrive. The traveller who resigns himself – quite contentedly – to being lost may stumble on the truth.

However, an imaginative realization of the world's true unity requires a relaxed helplessness through which defeat is admitted not only by the complacent tourist but also by the confident word-spinner. Wordsworth's invocation to imagination is partly a self-defeating attempt to describe how the older poet who is writing *The Prelude* feels when he actually abandons the attempt to describe his younger self's experience in the Alps. What Wordsworth here help-lessly calls 'Imagination' almost defines itself as the collapse of what critics often mean by a 'poetic' or 'creative imagination'. The 1850 version of *The Prelude* here is even more dauntingly explicit:

> Imagination – here the Power so called
> Through *sad incompetence of human speech*,
> That awful Power rose from the mind's abyss
> Like an unfather'd vapour that enwraps,
> At once, some lonely traveller. I was lost;
> Halted without an effort to break through;
> But to my conscious soul I now can say –
> 'I recognise thy glory:'
>
> (The Prelude (1850), 592–9, my italics)

Wordsworth wishes to write about the value of being 'Halted', about the discoveries available to one who abandons his own distracting 'struggle to break through'; but his dilemma is that writing itself involves that struggle, that the 'progress' of his 'Song' would be halted too if he were to be loyal to the state of mind he is espousing, that glory is discovered in a responsive silence which is hardly conveyed by words like 'Imagination'. The sad incompetence of human speech restlessly seeks the right word, earnestly journeys towards a truth that as a destination cannot exist.

So *The Prelude* momentarily advances to express its liberation from the temptation to advance, only to discover the overidentifica-tion with the 'unfetter'd clouds' wraps all statement into silence. The subsequent 'effort, and expectation, and desire' are thus partly the 'recovering' poet's rededication to the almost impossible task of deploying language to discredit itself. The implication is that those apparent inconsistencies into which the verse must contort itself in confronting the Vale of Gondo are not the clumsy products of a feckless poet but the strenuously achieved paradoxes of a remarkably industrious one. The intellectual laziness is presumably in those who think it easy to discriminate:

> to class the cabinet
> Of their sensations, and in voluble phrase,
> Run through the history and birth of each,
> As of a single independent thing.   (*The Prelude*, II. 228–31)

The glib compartmentalizing of our feelings makes us fantasize that the world which we inhabit can also be split and sorted into pigeonholes. This is almost the opposite of the 'realism' it claims to be, and compared to Wordsworth's 'Imagination' it is a

> false secondary power, by which,
> In weakness, we create distinctions, then
> Deem that our puny boundaries are things
> Which we perceive, and not which we have made.
>   (*The Prelude*, II. 221–24)

Elsewhere Wordsworth admits to 'feeble' moments when he himself weakened into 'sitting thus in judgement' so as to discriminate reality into a series of illusory pictures:

> pleas'd
> Unworthily, disliking here, and there,
> Liking, by rules of mimic art transferr'd
> To things above all art. . . .

> . . .

> giving way
> To a comparison of scene with scene
> Bent overmuch on superficial things,
> Pampering myself with meagre novelties
> Of colour or proportion,   (*The Prelude*, XI. 148–65)

At such times he was absurdly trying to contain forces whose nature he admits is to 'overflow with passion and with life'. It seems inevitable that a poet who saw the earth in such terms should describe the poetry in which he tries to do it justice as 'the spontaneous overflow of powerful feelings'.

The constant references to water in Wordsworth's imagery, like those to music or to breath, try to force implications of indissoluble fluidity from a verbal medium which tends to fixed definitions. The poet who crosses the Alps finds that verbalization may satisfy the mind's desire to 'attest its prowess', but tends to confine apprehensions to a falsely narrow channel. At its most potent the mind floats beyond these 'puny boundaries': 'Strong in itself, and in the access of joy / Which hides it like the overflowing Nile.' The final image is powerful indeed. The river that loses its identity, bursting through the defining banks that usually mark its individual course, is at its strongest. The earth which surrenders itself to the flood releases its own latent fertility. Abandoning all sense of its own landmarks, the mind, in its very lack of self-consciousness, discovers its own glory and that of the world which flows through it. No longer trying to confine itself within the usual 'incompetence of human speech', it joins 'the types and symbols of Eternity'. It expands to enjoy 'thoughts that are their own perfection' and seek no further definition. It merges apparently distinct observations into 'workings of one mind', and itself achieves the fluent stasis of the waterfall's stationary blast.

IV

It is something of a shock after all this to remember that Wordsworth had at his side, throughout his descent from the Simplon, the man who was then his closest friend. Robert Jones – 'fat and roundabout and rosy', according to Dorothy,[15] and 'a most affectionate man', according to William[16] – must have been a fairly palpable presence at the time. Yet he is barely visible in *The Prelude*'s description. Of course, the person chosen as the most likeable companion with whom to share a holiday could hardly be represented as just another inseparable aspect of the unified cosmos. He had been singled out from all those students who happened to be the right age to be up at Cambridge at the same time as Wordsworth. The affectionate instinct to make such a choice is very different from that inclusiveness of vision which Wordsworth learns to accept on discovering that they had already crossed the Alps. In claiming that 'the brook and road / Were fellow-travellers in this gloomy Pass', the poet's anthropomorphism implies analogies that simply will not hold. The feelings that lead the two men to keep each other company are essentially unlike the impersonal patterns of geography which cause the routes

of river and road to sometimes coincide. The poetry of indistinguishable 'Tumult and peace' has to forget Wordsworth's own
choice of a compatible 'fellow-traveller'.

Moreover, Jones could not be mistaken for a type or symbol of
eternity because the mortality of a person for whom one particularly
cares is hard to ignore. Preciousness evokes fragility, and the Alpine
landscape, for creatures whose survival depends on warmth and food
and shelter, is strikingly inhospitable. Indeed a rejected manuscript
version acknowledges incontrovertible evidence that the route followed by the two friends was downright dangerous:

> And ever as we halted, or crept on,
> Huge fragments of primaeval mountain spread
> In powerless ruin, blocks as huge aloft
> Impending, nor permitted yet to fall,
> The sacred death-cross, monument forlorn
> Though frequent of the perish'd Traveller,

The 'sad incompetence of human speech' with its finite tendency to
trail away into a full stop may be woefully inappropriate to the joy of
natural forces whose relationships are 'without end'; but there is an
equally saddening competence about our ability to mark with
wooden cross or verbal elegy the one point on a man's journey where
he ceased. The lines were presumably cut because they had found it
so easy to articulate that poignantly clear distinction between an
eternal earth and the vulnerable human beings who so briefly travel
upon it.

Yet the 'monument forlorn' to each forgotten individual who has
lost his life does intrude its surviving echo upon the published poem
where it is 'Winds thwarting winds' that sound 'bewilder'd and
forlorn'. This, of course, tells us more about the poet's ear than the
winds' intention. What such natural forces actually assert is no more,
if no less, than the fact of their own eternal life. It is not the resident
winds but only the intruding human beings who can feel 'bewilder'd
and forlorn'. Only *homo sapiens* needs that sense of direction which,
when it is defeated, can make us feel that we have been abandoned in a
confusing wilderness. Only human minds are so alert to pathos that
they can sense in the random collision of strangers a 'thwarting' of
those highly personal relationships for which we yearn. Only human
ears are so attuned to affection that they can hear 'forlorn' echoes of
that loneliness which seems so often to be both the origin and the

aftermath of our attempts to meet each other. So the forlorn winds, like the 'gloomy Pass' itself, are indeed pathetic fallacies: they admit the actual pathos of humanity while falsely suggesting that the natural world can share it.

The pathetic fact is that our tenderness for each other finds no support in the world where our bodies have to dwell and where our minds may as well try to feel at home. Winds and waterfalls can remain 'symbols of Eternity' because their all-embracing voice is never distracted by the wish to mark one particular spot as the place where some irreplaceably individual traveller perished. To keep pace with such a world, *The Prelude* passage not only needs to leave behind any reference to those 'frequent' crosses; it also needs to abandon any audible concern for the present travelling companion and his friendship: to have kept Jones in mind might have evoked how much more vulnerably we care about each other than do the trees of one wood, or the 'blossoms upon one tree'. So Jones is perhaps ignored in the Alps passage not because Wordsworth cared so little for him but because he cared so much. Calm acceptance of the larger love could hardly have survived too much attention to that more selective affection which sees another person as precious because he is different. Serene faith in the universal harmony is not wholly consistent with protectively ensuring that your friend does not break his neck on some inconveniently dangerous Alpine crag. Doing justice to his feelings for Jones would have required a second voice, and for once Wordsworth chose to confine himself to one.

'Crossing the Alps' chooses to see the natural world as the site of everything except human relationships, which have been comfortably forgotten. In a converse poem, Wordsworth's character wishes to see that world as nothing but the graveyard of a love affair which is obsessively remembered. Standing where he and the woman whom he loved used to stand together, the bereaved lover demands that the scene should reflect the loss which he feels. It is a demand which, by definition, must fall on deaf ears:

> 'Ye leaves,
> When will that dying murmur be suppress'd?
> Your sound my heart of peace bereaves,
> It robs my heart of rest'.
>
> ('*'Tis said, that some have died for love*',
> 21–4; *PW*, II.33: *app. crit.*)

The wood which superficially seems to be 'dying' through its leaves is, of course, 'never to be decay'd'. By its very nature, and by the nature of everything else except humanity, it cannot record the defeat of affectionate hope. Those natural laws which we long to see as supportive can speak only to the 'hope that can never die'. To demand otherwise is to ask for the impossible:

> 'Roll back, sweet Rill! back to thy mountain bounds,
> And there for ever be thy waters chain'd!
> For thou does haunt the air with sounds
> That cannot be sustain'd;
> If still beneath that pine-tree's ragged bough
> Headlong yon waterfall must come,
> Oh let it then be dumb! –
> Be any thing, sweet Rill, but that which thou art now.'
>
> (29–36)

The river 'of first and last, and midst, and without end' whispers promises which, for mortal lovers, 'cannot be sustain'd'. The 'stationary blast' can never speak to the dumb stasis of human grief because a waterfall's stability is compelled to thunder an eternity of movement.

Yet the poem tries to offer more than the bleak certainties of the bereaved lover's monologue. The speech-marks close and the poet's own voice supplies an interestingly uncertain comment. Wordsworth notes that, although ' 'Tis said, that some have died for love', nature can sustain our physical lives long after it has deprived our affections of their object: 'The man who makes this feverish complaint' is still vigorously healthy, and will clearly have many years in which to waste the gift of life mourning his beloved's death. So Wordsworth prays that he himself can learn not to care even about the woman with whom he had enjoyed 'Such happiness' that very day:

> Ah gentle Love! if ever thought was thine
> To store up kindred hours for me, thy face
> Turn from me, gentle Love, nor let me walk
> Within the sound of Emma's voice, or know
> Such happiness as I have known to-day.   (45–52)

The 'if' clause tries to make conditional what, for at least one of any pair of lovers, must be a certain destiny: Wordsworth or Emma will be left to mourn the other, unless of course they learn in time how not to love.

The 'feverish complaint' against mortality by the bereaved lover and the serene celebration of eternity which Wordsworth arrives at after 'Crossing the Alps' are both untypical. Each allows us to hear one of Wordsworth's two voices speaking in lucid isolation. In ignoring each other's claims, each is able to achieve an uncharacteristically unified, and less disturbingly complex, voice.

So many other Wordsworth poems do indeed offer two voices because they, with courageous honesty, insist on saying two quite different things. One of the Lucy poems – *Three Years She Grew* – is openly a dialogue. Nature's voice, serenely inclusive, summons Lucy to unity with the living universe:

> And hers shall be the breathing balm
> And hers the silence and the calm
> Of mute insensate things.   (*PW*, II. 215, 16–18)

'Even in the motions of the storm' there will be forces to 'mould' her individuality until it merges with the world. She will join the clouds and rivers whose 'beauty born of murmuring sound / Shall pass into her face' (29–30). She will relapse in fact into her proper role as just one of 'the features' on the living landscape's 'same face'. But nature's voice is interrupted by another. The second voice speaks with a poignantly human awareness of Lucy as one whose preciousness was dependent on her being individual and irreplaceable:

> Thus Nature spake – The work was done –
> How soon my Lucy's race was run!
> She died, and left to me
> This heath, this calm, and quiet scene,
> The memory of what has been,
> And never more will be.   (37–42)

'She died'. If wise passiveness does mean Lucy's sinking back into 'the calm / Of mute insensate things' then it is a kind of suicide. Becoming a type or symbol of eternity may benefit the beloved, but it leaves the lover unhappily aware 'of what has been / And never more will be'.

The difficulty is confronted in another of the Lucy poems, *Strange Fits of Passion Have I Known*. Here Wordsworth, though riding to visit his girlfriend, is initially in a very different frame of mind from the anxious protectiveness of the young lover. He seems much closer to *Tintern Abbey*'s 'serene and blessed mood' in which

> we are laid asleep
> In body, and become a living soul:
> While with an eye made quiet by the power
> Of harmony, and the deep power of joy,
> We see into the life of things.   (*PW*, II. 260, 45–9)

The young lover in wise passiveness allows himself to be carried along by his horse: 'My horse moved on; hoof after hoof / He raised and never stopped' (*PW*, II. 29, 21–2). He seems dozily unaware of where he is going, content to let the horse determine the pace: Wordsworth even has 'My horse *trudg'd* on' in early versions. There is none of the urgent impatience that one might expect of such a love-poem; Browning's *Meeting at Night* is one obvious contrast. Few mistresses would be flattered by this account of their lover's mood as he travelled towards them: 'In one of those sweet dreams I slept, / Kind Nature's gentlest boon!' (17–18). The profitably lost traveller of the Alps would understand. Focus on a specified destination would only mean failure to arrive at imaginative experience. But this is only one voice. It is suddenly interrupted by another, a voice which sees reality's once precious gift as the – until now ignored – Lucy: '"O mercy!" to myself I cried, / "If Lucy should be dead!"' (27–8). The voice 'made quiet by the power of harmony' may 'see into the life of things'; but the cry of human tenderness is painfully aware of the death which seems to reduce, rather than exalt, the beloved to a thing.

   In yet another Lucy poem she ends up 'Rolled round in earth's diurnal course, / With rocks and stones and trees'. Here the profound duality of Wordsworth's position turns on the ambiguity of the one word 'She'. Does it refer to his own potentially fretful ego blessedly laid asleep or to the beloved Lucy cruelly being exterminated?

> A slumber did my spirit seal;
>   I had no human fears:
> She seemed a thing that could not feel
>   The touch of earthly years.
>
> No motion has she now, no force;
>   She neither hears nor sees;

> Rolled round in earth's diurnal course,
> With rocks, and stones, and trees.
> *(A Slumber did my Spirit Seal; PW,* II.216)

If the 'She' of the third line refers to Wordsworth's 'spirit', then the poem celebrates a triumphant reunion with the trees and rocks of the Simplon Pass revelation. His spirit's inability to hear and see is in that case part of the positive paradox in which we must be 'laid asleep / In body' before we can 'become a living soul', in which we must have 'an eye made quiet' before we can 'see into the life of things', in which greedily gaping tourists must admit defeat before they can join the Alps as triumphant symbols of eternity. If, on the other hand, 'She' is a person loved by the speaker, then the poem mourns the loss of someone seen as far more valuable than the trees and rocks to which death reduces her. In that case her inability to hear and see matters partly because of the speaker's egocentric regret that she can no longer be aware of *him*, that her love can no longer function to limit his loneliness. The greatness of the poem is that its two voices articulate both as feelings which coexist in the speaker.

Wordsworth's best verse speaks to both instincts. It insists that the strength of feeling which accompanies them proves that neither can be dismissed in favour of the other. At the most instinctual level, we recognize both the magnificence of the integrated universe *and* the preciousness of the few people that we set apart from it:

> Two feelings have we also from the first,
> Of grandeur and of tenderness;
> We live by admiration and by love.
> *(The Prelude,* p. 571, 1–3)

❋ 2 ❋

THE WEAKNESS OF
HUMANITY

'THE RUINED COTTAGE' AND 'THE PEDLAR'

I

Wordsworth's greatest narrative poems are about people whose love
for each other threatens to make them blind and deaf to everything
else. In looking to just one person, they put at risk 'all the mighty
world / Of eye and ear, – both what they half create, / And what
perceive' (*Tintern Abbey*, 105–7; *PW*, II. 262). The infinitely various
'symbols of Eternity' may be obliterated by pain about the mortality of a single human relationship.

The Ruined Cottage, *The Idiot Boy* and *Michael* are all ambivalent
towards the value of living so intensely, and yet so dangerously. But
they vary enormously in plot, structure and tone, debating the
paradox with quite different effects. *The Idiot Boy* is a comedy,
where a mother's surrender to blind anxiety is sufficiently temporary
to be funny. Its title amusedly tolerates her own doting view that the
centre of the universe is her subnormal son. But the title also asserts
the significance to the reader of a child who, through being undistracted by normal human relationships, may be able to see more than
any other character in the poem. *Michael*, though its story is potentially tragic, records the triumph of a wider vision over the latent
destructiveness of love between people. Its title does not centre on
Luke, the beloved son who is lost, but identifies with the father's
survival, his strength – based on a larger love – to go on being Michael
even without Luke. By contrast *The Ruined Cottage* is bleakly
centred on a broken home. Its title – like its heroine, Margaret – is
confined to a place which appears to exclude the possibility of values
which survive, and to evoke only the sense of loss to which she has
reduced her vision of the world. So the earliest of Wordsworth's
great narrative poems confronts an extreme which sets it apart
from those that followed. It expresses a solemn fear that the very

tenderness it respects can become utterly destructive – a chilling defect in our nature, to be seen, in the gravest sense, as 'the weakness of humanity'.

The Ruined Cottage tells the story of a woman who lives only for the man she loves. Abandoned by him, she gradually loses the will to care for all that in happier times they had together cherished. In her distracted imagination the landscape dwindles to a sterile vacuum. But in fact its fertility grows even more potently dynamic. Its weeds engulf her untended garden. Its weather reaches within her neglected house. Yet still Margaret clings to the place because of the 'one torturing hope' of her husband's return. She stays to die of exposure to a world which she ignores, sacrificing literally everything to her baffled love. Her defiance of reality has the noble pathos and the frightening impracticality of a fight against hopeless odds. So the pity and fear aroused by classical tragedy could give Margaret our awed respect. But, as Jonathan Wordsworth says in the fullest published commentary on the poem, *The Ruined Cottage* records 'a relationship pointlessly destroyed, a relationship which one is convinced could have made for great happiness'.[1] Thus Margaret's story is also potentially a more modern tragedy of waste.

However, this approach can confuse the poem itself with Margaret's story, a story which it in fact carefully contains within a dramatic framework. *The Ruined Cottage* is much more than a tragedy. Indeed it would be more accurate to say that it is *about* tragedy. It explicitly questions the value of interpreting human life in tragic terms. Although Margaret's grief is given a curious dignity by its squalid ruins, our own habits of feeling are unflatteringly challenged. Margaret's story, like most tragedy, is the exaggeration of humanity. It tells of someone driven to pathetic extremes or inspired to frightening excess, but such emotive hyperboles are more the stuff of the stories we tell than the lives we actually lead. Though we too can lose any sense of the realities that surround us, we are more often blinded by trivia than tragedy. It is more likely to be petty egotism than impassioned love which narrows the landscape of our minds. The relationship between that fatuous egotism with which we value our individualistic selves and the apparently admirable sympathy through which we try to identify with another individual's suffering is one of the more elusive issues probed by *The Ruined Cottage*. The poem compels us to approach Margaret's uncommon intensity of grief through a dramatic framework grounded in two kinds of common sense. Neither the Pedlar, who tells her story, nor the Poet, who listens to it, are tragic figures.

The poem opens with an irritable Poet who is fed up with the countryside through which he is wearily walking. His sulking disregard for all that surrounds him makes him doubly blind. He cannot pattern the landscape's features into 'the types and symbols of Eternity'. Nor can he spot amongst them the one isolated image of human mortality, the ruined cottage. His vision has the narrowed concentration of someone for whom life is no more than a psychic assault course:

> Across a bare wide Common I had toiled
> With languid feet which by the slipp'ry ground
> Were baffled still, and when I stretched myself
> On the brown earth my limbs from very heat
> Could find no rest, nor my weak arm disperse
> The insect host which gathered round my face
> And joined their murmurs to the tedious noise
> Of seeds of bursting gorse that crackled round.   (19–26)

The treacherous earth and sweltering air, the buzzing insects and the crackling gorse are all interdependent aspects of the same scene. The one, long sentence which deploys them stresses their shared and cumulative effect; but their unity is not so much a welcoming chorus as a hostile conspiracy. The natural world, instead of inviting participation, seems to reject the human intruder.

In feeling that the landscape is no more than a nuisance, the Poet trivializes its impact and his own emotions. The attempt to conquer nature, though shown to be a battle against hopeless odds, is almost laughably ignoble. There can be few heroics in fighting an 'insect host'. This pugnacious approach to the world diminishes human vision until man sees nothing but his own discomfort. How much is obscured by the Poet's egocentricity here is to be revealed in his meeting with the Pedlar, whose first words are: 'I see around me here / Things which you cannot see' (67–8). To some extent the process parallels 'Crossing the Alps'. The ear which hears only the discord of 'tedious noise' will be tuned into harmony. The eye, whose short-sightedness sees only 'a bare wide Common', will focus. Listening to the Pedlar, the Poet will learn to see the landscape as an elaborately energetic spectacle in which he belongs. The world, where his restless mind at first 'Could find no rest', will in the last

words of the poem be shown to supply on this day, as on all days,
'our evening resting-place'.

In 'Crossing the Alps' there is only this one, essentially unified,
point which blundering egotism has at first missed. The landscape of
The Ruined Cottage is less certainly integrated. As early as the title
we are warned to look beneath the grandeur of unified nature for the
relics of individual men and women. So here the Poet is to make
two, potentially conflicting discoveries, both of which have been
obscured by his initial peevishness. Unconsciously sensing that the
world must offer relief if rightly approached, the Poet stumbles
towards the shade of some elm trees and finds himself at the ruin of a
house. It is at first as blank an image to him as the rest of the scene:
'four naked walls / That stared upon each other' (31–2). In their
nakedness, these human signs seem as barren of meaning as did the
'bare' common over which he has just toiled. The walls that look only
at each other seem to be locked into some private game like that of the
flies who 'joined their murmurs' to the sounds of gorse. The living
landscape and the decaying artefact seem equally closed.

But then the Pedlar appears. He is an old and trusted friend and
will show two ways in which this apparently stultifying scene can be
powerfully emotive. Not only can it be seen as an accessible, and yet
infinite, game through which one can be relaxed from one's fretful
individualism. Paradoxically, it can also evoke the poignant concentration with which people do value each other as individuals. The
ruin in which the two men meet is remembered by the Pedlar as the
home of people he knew and liked. So he at first reveals the place's
significance not as a symbol of eternity, but as an intimation of
mortality:

> I see around me here
> Things which you cannot see. We die, my Friend,
> Nor we alone, but that which each man loved
> And prized in his peculiar nook of earth
> Dies with him, or is changed, and very soon
> Even of the good is no memorial left.
> The Poets, in their elegies and songs
> Lamenting the departed, call the groves,
> They call upon the hills and streams to mourn,
> And senseless rocks – nor idly, for they speak
> In these their invocations with a voice

> Obedient to the strong creative power
> Of human passion. (67–79)

The pathetic fallacy does misrepresent the natural world (rocks are in fact 'senseless', and incapable of suffering). Yet it also articulates a great truth about human emotion. Love longs for a world in which its needs are answered, rather than frustrated.

The value that people put on a particular person or a specific place may in fact be an anomaly in a vast and interdependent universe. But 'the strong creative power / Of human passion' transforms our vision of the world. Concentrating so much love on such frail specifics forces us to blur the truth that we, and those we love, must die. Love, based on the joyful hope that a relationship can last for ever, is itself a pathetic fallacy about the world in which it struggles to survive. When a relationship is defeated by death, we inevitably fantasize that our disappointment too is natural enough to have the world's support.

The Pedlar sees this fantasy about the natural environment as representing an essential fact about human nature. Because this 'peculiar nook of earth' reminds him of people for whom he cared, he does not wish to acknowledge that it is now an indistinguishable part of the general landscape. To do so would be to deny the truth of his own feelings:

> Beside yon spring I stood,
> And eyed its waters till we seemed to feel
> One sadness, they and I. For them a bond
> Of brotherhood is broken; time has been
> When every day the touch of human hand
> Disturbed their stillness, and they ministered
> To human comfort. When I stooped to drink
> A spider's web hung to the water's edge,
> And on the wet and slimy foot-stone lay
> The useless fragment of a wooden bowl.
> It moved my very heart. (82–92)

The Pedlar's own emotion is certain. But it is merely in his imagination that the environment shares that emotion. The spring only 'seemed to feel' the loss. In reality it now provides the home for 'A spider's web' with the same unwitting co-operativeness as it once 'ministered / To human comfort'. The undiscriminating waters never understood their relationship with people in the essentially human terms of a 'brotherhood'. So they cannot grieve over that relationship being broken as the Pedlar must. To him, everything in this place can seem reduced to a 'useless fragment' by the absence of the people who gave it value. But, unlike the artefact of a wooden bowl, the natural world never does perish into fragments: it simply reforms its endless life into new patterns.

The Poet has already noticed that as the spring closes to human use it is opening to the plants: 'a well / Half-covered up with willow-flowers and grass' (62–3). To man, the place for which he cares as the home of personal relationship may vanish. Yet it also demonstrably continues to exist in a changed form: 'his peculiar nook of earth / Dies with him, or is changed'. The alternatives cannot be mutually exclusive if we are to be true to both ourselves and our world. The pathetic fallacy articulates one truth. But the ecological shifts that benefit the spider, and the willow-flowers and the grass exemplify an equally accurate vision. The dramatic framework invites us to identify with a Poet who is at first doubly ignorant. Unaware of the tragedy that has happened here, he sees no human significance in the place. Irritated by heat and flies, he is equally oblivious of the natural harmonies which are maintaining life on the site of death. As he listens to the Pedlar's story, the eavesdropping reader is lured towards both ways of seeing.

II

The Pedlar begins the story of Margaret's life with a repeated emphasis on her death. The fact that she is dead is set in the context of nature's continuing energy:

> She is dead,
> The worm is on her cheek, and this poor hut,   *etc.*
> Stripped of its outward garb of household flowers,
> Of rose and sweet-briar, offers to the wind
> A cold bare wall whose earthy top is tricked
> With weeds and the rank spear-grass. She is dead,
> And nettles rot and adders sun themselves
> Where we have sate together while she nursed
> Her infant at her breast. The unshod Colt,
> The wandering heifer and the Potter's ass,

Find shelter now within the chimney-wall
Where I have seen her evening hearth-stone blaze
And through the window spread upon the road
Its chearful light. You will forgive me, Sir,
But often on this cottage do I muse
As on a picture, till my wiser mind
Sinks, yielding to the foolishness of grief.   (103–19)

The Pedlar gives fair warning of the poem's ultimate duality by
describing grief as 'foolishness'. But the overriding impression at this
point is of unambiguous respect for humanity. The non-human
world's disrespect ('The worm is on her cheek') only emphasizes the
almost reverent intensity with which people can care for each other.
The plurals of more impersonal species seem excessively fertile and
self-indulgent: 'nettles rot and adders sun themselves'. By contrast
the singularity of human tenderness is epitomized in 'she nursed/
Her infant at her breast'. The 'weeds and the rank spear-grass' will
reappear at the end of the poem with explicitly opposed connotations. But here they suggest only an irreverence which, on Margaret's
and our own behalf, we resent. Because of them, the cruelly 'stripped' wall is not just anthropomorphically exposed to a rapist wind,
but tricked out with grotesquely gay decorations as if compelled to
celebrate its own humiliation.

   Yet nature, which now seems so callous, once had a very different
image in this place. The Pedlar remembers a time when it was the
palpable source of the family's livelihood, and of Margaret's pride in
her husband. From the wool of sheep and the produce of the garden,
Robert's work built happiness:

                    I have heard her say
That he was up and busy at his loom
In summer ere the mower's scythe had swept
The dewy grass, and in the early spring
Ere the last star had vanished. They who passed
At evening, from behind the garden-fence
Might hear his busy spade, which he would ply
After his daily work till the day-light
Was gone, and every leaf and flower were lost
In the dark hedges. So they passed their days
In peace and comfort,   (121–31)

Robert matters to the Pedlar because he mattered to Margaret. The narrative framework extends this pattern in which the significance of one person depends on his preciousness in the eyes of another. Just as the Pedlar remembers only what he 'heard her say' about Robert, so we hear only what the Pedlar's affection leads him to say about Margaret.

Such selective tenderness must struggle to function in a world swayed by hugely undiscriminating forces. The weather, for instance, is innately fickle. The agricultural economy on which Robert and Margaret depend is rocked by 'Two blighting seasons when the fields were left/With half a harvest' (134–5). The larger human society (or the God who is supposed to oversee it) conspires with the vagaries of nature: 'It pleased heaven to add / A worse affliction in the plague of war' (135–6). The ensuing recession drastically reduces Robert's earning power as a weaver, and an illness forces him to spend what little savings he had prepared against such times. Retreating from the humiliation of not being able to support his family, he withdraws into neurosis.

His madness is revealed partly by behaviour that defies the natural world, and partly by wild treatment of the people he loves. He muddles up 'the various tasks/Of summer, autumn, winter, and of spring', searching for 'any casual task/Of use or ornament' with an 'uneasy novelty' (166–71). To his family he is equally inconsistent. He lurches between growling at his children and entertaining them with manic games: 176 – 85.

> And he would leave his home, and to the town
> Without an errand would he turn his steps,
> Or wander here and there among the fields.
> One while he would speak lightly of his babes
> And with a cruel tongue, at other times
> He played with them wild freaks of merriment
> And 'twas a piteous thing to see the looks
> Of the poor innocent children. 'Every smile',
> Said Margaret to me here beneath these trees,
> 'Made my heart bleed.'   (176–85)

She speaks 'beneath these trees', trees which were as unmoved by her words then as they are by the Pedlar's now. They will maintain this aloofness until the end of the poem when the Poet offers his final thoughts 'beneath the trees', listening to birds singing in 'those lofty elms' (528–31). Jonathan Wordsworth convincingly argues that the 'imperturbability' of trees which are 'unconcerned and unaffected' by the suffering of people is meant to typify 'general Nature, into which both Margaret and her garden are assimilated'.[2] Here, however, Margaret's 'piteous' insight isolates her not only from the trees beneath which she lives but also from the people whom she loves. Like the Pedlar, we are compelled to see the children through Margaret's pain. Their happiness can seem to us either a pitiable ignorance or an enviable innocence, but as adults we are unable to share it. Robert, in regressing to do so, may persuade himself that he has no more need of a language for grief than his children; but his inarticulate 'freaks of merriment' also prevent any dialogue with his wife's love. Her painfully direct speech which sees 'Every smile' – whether the children's or Robert's – as cause for grief can only be made to a visitor who will try to remain as impassive as the surrounding trees.

It is at this point of looming tragedy that the Pedlar interrupts his story. He turns from the finally unbalanced Robert to his own precariously balanced responses. He has a tear for human tragedy, but also the sanity to question the value of tears amongst 'The calm of Nature': 185– 98

> At this the old Man paused,
> And looking up to those enormous elms
> He said, ''Tis now the hour of deepest noon.
> At this still season of repose and peace,
> This hour when all things which are not at rest
> Are chearful, while this multitude of flies
> Fills all the air with happy melody,
> Why should a tear be in an old man's eye?
> Why should we thus with an untoward mind,
> And in the weakness of humanity,
> From natural wisdom turn our hearts away,
> To natural comfort shut our eyes and ears,
> And, feeding on disquiet, thus disturb
> The calm of Nature with our restless thoughts?' (185–98)

He shares 'the weakness of humanity', the imaginativeness which not only feels for another's suffering, but also destructively infests the present calm with 'restless thoughts' about past misfortunes. But he is not resigned to that weakness. The 'insect host' that the Poet fought as enemies (23–4) can be recognized as contributing their own 'happy melody' to the harmonious 'calm of Nature'.

Other yearnings do balance our intense response to the preciousness of an individual human life. Such a life must always end in death. Even while it lasts, it may be overtaken by events which turn our concern to grief. So our equally intense capacity to long for 'repose and peace', for a calm beyond our 'restless thoughts' is properly recognized by the Pedlar here. The world is so vast that to concentrate on a single human relationship is to 'shut our eyes and ears'. Wordsworth's syntax for the time being limits the Pedlar to asking questions, but the assertions he will be allowed to make as the poem closes are already hinted. He fears that such tales turn our hearts away from a generously complex world where 'all things which are not at rest / Are chearful'.

III

Yet at this point the dramatic framework also invites us to approach Margaret's story from a quite different point of view. The Poet is already too emotionally involved with Margaret to allow the story to drop: 206-8

> In my own despite
> I thought of that poor woman as of one
> Whom I had known and loved.   (206–8)

In spite of the discomfort he is bound to feel if he hears the rest of the story, he feels Margaret's reality too intensely to restrain his curiosity. He can guess that her story will be tragic. So, in begging the Pedlar to continue, he is literally asking for trouble. Margaret's suffering is safely over, but if the Pedlar is persuaded to recall it in vivid narrative, it will come to life again in the sympathetic pain of the listening Poet. This resurrection of pain is what the Poet seeks. His position is in fact no stranger than that of the audience for any tragedy. We too, in reading the poem, choose to explore truths about human passion through this odd process of self-inflicted pain. 'Passion', as Wordsworth once observed, 'is derived from a word which signifies *suffering*' (*PW*, II. 427).

Wordsworth's one play, *The Borderers*, is subtitled as *A Tragedy*. In it he makes Oswald argue that

> Great actions move our admiration, chiefly
> Because they carry in themselves an earnest
> That we can suffer greatly.   (*PW*, I. 188, 1536–8)

Tragic action, according to Oswald, reveals emotions which seem to transcend mortality:

> Action is transitory – a step, a blow,
> The motion of a muscle – this way or that –
> 'Tis done, and in the after-vacancy
> We wonder at ourselves like men betrayed:
> Suffering is permanent, obscure and dark,
> And shares the nature of infinity.   (*PW*, I. 188, 1539–44)

But Oswald is the villain, and *The Borderers* is anyway one of Wordsworth's less coherent works. So we should be wary of how we apply this magnificent rhetoric. *The Ruined Cottage* chooses not to follow Robert after his disastrous decision to leave home. We learn nothing of how far 'in the after-vacancy' he has to live with the knowledge that his action has betrayed not only his family but also himself. The poem prefers to probe its terms more thoughtfully, and to challenge simplistic assertions like 'Suffering is permanent'. To Margaret, her own suffering may seem permanent: it lasts as long as her life. But to the Pedlar, her suffering can seem to have been ended by her death. Perhaps a human being shares 'the nature of infinity' most when least distracted by the preciousness of one person. Love, *The Ruined Cottage* suggests, is tragic precisely because it makes us need a fellow creature whose life is essentially finite. It is only a pathetic fallacy that love, or the suffering it causes, 'shares the nature of infinity'.

Yet it is, in the most precise sense, human nature to cling to that fallacy. We cling so tenaciously that tragedy can convince us of the value of human relationship in the very act of recording its inevitable destruction. *The Prelude* tries to verbalize the paradox offered by tragic literature:

> Sorrow that is not sorrow, but delight,
> And miserable love that is not pain
> To hear of, for the glory that redounds
> Therefrom to human kind and what we are.   (XII. 245–8)

But in *The Ruined Cottage*, Wordsworth faces the fact that sorrow really is sorrow and is thus forced to a more complex investigation of 'what we are'. There are other glories available to human kind, and we may lose them in our eagerness to hear of love intense enough to make us miserable. So the Pedlar is reluctant to satisfy the Poet's curiosity, and questions our faith in sympathy. Our human desire to care for each other's suffering could become a destructive masochism. If none of us put any restraints on our tenderness, even for dead strangers, an endless chain reaction of bereavement would engulf all human experience in misery.

Fortunately perhaps, full identification is impossible. The fierce selectivity of Margaret's love for Robert does echo against our own feelings. But an echo is a fading sound. Even the Pedlar's sympathy for a woman whom he knew is not so great as to fully duplicate her pain. The Poet may think that he feels with Margaret as someone he too 'had known and loved'. But his love is limited. The pain felt by Margaret in her rashly unlimited love for Robert cannot be fully shared. Even if we do all long to find and keep someone who seems uniquely precious, it is only for Margaret that Robert can be that irreplaceably valuable person. Her ruined cottage is an already crumbling image of a specific love which will eventually vanish from the earth.

Tragedy strives to build a positive generalization from the ruins of specifics. But its building resembles a museum whose faded collection of fragments insists on the mortality of all its preserves:

> We die, my Friend
> Nor we alone, but that which each man loved
> And prized in his peculiar nook of earth
> Dies with him, or is changed, and very soon
> Even of the good is no memorial left.   (68–72)

The Pedlar sees the ruined cottage not just as a place of death, but also of continuing, if changed, life. By the end of the poem he will argue that 'what we feel of sorrow and despair / From ruin and from change' can be 'an idle dream' (520–3). His terms are precise. Sorrow for Margaret becomes a delusion if it tends towards identification with her despair. What we may pity as ruin for her can also be for us an image of change; so the Pedlar agrees to continue the story. Though it is bound to stimulate the Poet's concern with one person, it may also reveal how much such tenderness obscures.

IV

The Pedlar recalls his visiting the cottage to find Margaret's love turned to grief. There is already only one way the world can answer to her needs: 254 - 7

> With fervent love, and with a face of grief
> Unutterably helpless, and a look
> That seemed to cling upon me, she enquired
> If I had seen her husband.   (254–7)

Robert has secretly sold himself into the army, leaving the one sum of money he has thus been able to earn where Margaret will find it after he has gone. This terrible miscalculation about what his wife really needs has not diminished her love. The Pedlar remembers her words as expressing more pity for Robert than for herself: 'Poor man, he had not heart/To take a farewell of me' (270–1). Robert cannot bear to face the woman he thinks he has failed. He does not recognize that he is in fact the victim of forces in the world about him. Once he has gone, Margaret herself begins to ignore the realities that surround her. She looks only for any sign that he may be returning.

The Pedlar, on his next visit, observes what she no longer cares to notice. Wandering far from home to find travellers who might have news of Robert, she has left her baby shut in the house, abandoning it to a solitude which for once in Wordsworth voices an unambiguous pain: 'From within/Her solitary infant cried aloud' (326–7). The garden, for which Robert cared, and which when he first left she had been motivated to maintain, now also reveals Margaret's dwindling will:

> It was changed.
> The unprofitable bindweed spread his bells
> From side to side, and with unwieldy wreaths
> Had dragged the rose from its sustaining wall
> And bent it down to earth.   (313–17)

The changed garden increases the anxiety with which the Pedlar – and the reader – awaits Margaret's return. Yet when she does come home, the Pedlar offers only an eye-witness's account of how she now looks: 'Her face was pale and thin, her figure too/Was changed' (338–9). It is Margaret herself who finally voices the change in her feelings: 348 - 55.

'Today
I have been travelling far, and many days
About the fields I wander, knowing this
Only, that what I seek I cannot find.
And so I waste my time: for I am changed,
And to myself', said she, 'have done much wrong,
And to this helpless infant. I have slept
Weeping, and weeping I have waked.'   (348–55)

It is Margaret's own pitiful speech which condemns her behaviour. It is she who admits that she has narrowed her mind until it knows only an endless frustration. It is she who speaks of waste, of wronging herself and her child, of abandoning each new day to tears before it has started. Margaret sees herself as already capable of only a partial return to the world of her child and the Pedlar. So he needs only to verbalize his sympathy, and confirm her statement by his own telling observations:

Sir, it would have grieved
Your very soul to see her: evermore
Her eye-lids drooped, her eyes were downward cast,
And when she at her table gave me food
She did not look at me. Her voice was low,
Her body was subdued. In every act
Pertaining to her house-affairs appeared
The careless stillness which a thinking mind
Gives to an idle matter.   (375–83)

This literal absent-mindedness is to grow remorselessly.

More and more her thoughts wander away to her search for Robert, and the distance from which she views what actually surrounds her increases. On a later visit the Pedlar sees that Margaret's vigilance no longer extends to even keeping the sheep fenced out of the garden:

Of her herbs and flowers
It seemed the better part were gnawed away
Or trampled on the earth. A chain of straw,
Which had been twisted round the tender stem
Of a young apple-tree, lay at its root;
The bark was nibbled round by truant sheep.
Margaret stood near, her infant in her arms,

And, seeing that my eye was on the tree,
She said, 'I fear it will be dead and gone
Ere Robert come again.'   (417–26)

Wordsworth is not imposing symbolism here. The unprotected apple tree is not meant to represent Margaret any more than was the rose parted from its sustaining wall. She never needed Robert to save her from being bitten by sheep or engulfed by weeds, but she did need Robert to make her feel that caring for the garden was worthwhile. Gardening requires faith in the future – it would presumably have been some years before the young apple-tree could have borne useful fruit – and for Margaret the only future worth working for is one shared with Robert.

Even more certainly, Margaret, though she speaks with 'her infant in her arms', is not making any conscious connection between the child's vulnerability and that of the tree. The words sound ominous to us precisely because their more sinister implications can no longer be recognized by Margaret herself. She clearly has no thought of what the Pedlar had anxiously noticed:

Her infant babe
Had from its mother caught the trick of grief
And sighed among its playthings.   (409–11)

The more Margaret focuses on trying to find Robert, the less she sees of all that together they had cherished. It is as if in her own obsessive need of his sheer physical presence, she can no longer imagine him as the real person who would wish to see his garden, and his child growing healthily.

Wordsworth brilliantly encapsulates this by juxtaposing the last things noticed by the Pedlar at the end of this visit with the disastrous news he hears at the beginning of the next:

Yet I saw the idle loom
Still in its place. His sunday garments hung
Upon the self-same nail, his very staff
Stood undisturbed behind the door. And when
I passed this way beaten by Autumn winds,
She told me that her little babe was dead,
And she was left alone.   (432–7)

Margaret has, of course, felt alone before the death of the child whom

she has been ignoring. What her words fail to express is fully articulated in the things she herself makes significant or insignificant, and
we feel that it is she, and not some labouring author, who deploys this
pathetically obvious symbolism. The passionate preference of
Margaret's love does not just make her pine for the man who could
fill out those waiting clothes. Her partial vision empties the living
universe of all other significance. It excludes from her consciousness
those energetic forces of growth and decay – the bindweed and the
rose, the sheep and the apple tree – by which she, and her baby, must
live or die.

By comparison 'Crossing the Alps' can seem almost tame in its
demands upon the reader. In *The Ruined Cottage* it is not just
transcendental serenities enjoyed by Alpine travellers which may be
diminished by human affection. Disconcertingly Wordsworth asks
us to witness the sacrifice to love of the beloved's own child. This is a
grimly literal demonstration of the way our discriminating minds
'murder to dissect' (*PW*, IV. 57, 28).

The ignored totality in which Margaret unwittingly exists is no less
dynamic for being unnoticed:

> Meanwhile her poor hut
> Sunk to decay; for he was gone, whose hand
> At the first nippings of October frost
> Closed up each chink, and with fresh bands of straw
> Chequered the green-grown thatch. And so she lived,
> Through the long winter, reckless and alone,
> Till this reft house, by frost, and thaw, and rain,
> Was sapped; and when she slept, the nightly damps
> Did chill her breast, and in the stormy day
> Her tattered clothes were ruffled by the wind
> Even at the side of her own fire. Yet still
> She loved this wretched spot, nor would for worlds
> Have parted hence; and still that length of road,
> And this rude bench, one torturing hope endeared,
> Fast rooted at her heart. And here, my friend,
> In sickness she remained; and here she died,
> Last human tenant of these ruined walls.   (476–92)

The writing here is delicately indirect, but its precision still imposes a
poignant lucidity. At first we are misled into connecting the cottage's
decline and Robert's absence in purely practical terms: 'for he was

gone' whose skills had repaired its roof 'with fresh bands of straw'. But if for Robert and Margaret this is innately man's work, then mending clothes must be a woman's and so the fact that they are 'tattered' insists on her despair. Even the energy to protect herself with needle and cotton is eventually sapped.

Robert had given her far more than his own labour. He had given her the will to value her own. The certainty that 'he was gone' is fatal to Margaret because it deprives her, not of an efficient home-handyman, but of the man she loves. The need to find him again excludes all other instincts. The 'wretched spot' is not important to her as a shelter in which she can at least physically survive. It has dwindled to nothing more than the place to which he might return. It is this utterly diminished spot which she would not trade 'for worlds'. The cliché is resonant in this context. All the infinite worlds of experience, 'Of first, and last, and midst, and without end', are rejected by Margaret in her fidelity to the 'one torturing hope' represented by these hopelessly ruined walls.

V

Viewed from the Alps, this is lunacy. Her bizarre blindness to the forces of the living universe is symptomatic of a diseased consciousness. The Pedlar to some extent sees her despair in this light. He speaks with the calm sympathy of a cosmic psychiatrist whose patient contracted fatal alienation:

> My Friend, enough to sorrow have you given,
> The purposes of wisdom ask no more:
> Be wise and chearful, and no longer read
> The forms of things with an unworthy eye.
> She sleeps in the calm earth, and peace is here.
> I well remember that those very plumes,
> Those weeds, and the high spear-grass on that wall,
> By mist and silent rain-drops silvered o'er,
> As once I passed, did to my mind convey
> So still an image of tranquillity,
> So calm and still, and looked so beautiful
> Amid the uneasy thoughts which filled my mind,
> That what we feel of sorrow and despair
> From ruin and from change, and all the grief

The passing shews of being leave behind,
Appeared an idle dream that could not live
Where meditation was. I turned away,
And walked along my road in happiness.   (508–25)

The Pedlar here disassociates himself from the delusions of Margaret,
and of the Poet who 'with a brother's love' has 'blessed her in the
impotence of grief' (499–500). The Pedlar remembers at least one
occasion when he felt sure that the individual is no more important or
separable from the world than those complacently flourishing weeds.
Reality has not perished with Margaret. It is alive and well and living
everywhere. Anxiety is thus 'an idle dream'. So presumably is the
passionate need Margaret felt for Robert. So is the tender identification with her grief which the Poet has just felt. A person – like a blade
of spear-grass – is but one of innumerable 'passing shews of being'.
That infinite 'being' evoked by the present participles of 'Crossing
the Alps' remains unaffected.

   Now we are not meant to accept such a response as adequate on its
own. We are expected to remember numerous moments when the
Pedlar has himself encouraged a more sympathetic response to the
story he tells – 'Sir, it would have grieved / Your very soul to see her'
(375–6). Even more certainly we are bound to have in mind the Poet's
reaction to the end of Margaret's story; a reaction which immediately
precedes the Pedlar's argument that he has given 'enough to sorrow'.

The old man ceased: he saw that I was moved.
From that low Bench rising instinctively,
I turned aside in weakness, nor had power
To thank him for the tale which he had told.
I stood, and leaning o'er the garden gate
Reviewed that Woman's sufferings; and it seemed
To comfort me while with a brother's love
I blessed her in the impotence of grief.
At length towards the cottage I returned
Fondly, and traced with milder interest,
The secret spirit of humanity
Which 'mid the calm oblivious tendencies
Of nature, 'mid her plants, her weeds and flowers,
And silent overgrowings, still survived.   (493–506)

To some extent the Poet here prepares the way for the Pedlar's quietism. It is the Poet himself who regards his being so 'moved' as a 'weakness', and makes the judgement concrete by having to clutch at the 'comfort' of the garden gate for support. He admits the 'impotence' of his grief, its uselessness to Margaret. He does force himself to calm down and approach the cottage with a 'milder interest'. But what he seeks there is still the 'spirit of humanity'. He focuses on the evidence that it has 'still survived' amongst the 'silent overgrowings'. He still identifies with Margaret rather than with the world's 'calm oblivious tendencies'. He is still audibly the man who 'thought of that poor woman as of one' whom he 'had known and loved' (207–8).

I suspect that most readers find the Poet's reaction more appealing than the Pedlar's. If asked to make literary judgements, they might describe the Pedlar's language as pompous, even smug. But consider Wordsworth's problem here. The English language and the habits of thought it fosters are as well suited to the Poet's explicitly personalized comments as they are ill suited to the Pedlar's essentially inclusive view. The Poet's use of 'I' five times in fourteen lines cannot be mistaken for comfortable self-regard since it is openly tending to identification with Margaret. The Pedlar uses 'I' only three times in sixteen lines. Yet it sounds more culpably egotistical because he is required to articulate the relative triviality of Margaret as an individual. Wordsworth does his best. He tries to show that the Pedlar relegates not just Margaret, but also himself, to equality with weeds. 'As once I passed' does help to make his own journey through life no more than one of 'the passing shews of being'. But the effect of personal pronouns can only be reduced, not eliminated. Personal pronouns are personal. As such they are essential to the Poet's grief but disastrously suggestive of hypocrisy when used in the Pedlar's humble philosophizing.

Our language values the concrete and specific, which it associates with 'real things'. It mistrusts the abstract and the generalized, which it finds too nebulous for clear focus. In a narrative work it can render 'that Woman's sufferings' almost too distinctly. It can convey the Poet's sympathy as he clings to the garden gate for support in a world which suddenly seems to have been emptied by Margaret's death. In the same context the Pedlar's serenely inclusive nouns – 'peace', 'tranquillity' and 'meditation' – seem unconvincingly vague. But how can language reveal that the Pedlar's apparent vagueness is caused not by blindness to the specific but by awareness of all specifics, that his generalizations are not designed to exclude Margaret but to include everything? Only a speech that never ceased would begin the task. Wordsworth, in trying to maintain a balance between his two voices, is often threatened by the limits of language operating more harshly on one than on the other.

The greatness of *The Ruined Cottage* lies in other moments where Wordsworth does force language to overcome its own limitations. At such moments justice is done to both points of view, and words function with complex economy. Consider for instance the force of Wordsworth's insisting at the moment of Margaret's death on her humanity: 'And here she died, / Last human tenant of these ruined walls' (491–2). This moves us in two, quite different, ways. We are touched by the hint of human emotion having a value that lingers beyond the fact of death. The surviving importance of Margaret is partly that she epitomizes and inspires an essentially human capacity for personal affection. There are unmistakable echoes here of the crucial contexts in which the word human has been used earlier in the poem. There is, for instance, the tender fantasy to which the Pedlar is moved by his own telling of the tale:

> I seem to muse on one
> By sorrow laid asleep or borne away,
> A human being destined to awake
> To human life, or something very near
> To human life, when he shall come again
> For whom she suffered.   (370–5)

The Pedlar here prays for a second coming, yet his longing invokes not a God but a human being. His sympathy leads him to wish on Margaret a resurrection which only Robert can supply. Being 'awake / To human life' is here defined as consciousness of that need. Yet to feel such need is to be vulnerable to the suffering which eventually kills Margaret. So the Pedlar's own affection makes him momentarily hesitate as to what he does wish for Margaret. Retreating with 'or something very near / To human life', he tries to blur the paradox of yearning that a person he liked should again endure love's pain. But the hesitation cannot mask what Margaret's being 'human' in the Pedlar's fantasy must mean. It is to love the man 'for whom she suffered'. These last words make Robert at once the object of her loving pity and the sole cause of her own pain. They record a capacity for sympathetic identification which is shared by Margaret witnessing Robert's suffering, by the Pedlar remembering hers, and by the Poet hearing his. It is that capacity which the poem invites us here to recognize in ourselves and acknowledge as one definition of 'human life'.

Margaret's own emotional and imaginative life grows more intense even as her other energies decline. So Mary Jacobus argues that as 'the last human tenant' Margaret is an image 'not so much of hope's vainness, as of its tenacity':

> 'The Ruined Cottage' turns on the paradox of Margaret's despairing apathy and her heightened inner life. Ever seeing and failing to see her returning husband, her eye is 'busy in the distance, shaping things / That made her heart beat quick,'; her pathetic questioning of each passer-by reveals her consuming hope while accentuating its futility. As Margaret herself grows weaker, her feelings seem to intensify.[3]

It is certainly because we are alive to such feelings that we focus on the 'secret spirit of humanity' in the ruin, rather than on the impersonal vegetation which threatens to obscure it. It is Margaret's love which makes us see the overgrown spring as mattering only because there 'the touch of human hand' once ministered 'To human comfort' (86–7). Margaret as the 'last human tenant' may be the last tenant in whom we can take an interest.

But to see the ruin as only a fading image of love between two people who are now dead is a kind of blindness. In calling Margaret the 'last human tenant', the Pedlar also reminds the Poet that 'these ruined walls' have other tenants now. The nettles, the adders, 'The unshod Colt, / The wandering heifer and the Potter's ass' all 'find shelter now within the chimney-wall' (109–13). So Margaret's death points not only to the strength of human love, but also to what the Pedlar calls 'the weakness of humanity', the 'untoward mind' with which we 'turn our hearts away' from all the other forms of life with which we share our world. Our yearning to feel 'The calm of Nature', our response to its 'image of tranquillity' are also part of our humanity. We long to feel that the earth is itself our home. The frail houses in which we try to shelter those we love seem to offer only a precarious security. Such homes can become centres of anxiety, and deserve *The Prelude*'s description of 'the fretful dwellings of mankind' (1. 283). Caring for a house can be all too evocative of cowering amongst already 'ruined walls'.

Witnessing Robert and Margaret's helpless struggle for independence, we share the Pedlar's view:

> happier far
> Could they have lived as do the little birds
> That peck along the hedges, or the kite
> That makes her dwelling in the mountain rocks.   (157–60)

Being human, we feel the tenderness which compels Margaret to
cling to her crumbling home. But we are also human in sharing the
Pedlar's and the Poet's sense of relief as they turn from that home's
chillingly inevitable collapse to face, in the poem's last lines, the
endlessly regenerating warmth of a larger world: *526 – 58.*

> He ceased. By this the sun declining shot
> A slant and mellow radiance, which began
> To fall upon us where beneath the trees
> We sate on that low bench. And now we felt,
> Admonished thus, the sweet hour coming on:
> A linnet warbled from those lofty elms,
> A thrush sang loud, and other melodies
> At distance heard, peopled the milder air.
> The old man rose and hoisted up his load.
> Together casting then a farewell look
> Upon those silent walls, we left the shade;
> And, ere the stars were visible, attained
> A rustic inn, our evening resting-place.   (526–38)

The linnet and thrush here, like 'the little birds / That peck along the
hedges', enjoy an ignorance of suffering which distinguishes them
from people. Their song places them securely amongst the 'lofty
elms' which remain long after the sound of Margaret's sorrow has
died away. Yet Wordsworth insists that the singing birds, along with
the 'other melodies' of a harmonious landscape, 'peopled the milder
air'. The choice of 'peopled' can at first seem jarringly inappropriate.
The human voices are stilled – 'she died', 'he ceased'. The 'silent
walls' lack the voices of people whose lives they once sheltered. The
Pedlar and the Poet could feel that as people, sharing the vocabulary
of grief, they are doomed to remain wholly separate from the inarticulate birds.

But just as the place has only been changed, not destroyed, by
Margaret's death, so the Pedlar, in ceasing to speak of her suffering,

has not perished. He has merely altered the way in which he makes sense of the world. That world is not reduced to a vacuum by the loss of one human love affair. The story of Margaret's love – like all personal stories – has led literally to a dead end. But the Pedlar who has told it, and the Poet who has listened, remain alive to the possibility of fresh starts. The ever-changing world makes all endings inseparable from new beginnings. The 'sun declining' was, and will be again, the rising sun of a new dawn. Both men have had 'restless thoughts' in which they narrowed their minds to identify with Margaret's vigil. But now both achieve an 'evening resting-place'. In it their minds will sleep at the end of one experience and wake at the beginning of another. So they acknowledge that as people they do not belong only with Margaret whose pained love allowed the baby which she and Robert had created to die. They also belong in the infinitely larger world whose fertility is inexhaustible. It is explicitly when he is no longer distracted by Margaret's story that the Poet is able to hear the air he breathes as 'peopled' by sounds of life. The grandeur of the earth's unfailing music need not be an alien chorus from which we feel excluded. We can recognize it as an essentially 'peopled' orchestration in which our human eyes and ears have crucial parts to play.

People are home-builders and they are travellers. It is human to try to hold a place for oneself, and for those one loves, in defiance of the natural laws of change and decay. But it is equally human to accept one's life as a journey, whose shifting movements match the end-lessly changing world through which we pass. The poem is centred on a cottage to which Margaret is tied by 'one torturing hope', yet it also moves towards a wayside inn where people can relax into an essentially temporary and impersonal 'resting-place'. The bird-song that 'peopled the milder air' rouses Pedlar and Poet to feel that people belong not only here but elsewhere. Both linger for 'a farewell look / Upon those silent walls', and we can assume that the Pedlar, at least, is bound to one day return – his compulsion to visit Margaret's old home is a 'weakness of humanity' from which there is no perma-nent escape. But for the time being he is strengthened by 'melodies / At distance heard' to look to wider horizons.

VI

Bird-song is often in Wordsworth both an invitation to which we are bound to respond and, paradoxically, the alienating din of a party to which we can never be admitted. In *Lines Written in Early Spring*, the 'thousand blended notes' of the birds impose an ambivalent mood in which 'pleasant thoughts/Bring sad thoughts to the mind' (*PW*, IV. 58, 1–4). The lyric recognizes the indissoluble bond between what Wordsworth hears in the world and what he is as a person: 'To her fair works did Nature link/The human soul that through me ran;' (5–6). He acknowledges his own innate capacity to believe in the 'pleasure' with which the landscape is alive. Watching the ways in which 'The birds . . . hopped and played', he senses 'a thrill of pleasure' in 'the least motion' (13–16). He 'cannot measure' what 'thoughts', if any, the birds have (14). But the human world is known to be – to its cost – much more than such unthinking games. So Wordsworth feels an equally strong tendency 'to lament/What man has made of man' (23–4).

The damage that man does to himself is spelt out more clearly in the group of short lyrics known as the Matthew poems. It seems never to have been noticed that in these poems Wordsworth explores what is recognizably the problem of *The Ruined Cottage* from an illuminatingly different angle. Matthew has lived to be an old man, but his son and daughter have died as children. He must try to survive without the people he loves, and so his situation resembles Margaret's. Yet, unlike her, he still often feels the delight in life articulated by the Pedlar. In her biography of Wordsworth, Mary Moorman suggests that the same Hawkshead packman whom he knew as a teenager may have inspired the portraits of both Matthew and the Pedlar.[4] Certainly the two figures are deployed to evoke a remarkably similar duality. For Matthew too, bird-song can both epitomize the serene sanity of living in the present and define by contrast the wastefulness with which people struggle against the natural law that things change.

Matthew in *The Fountain* observes:

'The blackbird amid leafy trees,
The lark above the hill,
Let loose their carols when they please,
Are quiet when they will.

'With Nature never do *they* wage
A foolish strife; they see
A happy youth, and their old age
Is beautiful and free:'   (*PW*, IV. 72, 36–44)

The birds are free to live in the present, but Matthew himself is sometimes forced by the 'heavy laws' of human nature to remember a past (45–8). He cannot at first respond to an invitation to identify with what is now available. The young poet asks him to join in and sing some 'border-song, or catch / That suits a Summer's noon', to match the pleasant tune presented by the immediate landscape (9–12). But Matthew is too distracted by his sense of what is gone. He measures what he is by memories of what he once was – 'a vigorous man' (25–8). He sees in the young man before him only the absence of his own children who have died. Far from lending his voice to the suggested song, he uses it to:

> bemoan
> His kindred laid in earth,
> The household hearts that were his own;   (49–51)

He is not straightforwardly lonely. He is surrounded by people who care for him. But people are not interchangeable, and so in the presence of love, he feels its absence: 'many love me; but by none / Am I enough beloved' (55–6).

His young friend rebukes this as a wretched example of what man has made of man:

> 'Now both himself and me he wrongs,
> That man who thus complains!
> I live and sing my idle songs
> Upon these happy plains;
>
> 'And, Matthew, for thy children dead
> I'll be a son to thee!'
> At this he grasped my hand, and said,
> 'Alas! that cannot be.'   (57–64)

For the anonymous birds, of course, life is more painlessly undiscriminating. Wordsworth's grammar carefully makes blackbird and lark indistinguishably equal subjects of no less than seven verbs. Their life is an interchanged song. But for a father there can be no substitute for his son.

An enticingly lucid and thoughtful summary of the poem is offered by David Ferry:

> The 'heavy laws' that oppress man are the laws that compel him to feel a sorrow corresponding to the joy his human relationships

once gave him, since those relationships are inevitably altered by inconstancy or death. This is also his 'foolish strife' against nature, but the poem has no bland assumptions that it would be easy for him to be at one with nature, easy not to be human. Man's folly is indigenous to him. . . . To be at one with nature would be not to be human, so that one would neither have to grieve at bereavement nor experience the anterior joy which causes such grief. The old man is mourning for his humanity.⁵

But Wordsworth's stance is more judiciously balanced than this suggests. What Ferry omits to mention is that the poem closes with Matthew agreeing after all to join the young man in a song whose jollity matches the landscape's. Matthew finally manages to laugh away his sobering sense of time:

> He sang those witty rhymes
> About the crazy old church-clock,
> And the bewildered chimes. (70–2)

So the old man, when 'mourning his humanity', was not just acknowledging a real difference between birds and men: he was denying an equally real similarity which is just as much a part of human nature. The instinct to join the world's carefree song is as 'indigenous' to man as his need to tell the tale of his individual loss.

Moreover Ferry gives too little weight to Wordsworth's insistence that human love is so peculiarly specific. Matthew is literally at pains to reveal that for him affection is about irreplaceably personal relationships. In a companion poem, *The Two April Mornings*, Matthew meets a beautiful child who reminds him of his dead daughter, Emma. The living child seems to have the secure loveliness of the imperishable landscape, but Matthew is not to be gulled into giving hostages to fortune a second time:

> 'No fountain from its rocky cave
> E'er tripped with foot so free;
> She seemed as happy as a wave
> That dances on the sea.
>
> 'There came from me a sigh of pain
> Which I could ill confine;
> I looked at her, and looked again;
> And did not wish her mine!' (PW, IV. 71, 53–6)

The poem is not just about what life is, but also about what it seems to be. The living girl seemed at first destined to enjoy the perpetual vivacity of a fountain or a wave, but she is in fact as mortal as any other child. Matthew at the grave-side of his daughter has just suffered the torment of feeling his love for Emma more intensely than ever before, or as Wordsworth precisely adds, 'so it seemed'. David Ferry ignores this crucial qualification and sees Matthew as literally loving Emma more than he did when she was alive. So Ferry concludes that love for Matthew is not so much a need of one particular person, but a sweeping preference for corpses:

> He does not wish her his, and for the same reason that, in the other poem, he refuses the poet's offer to be like a son to him. In either case, it would be taking up again the burden of human relationships with their joy and attendant sorrow. . . . He loves Emma in her grave more than he had loved her while alive. When he sees the living girl it is as if he were offered a choice between the living and the dead, and he chooses the dead.
>
> For a relationship with the dead is, by that much, more stable than a relationship with the living: the dead are dead. . . . This helps explain why so many of the poems of Wordsworth which dramatise human feelings are poems about bereavement.[6]

But Matthew surely rejects the idea that the young man should become his son and the young girl his daughter less because it is undesirable than because it is impossible. Human love is almost by definition about our not being able to substitute for each other: the beloved is unique. Far from being faced by a choice between the living and the dead, Matthew essentially cannot choose whom he loves. He explicitly calls his daughter 'my Emma', defining her significance as a named individual (37). The living girl he meets – who has presumably been given a different name by her own parents – is no more capable of answering to the needs of Matthew's untransferable love than she is likely to answer to his addressing her as Emma. To wish that the living girl could be his is really to wish that Emma could come back to life, and to face the pain of knowing that such wishes can never be fulfilled.

In both poems Matthew is offered only the fantasy of a resurrected relationship. It can no more be fulfilled than the Pedlar's fantasy in *The Ruined Cottage* that Robert comes again to resurrect Margaret. Moreover both men sense in their hopeless longing for an irrevocably dead past that they may be throwing away their opportunity to enjoy all that the real world still offers. The stanzas of *The Two April Mornings* that Ferry does not quote make it clear that Matthew is usually sane enough to forget his longing for a daughter. Normally he is 'As blithe a man as you could see/On a spring holiday' (7–8). The poem opens with an April morning being enjoyed by Matthew who travels 'merrily' through the landscape with the young poet. It is the very act of relishing the colours of cornfield and hillside in the April sunlight which triggers his mind back to a similar spring morning of thirty years ago when he had met the girl in the graveyard (25–8). He remembers that on that day too he had set off cheerfully enough, even though then his bereavement must have been a much fresher memory. He had started out 'with rod and line' to enjoy some fishing, already able to make the most of what was offered by the natural world's cyclic changes: he had looked forward to 'the sport/Which that sweet season gave' (29–32). When he paused to look at his daughter's grave, he was obviously not expecting to be so overwhelmed by his sense of loss as to be prevented from enjoying all that remained.

So 'the burden of human relationships with their joy and attendant sorrow' in fact threatens to reimpose its intensities on a relatively happy man. Matthew has come positively to enjoy a more casual existence in which there is mercifully little felt 'relationship with the dead'. In fact, if there is a soothingly 'stable' relationship which Matthew wants to protect, it is not love for a dead person but delight in a living universe. When David Ferry deduces that 'the ideal relationship' implied by the poems 'would be the dead speaking to the dead',[7] he is discovering in the verse a very different voice from the one I hear. Wordsworth seems to me to explore death and bereavement only to discover what it is like to be alive. The life thus revealed is complex. It is partly the vivacity of a singing landscape with which men like Matthew and the Pedlar can identify. It is partly the vitality of regrets and hopes with which both men, as imaginative human beings, can distract themselves from the present into memories of the past and fantasies about the future. Instead of 'the dead speaking to the dead', Wordsworth offers a dynamic dialogue between different ways of living.

In both *The Fountain* and *The Two April Mornings*, Matthew eventually resists the temptation to narrow his world to 'the one torturing hope' that is Margaret's life. Where Margaret ignores the present in looking for a past that cannot return, Matthew – however distracted on occasion by memory – does manage to go on living in the present. Both Matthew and Margaret function in poetry that insists on the duality of human life, on the strange intensity with which we can respond both to the 'thousand blended notes' of anonymous bird-song and to the story of one named person's bereavement. Such intensity runs risks. Matthew's love for Emma could, like Margaret's for Robert, become a deranged suppression of his other latent life as part of a larger world which embraces corn fields and hills, fishing and funny songs. Conversely the Pedlar's identification with the landscape could grow until he was deaf to the call of human sympathy. For both men one kind of liveliness is challenged by another. Yet their disconcerting compulsion to be alive both to general nature and particular people remains.

VII

Unfortunately Wordsworth did not always muster the precision to maintain the debate's energy. Elsewhere he himself asserted 'Love of Nature Leading to Love of Man' and thus provided the two ponderous abstracts which can still the great verse's seesaw. David Ferry argues that one is so top-heavy that it is only a complacent tautology: 'The formula that the love of nature leads to the love of man can be reduced to the formula that the love of nature leads to the love of nature.'[8] Stranded in the air at the other end of the seesaw is, then, what Ferry regards as Wordsworth's 'enmity to man, which he mistook for love'.[9] These lofty generalizations can allow even the most carefully poised poems to be falsely accused of imbalance. *The Ruined Cottage* itself has been offered as evidence that 'Nature was loved as a reality, man as an idea'. David Perkins complains that, after 'the pathetic history of Margaret's life', we are asked 'to quit the poem not with vibrant feelings of grief or protest, but with "meditative sympathies"', inspired by 'the final, vivid image of "spear-grass . . . by mist and silent rain-drops silvered o'er"'. For Perkins there is no challenge of invigorating conflict, only the acceptance of a consistent hierarchy:

> Throughout Wordsworth's poetry there is a striking difference between the presentation of natural objects, so vivid, concrete, and detailed, and the presentation of human beings, so often mere, stark abstractions. Nature was loved as a reality, man as an idea.[10]

But the concepts, and even some of the terms, which are used so confidently here are the very ones which *The Ruined Cottage* questions. Should we feel cheated by the way 'vibrant feelings of grief' are finally contained when Wordsworth exposes 'the impotence of grief', the uselessness to Margaret of the 'brother's love' felt by the Poet?

What Poet and Pedlar are tempted to 'feel of sorrow and despair' can indeed seem inadequately 'stark abstractions', irrelevant to the dead woman who wanted only Robert. If so, it is because Wordsworth has made not only the natural world but also Margaret's need of Robert 'vivid, concrete and detailed'. On occasion he does both simultaneously. The world she disregards and the love with which she is obsessed are made equally palpable in the unsupported rose or the abandoned apple tree. But many of the most telling concrete details – the broken wooden bowl or Robert's Sunday clothes – are essentially human artefacts, moving precisely because they are not natural objects. Far from valuing only nature as a reality, the poem makes landscape and cottage, the power of the world and the weakness of humanity, equally real. Our own comfortably compartmentalized ideas of how we respond to these two realities, our lazy assumptions that we know what we mean by 'natural' or 'human', our complacent acceptance of the pleasure we take in tragedies like 'the pathetic history of Margaret's life' – all these the poem challenges.

So the emphasis placed by some critics on the tragedy inherent in Margaret is potentially as misleading as Perkins's stress on the 'meditative sympathies' attempted by the Pedlar. Jonathan Wordsworth, for instance, after an often brilliant commentary on the poem's fluctuations, decides that *The Ruined Cottage* is important in the end because of its pathos: 'It shows in Wordsworth, a humanity, an insight into emotions not his own, that is wholly convincing – places him, perhaps unexpectedly, among the very few great English tragic writers.'[11] But surely the poem's own varying use of the word 'human' insists that the ability to care about someone else's personal tragedy is but one aspect of our equivocal 'humanity'. The Pedlar's 'insight into emotions not his own' allows him to recognize not only the pain of Margaret but also the cheerfulness of the birds.

Some readers shrewdly identify a dichotomy in the poem, but then represent it as involving alternative options: Paul D. Sheats claims that the Pedlar 'is forced to choose between relationship to man and relationship to nature, between a shared consciousness of grief and mortality and a psychological identification with nature that offers timeless joy'.[12] But of course it is not the confused Pedlar, but coherent critics who feel able to exercise such absolute options. Then, having picked out one half of the poem, they tend to complain that they have been given short measure. Sheats objects that 'the pedlar's reverent naturalism does not permit a full and generous response to Margaret's plight, or, more broadly to the plight of man.'[13] But the Pedlar, describing Margaret's plight, moves himself to tears. As Jonathan Wordsworth so neatly says, 'He can ask the question, "Why should a tear be in an old man's eye?" but the tear remains.'[14] In fact it is partly because his response is so 'full' that he is compelled to distance the site of her pain into an 'image of tranquillity'. Far from being forced to choose, the Pedlar is prevented by human nature from ever finally choosing. He cannot always restrain himself from sharing Margaret's dream of Robert's return. Nor can he elect to withdraw as she does into permanent blindness to all that remains.

Choices are indeed forced on others. Margaret, in her almost dehumanized despair, is finally forced to choose 'grief and mortality'. Her fevered imagination ties her to a dying past. The birds, in their animal delight amongst 'those enormous elms', have to choose 'timeless joy'. Their mindless instincts lock them into an eternal present. But the Pedlar, with the bewildering inconsistency of a fully alive human being, will fluctuate between tenderness for all that has passed at the cottage and identification with the grandeur that now, and for ever, contains it. Sometimes he will feel 'all the grief / The passing shews of being leave behind'. Sometimes he will feel it as no more than 'an idle dream' from which he wakes to recognize 'the types and symbols of Eternity'. The strength of human pity will remain bafflingly entangled with 'the weakness of humanity' which resurrects past pain to the destruction of present joy. But the Pedlar is stretched on the tensions of a great poem which requires him to have the courage of his contrary convictions.

VIII

Wordsworth himself had difficulty in keeping his nerve. The working drafts of *The Ruined Cottage* record various efforts to build bridges across the chasm that the poem threatens to expose. The textual history is complex but the essential point is this: Wordsworth composed an extra 350 lines which attempt to demonstrate that, after all, there need be no conflict between joy in nature and compassion for people. He was more than once tempted to force this sequence into the poem. The very notebook which contains the first fair copy manuscript of *The Ruined Cottage* also contains, amongst other poems and fragments, a fair copy of these extra lines. So, as early as 1799–80 when he produced what is now the generally accepted text of the complete *Ruined Cottage*, he was unwilling to abandon completely the extra sequence. In 1815 he decided to insert a revised version of *The Ruined Cottage* into the longest poem he ever wrote, *The Excursion*. In doing so he chose to use the emergency exit prepared fourteen years earlier and included, albeit in a considerably altered form, the extra lines. In their original form of the 1800 manuscript they have been published recently under the title of *The Pedlar*.[15] The additional lines are indeed about a Pedlar, but a significantly different one from the narrator of *The Ruined Cottage*, and Wordsworth was undoubtedly right to decide at first that their intrusion into the poem could only be damaging. They are a fascinatingly clear account of how Wordsworth – even while he was writing his greatest poetry – sought to evade the dilemma he was revealing.

The Pedlar attempts a synthesis based on the wild hopes raised by Coleridge's ideas. In 1796 Coleridge had published his confident assertion that pantheism was not just compatible with humanitarianism, but actually the source of human sympathy:

> 'Tis the sublime of man,
> Our noontide Majesty, to know ourselves
> Parts and proportions of one wond'rous whole!
> This fraternises man, this constitutes
> Our charities and bearings.[16]

Infected by Coleridge's confidence, Wordsworth in *The Pedlar* gives his own intuitions the authority of biblical rhetoric:

> He was only then
> Contented when with bliss ineffable
> He felt the sentiment of being spread
> O'er all that moves, and all that seemeth still,
> O'er all which, lost beyond the reach of thought

And human knowledge, to the human eye
Invisible, yet liveth to the heart;
O'er all that leaps, and runs, and shouts, and sings,
Or beats the gladsome air; o'er all that glides
Beneath the wave, yea, in the wave itself,
And mighty depth of waters. Wonder not
If such his transports were; for in all things
He saw one life, and felt that it was joy.

(*The Pedlar*, 206–18)

Out of context this can be magnificently convincing. One is almost persuaded that the Pedlar serenely maintains the joy of seeing all things as 'one life'. Neither 'meddling intellect' nor any instinct towards a more discriminating tenderness seems to threaten his sense of shared security with the animals and birds and fishes. He seems to have transcended the limits of his species, reaching above 'human knowledge' to a vision beyond that of the 'human eye'. We hardly need Wordsworth's appeal of 'Wonder not'. Temporarily we join the Pedlar in his 'transports' and forget the existence of the human world. Or perhaps we momentarily feel that, even if we do see 'all things' as necessarily including people, we can dismiss their apparent suffering as an illusion in which they cut themselves off from the one true life of shared joy, and imagine themselves to be poignantly isolated individuals. At certain moments *The Ruined Cottage*'s Pedlar saw things this way, so we might hope that *The Pedlar* too will accept that this is only one way of seeing and offer other moments in which a more tragic insight pulls our feelings in an opposite direction. There seems to be such a hint of more restless moods in the phrase, 'only then / Contented'.

But the other moments Wordsworth has in mind here turn out to be unimaginably odd. They are occasions when the Pedlar turns from his joy in things to confront the pain of people and yet remains in precisely the same mood. He is able to keep his undiscriminating delight in an inclusive world at the same time as identifying with the specific unhappiness that other people endure in their selective relationships. Indeed it is his own pleasure in solitude that allows him to identify with other people in the pain of their loneliness:

there he kept
In solitude and solitary thought,
So pleasant were those comprehensive views,

His mind in a just equipoise of love.
Serene it was, unclouded by the cares
Of ordinary life; unvexed, unwarped
By partial bondage. In his steady course
No piteous revolutions had he felt,
No wild varieties of joy or grief.
Unoccupied by sorrow of its own,
His heart lay open; and, by nature tuned
And constant disposition of his thoughts
To sympathy with man, he was alive
To all that was endured; and in himself
Happy, and quiet in his chearfulness,
He had no painful pressure from within
Which made him turn aside from wretchedness
With coward fears. He could afford to suffer
With those whom he saw suffer.   (265–84)

He has never experienced the emotions of human relationship with
all its 'wild varieties of joy or grief', yet, incredibly, he can recognize
them in others and indeed identify with them. His 'just equipoise of
love' cannot distinguish the human species in general as distinctly
more precious than fish or birds. He has certainly never known what
it is to value one person more highly than another. Yet having never
known the 'painful pressure' of such 'partial bondage', his heart is
somehow open to feel with those who do. The mind sheltered in
solitude has not only learnt to recognize the harmonies of landscape;
in its very isolation it has been 'by nature tuned . . . To sympathy
with man'.

So, even in this early manifestation, the doctrine of love of nature
leading to love of man reveals itself as nonsense. It can only express
itself in words stripped of meaning. The man who saw everything as
'one life, and felt that it was joy' can only be said 'to suffer' in a lazy
language which no longer values human emotion as worth disting-
uishing. Wordsworth in fact suggests that the Pedlar is not so much
compelled to feel sympathy, as free to charitably distribute it: 'He
could afford to suffer/With those whom he saw suffer'. But such
comfortable largesse only exposes how far the word 'suffering' is
abused here.

The Pedlar's mind – 'serene it was, unclouded by the cares/Of
ordinary life' – seems to be at a safe distance from the suffering it

observes. Indeed the next lines credit him with an almost scholarly detachment:

> For hence, minutely in his various rounds
> He had observed the progress and decay
> Of many minds, of minds and bodies too;
> The history of many families,
> And how they prospered, how they were o'erthrown
> By passion or mischance, or such misrule
> Among the unthinking masters of the earth
> As makes the nations groan.   (285–92)

The general suffering imposed by an unjust society may well be visible to the Pedlar in the impersonal clarity of his 'comprehensive views'. But whether a joyful pantheist would feel motivated to do much about the peculiarly human, as opposed to the broadly ecological, effects of political 'misrule' seems debatable. Even more damaging is the Pedlar's acknowledgement that the 'decay' of many 'minds and bodies' is due to 'passion or mischance'. 'The history of many families' is indeed the story of personal emotions and particular events, of specifics which must be separated from the 'one life' if they are to be valued.

Family life and the 'one life' are in fact innately opposed. The Pedlar, to achieve his solitude, has left his home. Wordsworth does not dwell on the painful gap this may have caused in the family, but he does record that 'The Father strove to make his son perceive . . . With what advantage he might teach a school/In the adjoining village' (227–30). The idea, though clumsily tactful in its restraint, disguises neither the father's sorrow nor Wordsworth's embarrassment at guessing it. The father is at least one man who does not believe himself to be more loved as a result of his son's enthusiasm for nature. Wordsworth is honest enough to imagine that at parting

> The old man
> Blessed him and prayed for him, yet with a heart
> Foreboding evil.   (236–8)

There is no hint that the father fears immorality. He is simply afraid that his son will not want to end his solitary wandering and come home again. The 'evil' that he dreads is no more – and no less – than the loss of the son he loves.

What Wordsworth exposed in working on the manuscripts that

became *The Pedlar* was a conflict which rhetoric could not disguise. A solitary man, dwelling permanently in a vision of nature's grandeur, could not also feel the 'partial bondage' of tenderness for an individual. When all life is seen as joyful, a pitying concentration on human suffering must seem a wasteful delusion. Feeling closer to people splits the unified world into a background landscape and the human figures who dominate it. Conversely, to travel into nature is to journey away from home. So, if author and reader feel moved in both directions, a credible narrator must commute.

For the facts of our own confusion we should turn back to the narrator of *The Ruined Cottage*. Trying and yet failing to suppress the 'tear in an old man's eye', he can movingly enact our own inconsistency. He knows he must struggle to preserve his joy in the 'one life' against a compassion that threatens it. Unlike his inhumanly comfortable counterpart in *The Pedlar*, he fears that whenever he has allowed himself 'to suffer / With those whom he saw suffer' he may have been breaking a natural law – 'all things which are not at rest / Are chearful'. So when Wordsworth decided to keep *The Ruined Cottage* separate from *The Pedlar*, he saved a great poem from a far shallower one. Even critics who believe Wordsworth's greatness to rest in the consistency of his vision rather than its admission of conflict have never argued that *The Pedlar* is as good a poem as *The Ruined Cottage*. My own view is that the comparison is typical in suggesting that where Wordsworth dares to equivocate he writes at his best, and that where he attempts a tidily singular vision he is at constant risk of sounding silly.

When the ageing Wordsworth did force the works together, he made them part of *The Excursion*, perhaps the most unreadable poem ever written by a major writer. There, he retreats into an orthodox piety where the earth seems only a pale reflection of the 'one life' to be found in heaven, and love between human beings is little more, even at its best, than a dress rehearsal for meeting God. From such a perspective, both the grandeur of the earth and the tenderness we feel for a few of the people who are passing through it dwindle into a less tense coexistence. The Pedlar of *The Excursion* settles into 'gratitude and reverential thoughts' towards 'The Scottish Church', and is guarded by 'The strong hand of her purity' (1.397–402). The 'meditative sympathies' he feels with the landscape now 'repose / Upon the breast of Faith' (1.954–5). His joy in the beauty of God's creation thus fits comfortably enough with his desire to help Margaret. He tells her 'to place her trust / In God's good love, and seek his help by prayer' (1. 807–8).

The importance of Robert's love is obviously reduced by comparison with God's. Margaret ceases to be inconsolably lonely, and becomes:

> One
> Who in her worst distress, had ofttimes felt
> The unbounded might of prayer; and learned, with soul
> Fixed on the Cross, that consolation springs
> From sources deeper far than deepest pain,
> For the meek Sufferer.   (1. 934–9)

The Pedlar of *The Ruined Cottage* may doubt Margaret's wisdom in looking so hard for Robert that she sees nothing else, but he is often compelled to see things from her own anguished point of view. Sometimes his identification is such that he and Margaret almost reverse roles:

> I had little power
> To give her comfort, and was glad to take
> Such words of hope from her own mouth
> As served to cheer us both.   (275–8)

The Pedlar's wandering life, with its lengthy intervals between each visit to Margaret, parallels his fluctuating awareness of all that she, in her unchanging grief, forgets. This dynamic movement to and from human suffering loses all meaning in *The Excursion*. There, in a tableau of lifeless consistency, the Pedlar and Margaret end standing side by side, their gaze equally 'Fixed on the Cross'. He may still glimpse, out of the corner of his eye, earth's grandeur as an alternative example of God's generosity, but the crucifix reminds us that it was a self-sacrifice on God's part to visit this vale of tears. Margaret may glimpse in the God who died for love of man a dim reflection of human tenderness. But she must feel it would be blasphemous to compare her 'torturing hope' that 'he shall come again / For whom she suffered' either with Jesus' own torture or the hope of His followers that He will return. Wordsworth's later verse never openly abandons either love of nature or love of man. It merely damns both with faint praise.

But the mystery is not really that he eventually retreated. He lived for a very long time. He was twenty-five years old, and already a published poet, when Keats was born, and yet he survived Keats by nearly thirty years. Wordsworth died, at the age of eighty, after more than forty years of being battered by private bereavements and pampered by public adulation. During such a span he had inevitably accumulated much poetic junk to bequeath to posterity. The self-indulgence – if not the stamina – required to write *The Excursion* needs little explanation. Far more puzzling is the self-discipline with which his earlier verse boldly explores conflict, probing the 'weakness of humanity', and resisting the temptation to tidy thought-provoking inconsistency into thoughtlessly coherent didacticism. The mysteries, whose origin no scholar will ever fully uncover and whose achievement no critic fortunately can explain away, are *The Ruined Cottage* and the other great poems he was still to write.

THE STRENGTH OF LOVE

'MICHAEL'

I

As a narrative poet, Wordsworth tries to express the feelings of people who themselves say remarkably little. He claimed that *Michael* was written 'to shew that men who do not wear fine cloaths can feel deeply',[1] and none of his major characters belongs to that educated class which finds verbalization easy. Moreover Wordsworth's plots tend to deprive his characters of the person to whom they would be most likely to talk. He exposes Margaret's love, for instance, largely by depriving her of Robert. So we eavesdrop, not on the central dialogue of her life, but on the silence of its aftermath. Similarly we feel most sympathy for the mother in *The Idiot Boy* and the father in *Michael* when the loss of a beloved son persuades each that conversation with anybody else is no longer worthwhile.

Of course, there are moments of crucial direct speech. Wordsworth sometimes allows his characters to achieve startlingly powerful effects in a vocabulary which is still narrow enough to seem convincingly their own. But they do so in ways which actually reinforce our sense that they now cannot speak to the person they love. Margaret feels for her neurotically evasive husband a pity which he cannot bear to hear. So it is to the Pedlar that she has to speak:

> 'Every smile,'
> Said Margaret to me, here beneath these trees,
> 'Made my heart bleed!'

In *The Idiot Boy* it is not even to another person but to a dumb animal that Betty has to appeal:

> 'Oh dear, dear Pony! my sweet joy!
> Oh carry back my Idiot Boy!
> And we will ne'er o'erload thee more.'
>
> (*PW*, II.76, 299–301)

In *Michael* the old shepherd finally loses a son who will never return, and so is more permanently forced back into relationship with the 'dumb animals, whom he had saved,/Had fed or sheltered' (*PW*, II. 82, 71–2). He ends 'Sitting alone, or with his faithful Dog' (468).

But Michael is at first a far more ambiguous figure than Margaret or Betty Foy, and for him animals do not always seem a forlorn second best to people. Betty on her lonely search strains to hear the pony's hoof-beats only because the sound may lead her to the missing child: 'She listens, but she cannot hear/The foot of horse, the voice of man;' (*PW*, II. 76, 282–3). When Margaret is abandoned, she too has ears only for news of the one person who is not there. But Michael is at first happy to work in solitude, listening to the language of his landscape, and speaking only to himself:

> Hence had he learned the meaning of all winds,
> Of blasts of every tone; and oftentimes,
> When others heeded not, He heard the South
> Make subterranean music, like the noise
> Of bagpipers on distant Highland hills.
> The Shepherd at such warning, of his flock
> Bethought him, and he to himself would say,
> 'The winds are now devising work for me!'   (48–55)

Instead of clinging tenaciously to one chosen person, Michael accepts easy-come and easy-go relationships with the fluid forces of his world:

> he had been alone
> Amid the heart of many thousand mists,
> That came to him, and left him, on the heights.   (57–9)

Love for Michael is at first not singular and selective, but plural and inclusive. It embraces not only the 'dumb animals' but also 'the green valleys, and the streams and rocks' (63).

'Fields, where with cheerful spirits he had breathed/The common air' (65–6) give him life and livelihood. So Wordsworth is almost apologetic about offering such an obvious truth as the shepherd's feeling of love:

> Those fields, those hills – what could they less? had laid
> Strong hold on his affections, were to him
> A pleasurable feeling of blind love,
> The pleasure which there is in life itself.   (74–7)

This love is blind partly in the paradoxical sense that the 'eye' of *Tintern Abbey* has to be 'made quiet' before we can 'see into the life of things' (*PW*, II.260, 47–9). But the blindness of Michael's early love is also its inability to recognize the intensities of human relationship. Michael begins, and to some extent ends, as a man so unusually conversant with his world that he feels little need of conversation with other people. Yet it is on his brief hopes of one other person that his story centres.

The unexpected birth of a son in Michael's old age threatens its own kind of blindness. Parents can be distracted by 'instinctive tenderness, the same / Fond spirit that blindly works in the blood of all' (144–5). Michael has had no other children. In his own terms he has reached the age when he could not hope for such an event: 'he was old – in shepherd's phrase, / With one foot in the grave' (89–90). A precious child can be a dubious blessing to an old man who had been peacefully resigned to his own mortality:

> a child, more than all other gifts
> That earth can offer to declining man,
> Brings hope with it, and forward-looking thoughts,
> And stirrings of inquietude, when they
> By tendency of nature needs must fail.
> Exceeding was the love he bare to him,   (146–51)

Michael's love for Luke could indeed become, like Margaret's for Robert, excessive. With hope, comes anxiety. The 'forward-looking thoughts' disturb the potential calm of old age with 'stirrings of inquietude' which would otherwise – by a perhaps merciful 'tendency of nature' – have faded away. Michael could have moved resignedly towards the death already accepted by his own parents:

> Both of them sleep together: here they lived,
> As all their Forefathers had done; and when
> At length their time was come, they were not loth
> To give their bodies to the family mould.   (367–71)

But, for Michael, the 'stirrings of inquietude' born with Luke raise a restless 'hope' which echoes disturbingly throughout the poem.

His son becomes his 'daily hope' (206). When economic disaster threatens the farm, Michael feels that it takes: 'More hope out of his life than he supposed that any old man ever could have lost' (219–20). He tries to convince himself that Luke leaving to earn money in the city is a solution; but his words to Isabel, his wife, audibly protest too much: 'this hope is a good hope' (278). Isabel fears the worst:

> for, when she lay
> By Michael's side, she through the last two nights
> Heard him, how he was troubled in his sleep:
> And when they rose at morning she could see
> That all his hopes were gone.   (289–93)

Parting with Luke, Michael still manages to speak of 'good hope' and 'many hopes' (388–98), but by now the more we hear the term, the closer it sounds to fear. Looking to the imagined future can be an exile from all that is actually present. So perhaps the 'instinctive tenderness' which 'blindly works in the blood of all', the irrational lovability of one's own child by which Michael finds himself 'enforced / To acts of tenderness' (156–7), does threaten the old man's place in the grandeur of that very different 'blind love, / The pleasure which there is in life itself' (76–7).

Anticipation becomes audibly destructive on the day before Luke leaves, when his father takes him to the sheep-fold they had hoped to build together. Michael then so powerfully feels the pain of looming separation that dialogue threatens to collapse into soliloquy:

> 'This was a work for us; and now, my Son,
> It is a work for me. But, lay one stone –
> Here, lay it for me, Luke, with thine own hands.
> Nay, Boy, be of good hope; – we both may live
> To see a better day. At eighty-four
> I still am strong and hale; – do thou thy part;
> I will do mine. – I will begin again
> With many tasks that were resigned to thee:
> Up to the heights, and in among the storms,
> Will I without thee go again, and do
> All works which I was wont to do alone,
> Before I knew thy face. – Heaven bless thee, Boy!
> Thy heart these two weeks has been beating fast
> With many hopes; it should be so – yes – yes –
> I knew that thou couldst never have a wish
> To leave me, Luke: thou hast been bound to me
> Only by links of love: when thou art gone,
> What will be left to us!'   (385–402)

The frequent vocatives, and even the repeated 'yes', do not function positively to suggest Luke's closeness. They point by contrast to Michael's fear of how much may already be incommunicable between father and son.

For eight years Luke has lived exactly his father's life:

> soon as Luke, full ten years old, could stand
> Against the mountain blasts; and to the heights,
> Not fearing toil, nor length of weary ways,
> He with his Father daily went, and they
> Were as companions,   (194–8)

Now, on the day before they part, Luke is anticipating a wholly different way of life from that to which his father must return – 'Up to the heights . . . alone'. Michael's affection makes him pleased that Luke is looking forward to city life with 'many hopes,' but this immediately triggers an anxiety: those who do not regret going may not return. So Michael needs to persuade himself that the boy 'could never have a wish to leave'. Such undisguised fluctuations suggest the privacy of monologue. Michael is already anticipating the time when he will again have to talk only to himself. The speech which begins with 'This was a work for us; and now, my Son, / It is a work for me,' falters into a soliloquy where 'us' suggests only Michael himself and Isabel. It has already dwindled to exclude Luke: 'when thou art gone, / What will be left of us!'

Eventually the pretence of dialogue becomes too great a strain:

> The old Man's grief broke from him; to his heart
> He pressed his Son, he kissed him and wept;
> And to the house together they returned.
> – Hushed was that House in peace, or seeming peace,
> Ere the night fell: (421–5)

The family is 'hushed' into a 'seeming peace', a silence which already threatens to freeze into the tableau of Michael's final wordless isolation. Into this encroaching silence, the narrative poems' rare moments of direct speech reverberate. Their fading echoes are thus made to sound at once compellingly distinct, and yet pathetically frail.

II

Wordsworth's more usual method is to allow his characters to show us, rather than tell us, what they are feeling; but the poetry is not straightforwardly 'symbolic'. It does not impose a patronizing structure of literary images whose significance could only be comprehended by author and reader, and not by the characters. On the contrary, the poems respect what the characters themselves choose to make significant. In *The Ruined Cottage* Margaret articulates her despair by allowing her house and garden to collapse. But her preservation of Robert's more personal belongings precisely conveys her sense that she herself belongs here only – and yet absolutely – because Robert may come once again to treat it as his home. We feel it is Margaret who chooses what to do, and what to leave undone, so as to signal her priorities to the Pedlar and – should he ever return – to Robert.

Michael is explicitly about a far more conscious choice of symbol. The shepherd makes his son lay the cornerstone for a new sheep-fold before he leaves the farm. The scene may turn out in practice to falter from an optimistic dialogue into a tacit admission that the ritual could prove powerless. But Michael's intention is clearly to demonstrate faith. Luke is told that this act is to form 'a covenant' between father and son, representing the shared hope that they will 'live/To see a better day' (414, 388–9). Michael promises to complete the sheep-fold, and maintain the farm and flock it epitomizes, so that all will be ready for Luke's return (412–14, 391–6). Luke's side of the bargain is to look after himself so as to be able to return, and to remember this moment which binds him to do so, defining him as the cornerstone of the farm's future, and of his father's hopes (405–15).

The hill farmer's way of life had the great advantage to Wordsworth of being innately symbolic. To Michael, the landscape of his work 'had impressed/So many incidents upon his mind/Of hardship, skill or courage, joy or fear' that the scenery seemed to have 'preserved the memory' and to be 'like a book' (67–70). Wordsworth makes a similar point about independent shepherds in a letter to James Fox:

> Their little tract of land serves as a kind of permanent rallying point for their domestic feelings, as a tablet upon which they are written which makes them objects of memory in a thousand instances when they would otherwise be forgotten.[2]

At first the two points may seem distinct. The lines from the poem see land as triggering memories of a working life, 'Of hardship, skill or courage'. Wordsworth's letter describes land as a preserver of family values, a 'rallying point' for 'domestic feelings'. But, of course, the independent hill farmer's way of life appealed to Wordsworth precisely because there the two might be compatible to the point of being interdependent.

Early in the poem we are offered two apparently quite different definitions of love. There is 'The pleasure which there is in life itself' which, for Michael, is 'A pleasurable feeling of blind love' for the landscape where he works (76–7). There is also the 'instinctive tenderness' of father for child which 'blindly works' in the blood of all men (144–5). Because the land is passed on from father to son, hill farming offered Wordsworth an image in which these two partial visions could be mutually supportive. The hill farmer's love for the land, and for the flock it feeds, is a practical expression of his love for his family – his respect for the values of his forefathers, and his concern for the future of his children. The flock is maintained by the annual retention of the best female lambs to replace ewes which have grown too old to breed. It thus has the permanence of the 'woods decaying, never to be decay'd' in 'Crossing the Alps'. Endless generations of the same flock graze upon the same pastures. There is no stock-proof fencing. Each lamb learns the habit of keeping to the farmer's land from its mother. So sheep, like their shepherds, represent an innately traditional way of life. In one place, succeeding generations of the same flock sustain – and are sustained by – succeeding generations of the same farming family. Wordsworth can write in *The Brothers* of a flock which 'Had clothed the Ewbanks for a thousand years' (*PW*, II.9, 303). *Michael*, itself, he told Thomas Poole, was intended as

> a picture of a man, of strong mind and lively sensibility, agitated by two of the most powerful affections of the human heart; the parental affection, and the love of property, *landed* property, including the feelings of inheritance, home, and personal and family independence.[3]

If love for the land involves as many 'feelings of inheritance, home . . . and family independence' as does 'parental affection', then the two, far from being mutually exclusive, can seem almost indistinguishable. The land on which man works for flock and family seems to body forth an essentially integrated system of values.

This innate symbolism, however, is deployed by Wordsworth in poems which consistently record the collapse of such values. Even if there had once been a way of life in which a man need feel no conflict between his response to landscape and to people, Wordsworth sensed that it was now over. 'This class of men is rapidly disappearing,' he told Fox. In *The Brothers*, the bankrupt Ewbanks lose home and land and flock. The father, 'buffeted with bond, / Interest and mortgages' goes 'into his grave before his time' leaving his sons destitute (*PW*, II. 7, 214–16). Leonard has to enlist as a sailor, deserting his brother in order to support him financially.

In *The Last of the Flock*, Wordsworth describes his meeting with a hill farmer who, in a vicious circle of poverty, has been forced to sell the sheep which have allowed him to be a breadwinner. The parish authorities have said that, until the last is sold, they will regard him as 'a wealthy man' whose family cannot be given 'what to the poor is due' (*PW*, II. 44, 41–50). But to the shepherd the flock is not a mere financial asset: he sees it as the very source of commitment to his family. It was only his success in building up a flock which made him feel competent to support a wife and children:

> 'When I was young, a single man,
> And after youthful follies ran,
> Though little given to care and thought,
> Yet, so it was, an ewe I bought;
> And other sheep from her I raised,
> As healthy sheep as you might see;
> And then I married, and was rich
> As I could wish to be;
> Of sheep I numbered a full score,
> And every year increased my store.
>
> 'Year after year my stock it grew;
> And from this one, this single ewe,
> Full fifty comely sheep I raised,
> As fine a flock as ever grazed!
> Upon the Quantock hills they fed;
> They throve, and we at home did thrive:'   (21–36)

The personal pronoun, in which the shepherd refers to his original ewe as 'her', gives the animal no more than her due. Almost as much as his wife, she is the foundation of the shepherd's personal life. Without her fertility, he could never have felt able to 'number'

himself as 'rich' enough to marry, and to have children. The flock, in
feeding itself upon the hills, also feeds his family.

So the process of selling, 'in a time of need', his breeding sheep
deranges the shepherd into feeling that he is betraying not only them,
but also his family:

> 'To wicked deeds I was inclined,
> And wicked fancies crossed my mind;
> And every man I chanced to see,
> I thought he knew some ill of me;
> No peace, no comfort could I find,
> No ease, within doors or without;
> And crazily and wearily
> I went my work about;
> And oft was moved to flee from home,
> And hide my head where wild beasts roam.'   (71–80)

Self-confidence not only as farmer, but also as a father, rises and falls
with the numbers of the man's sheep;

> 'Sir! 'twas a precious flock to me,
> As dear as my own children be;
> For daily with my growing store
> I loved my children more and more.
> Alas! it was an evil time;
> God cursed me in my sore distress,
> I prayed, yet every day I thought
> I loved my children less;
> And every week, and every day,
> My flock it seemed to melt away.'   (81–90)

His love for his children, deformed by his pained sense that he is
failing them and selling their birthright, becomes hatred. Their needs,
which had made the expansion of the flock meaningful, now appear
cruelly voracious as they demolish all that he has lovingly built.

So selling the last of the flock is virtually synonymous with abandoning his roles as husband and father. It is a precise emblem,
admitting a total defeat:

> – 'This lusty Lamb of all my store
> Is all that is alive;
> And now I care not if we die,
> And perish all of poverty.'   (37–40)

The shepherd recognizes, in the lamb he carries to market, a symbol defining, equally and inseparably, the death of the flock and the end of family life. It is typical of Wordsworth's respect for his characters' own sense of significance that, in what is technically a dialogue poem, the shepherd himself has the last words, and that they form the title by which we guess the poem's meaning: 'It is the last of all my flock' (100).

In writing *Michael*, Wordsworth was faced by a temptation to make the sheep-fold carry significances which could seem meaningless to the old shepherd himself. We know from Dorothy's Journal that the actual sheep-fold which inspired the poem was 'built nearly in the form of a heart unequally divided'.[4] But Michael would not be sentimental enough to choose a shape for his sheep-fold on the basis that it could resemble a heart. Of course he means the building to express his love for Luke. But he hopes that such love belongs not in the precariously self-contained fictions of a Valentine's card, but in the securely interlocking facts of a hill farmer's job. The actual functions of sheep farming are so important to Michael, and to his plans for Luke, that the design of the sheep-fold's walls will be determined only by the specific 'kinds of labour for his sheep' that it is meant to facilitate (458). Even at the very end Michael still struggles to see it as 'the fold of which / His flock had need' (460–1).

Moreover Michael does not want to feel that his emotional commitments are 'unequally divided'. There should be no innate conflict between loyalty to the land bequeathed by his own father, and to the son who should eventually inherit it. Michael means to shape the sheep-fold into a binding agreement as to what the farm requires. Luke's return is to Michael partly what the fold is – something 'of which his flock had need'. It is these 'links of love' forged by the chain of inheritance that Michael's practical imagination strives to hold. He sees Luke's departure as threatening to impose a false symbolism, a denial of the interdependent values by which, since his son's birth, he has lived. So the covenant of the sheep-fold is intended as a counterweight to misleading metaphor. Just such a metaphor had been offered by the shape of the real sheep-fold which Dorothy describes. Wordsworth rightly kept it out of the poem. Michael cannot see his lovingly laborious life in either such decorative, or such discriminating, terms as 'a heart unequally divided'.

III

In the end, of course, Michael's symbolism is defeated. He had hoped that the laying of the foundation stone would help Luke to remember in the city that his true place was on the land:

> When thou art gone away, should evil men
> Be thy companions, think of me, my Son,
> And of this moment; hither turn thy thoughts,
>
>   . . .
>
>   that thou
> May'st bear in mind the life thy Fathers lived,   (405–10)

But 'in the dissolute city', Luke soon forgets the sheep-fold and all that it represents. Eventually he behaves so badly that he has to flee abroad.

Yet even now, when Michael knows the covenant is irreparably broken, he still uses the sheep-fold to express his feelings:

> And to that hollow dell from time to time
> Did he repair, to build the Fold of which
> His flock had need. 'Tis not forgotten yet
> The pity which was then in every heart
> For the old Man – and 'tis believed by all
> That many and many a day he thither went,
> And never lifted up a single stone.
>
> There, by the Sheep-fold, sometimes was he seen
> Sitting alone, or with his faithful Dog,
> Then old, beside him, lying at his feet.
> The length of full seven years, from time to time,
> He at the building of this Sheep-fold wrought,
> And left the work unfinished when he died.
> Three years, or little more, did Isabel
> Survive her Husband: at her death the estate
> Was sold, and went into a stranger's hand.   (460–75)

Trusting his unsophisticated characters to speak for themselves through gestures, Wordsworth does not confine them to expressing unambivalent feelings. Margaret is centred on 'one torturing hope', yet in the cottage she allows to collapse, we see her growing despair.

Michael knows his son will not return, but in the sheep-fold he still struggles to build, we see the painful flickering of a hope which threatens his calm resignation.

Michael ends up 'sitting alone' but, like the building of the sheep-fold, his isolation is his own choice – a wordless statement of the love he feels for his son. He does not have to be alone. He is surrounded by sympathetic witnesses who remember, years later, 'The pity which was then in every heart / For the old Man'. He is the subject of an affectionate community's gossip ("tis believed by all'), and the object of concerned eyes ('sometimes was he seen'). His wife's loyalty and physical strength as a survivor remain unquestioned. But she is evidently no more of a solution to Michael's potential tragedy than is 'his faithful Dog / Then old'. What Michael needs to express is not simple loneliness. Like Margaret, who lives with her children and is visited by the Pedlar, Michael is not isolated from people in general, but feels abandoned by one particular person. Luke has left a gap which other people – however numerous they are, however well intentioned they feel – cannot fill. They are kept at a distance, silently observing Michael's silence. They helplessly watch him articulate the fluctuations of his baffled love as he sometimes sat 'And never lifted up a single stone', and on other occasions 'at the building of this Sheep-fold wrought.'

Wordsworth never sees the rustic community as able to substitute for the intensity of more personal relationships. In *The Brothers* the priest recalls that once Leonard had gone, James 'drooped, and pined, and pined' (340). Yet the orphan was surrounded by love:

> He was the child of all the dale – he lived
> Three months with one, and six months with another;
> And wanted neither food, nor clothes, nor love: (343–5)

The priest believes he died largely because 'His absent Brother still was at his heart' (348). Similarly in *The Fountain* Matthew insists that others cannot substitute for his dead children – 'many love me; but by none / Am I enough beloved' (*PW*, IV. 73, 55–6).

But even if the bereaved can gain little comfort from other people, they are not exiled into some fantastical total vacuum. Luke may have gone, but Michael is still surrounded by a dynamic universe:

> There is a comfort in the strength of love;
> 'Twill make a thing endurable, which else

> Would overset the brain, or break the heart:
> I have conversed with more than one who well
> Remember the old Man, and what he was
> Years after he had heard this heavy news.
> His bodily frame had been from youth to age
> Of an unusual strength. Among the rocks
> He went, and still looked up to sun and cloud,
> And listened to the wind; and, as before,
> Performed all kinds of labour for his sheep,
> And for the land, his small inheritance.   (448–59)

At first we may well misinterpret the 'comfort in the strength of love'. We may remember that it was Luke who had earlier been called Michael's 'comfort and his daily hope' (206). We may struggle to believe that the very strength of Michael's need for Luke is what makes the boy's absence tolerable. But the line invites us to try only so that we will eventually dismiss the paradox as a cruel nonsense.

The comfort, of course, comes not from thinking of the absent Luke but from recognizing all that can never go away. Michael falls back upon that 'blind love' for his landscape which to him had been 'life itself' before Luke was born. Then Michael's 'bodily frame had been from youth to age / Of an unusual strength' (43–4). The verbatim echo of these early lines at the end of the poem stresses survival. What has survived is in many ways the very opposite of loneliness. Michael, though choosing to be apart from other people, confronts with his 'unusual strength' the still present forces of his world. He maintains that sense of relationship with recognized realities that – before he had dared to hope for a son – had taught him 'the meaning of all winds' (48). Then he had responded to the boisterous call of the storm which, both as a challenge and as an invitation, had 'summoned him / Up to the mountains' (57–8). It is that sense of belonging, that acknowledgement of his own inevitable involvement, which survives:

> Among the rocks
> He went, and still looked up to sun and cloud,
> And listened to the wind;   (455–7)

Michael still cares for his flock – 'the dumb animals, whom he had saved, / Had fed or sheltered' before Luke's birth (71–2). The neighbours report that, after Luke's loss, the shepherd, 'as before, / Performed all kinds of labour for his sheep' (458).

It is true that there are more poignant reverberations in the phrase: 'as before'. It recalls Michael's earlier reacceptance of 'many tasks' that had been 'resigned to' Luke:

> Up to the heights, and in among the storms,
> Will I without thee go again, and do
> All works which I was wont to do alone,
> Before I knew thy face.   (394–6)

Similarly Michael's surviving response 'to sun and cloud, / And . . . to the wind' (455–7) may recall the broken relationship with his son who, in happier times, had given him 'Feelings and emanations – things which were / Light to the sun and music to the wind' (201–2). There is pathos too in Michael's working 'for the land, his small inheritance' (459). What should have been destined to be Luke's is now recognized by Michael as only 'his', and so a more pathetically 'small inheritance' than it had once seemed.

But these closing paragraphs only hint at the father's unhappy tenderness for his son. What they assert is the grandeur of Michael's surviving sense of reality. The sun, the clouds, the winds, the hills along with the 'dumb animals' they support, are felt presences to Michael. They are visible to his 'blind love', and in the strength of that unfaded vision he takes comfort. To the concerned witnesses, Michael sitting alone at the sheep-fold is alone indeed. They may fear that without Luke he will find life so empty that he may go mad, or even die. But Michael himself still often feels surrounded by 'The pleasure which there is in life itself', among 'Those fields, those hills' which 'had laid strong hold on his affections' (74–7):

> There is a comfort in the strength of love;
> 'Twill make a thing endurable, which else
> Would overset the brain, or break the heart: (448–50)

Michael may have his temporary aberrations of thinking that the world could be well lost for love of Luke. But after them he goes home to the living universe glimpsed by Wordsworth in 'Crossing the Alps'. We are meant to find in ourselves feelings which validate not only Michael's sense of his son's preciousness, but also the old man's heroic rediscovery of the world about him. We may be impressed by a love strong enough to 'overset the brain, or break the heart'. But we must be alerted to the oddity of favouring a feeling

which – at its most impressively intense – will make us mad and
miserable.

IV

So in the end Michael's apparent isolation is presented in two quite
different ways. One is an inert image of loss – 'sitting alone'. The
other is a dynamic movement through a landscape which can never
be lost, a world which demands Michael's work as surely as it exposes
him to its weather:

> Among the rocks
> He went, and still looked up to sun and cloud,
> And listened to the wind; and, as before,
> Performed all kinds of labour for his sheep,   (455–8)

There are two distinct kinds of solitude. Michael, who can slump
beneath the tragic disorientation of one, achieves the triumphant
sanity of frequently rising into the other.

Wordsworth's own vision of the landscape acknowledges both.
He closes the poem with an evocatively depopulated solitude which
still speaks of the man who loved his son here years ago:

> The Cottage which was named the Evening Star
> Is gone – the ploughshare has been through the ground
> On which it stood; great changes have been wrought
> In all the neighbourhood: – yet the oak is left
> That grew beside their door; and the remains
> Of the unfinished Sheep-fold may be seen
> Beside the boisterous brook of Green-head Ghyll.
>   (476–82)

We remember the detailed domestic idyll of father, mother and son
working at their fireside, beneath a lamp which could be seen so far
away that the cottage 'was named the Evening Star' by all 'who dwelt
within the limits of the vale' (95–139).

The singular oak tree which survives at the end stands even more
specifically for the love between father and son. It recalls the lengthy
passage in which Michael insisted that Luke, 'ere yet the Boy / Had
put on boy's attire', should sit with him 'Under the large old oak'
while he sheared the sheep (159–76). Wordsworth had then stressed
that the tree's name – unlike the love that gave it its significance – had

survived: it 'was called/The Clipping Tree, a name which yet it bears' (168–9). The human language, which gives names to cottage and tree and stream, makes this final solitude reverberate to the echoes of love between people who are now dead.

But, of course, their deaths have only changed, not ended, the scene. Michael's sheep-fold, like Margaret's cottage, is a poignantly frail anomaly in a natural world whose own apparent decay is merely a figment of human imagination. The Clipping Tree of *Michael*, like the elms of *The Ruined Cottage*, survive long after the human buildings collapse. The trees belong in a world whose undiminished energy is as 'boisterous' as the brook which flows through the last line of *Michael*. They are like the woods of the Simplon Pass, 'decaying, never to be decay'd'. Even if a particular elm or oak had fallen, it would only have made a space of light in which saplings it had itself seeded could grow. It is in the human mind, not the external world, that a tree can be made so preciously specific as to become an elegy for a dead past:

> – But there's a Tree, of many, one,
> A single Field which I have looked upon,
> Both of them speak of something that is gone:
> (*The Immortality Ode, PW*, iv. 280, 51–3)

Michael himself turns out to have more in common with the natural world's resilience than Isabel's tenderness for him allows her to expect. He does not die of grief at Luke's departure as she fears he will (298). In fact he lives on for a full seven years after he knows that Luke will not return. Michael eventually dies of, precisely, natural causes.

In the last paragraph of the poem Wordsworth does make the isolated landscape speak, in nouns that are singular and specific, of the human tenderness that cares for a particular, and inevitably mortal, person. But he has already, in the poem's first paragraph, offered the reader an alternative view of the same scene, a view deploying the inclusiveness of plural nouns:

> around that boisterous brook
> The mountains have all opened out themselves,
> And made a hidden valley of their own.
> No habitation can be seen; but they
> Who journey thither find themselves alone

> With a few sheep, with rocks and stones, and kites
> That overhead are sailing in the sky.
> It is in truth an utter solitude;   (6–13)

Of course even here – though it is so explicitly made out of the mountains themselves – the hidden valley is singular. Wordsworth is, after all, about to notice the specific trigger of his story – 'a straggling heap of unhewn stones' (17). But this last vestige of the sheep-fold is as he says an 'object which you might pass by, / Might see and notice not' (15–16). It is easy to ignore this artificial distraction from the natural scenery's 'utter solitude', and it is not necessarily wrong to do so.

For the solitude is not an emptiness. The careful placing of the ending to line 10 gulls us into our normal assumption that to be away from people is to be in some kind of vacuum, to be really alone: 'they / Who journey thither find themselves alone' (9–10). But then as the eye moves to the beginning of the next line, the illusion is exploded. Self-discovery need not mean recognition of one's own alienated isolation. It can mean finding oneself to be surrounded by life, accompanied by a plural world: 'With a few sheep, with rocks and stones, and kites / That overhead are sailing in the sky.' So long as 'alone' remains unqualified, it suggests only a negative absence of human company. But the next lines reveal the positive presence of sheep, the palpability of the rocky ground, the visibility of a sky, whose serene vastness allows the kites to sail it as if it were a sea. A precisely similar effect is achieved at line 58 where Michael momentarily appears alone, before being revealed as at the centre of incalculably fluid energies: 'he had been alone / Amid the heart of many thousand mists' (58–9). In spite of our fantasies of alienation, we are never really alone. We may not notice it, but, like Lucy, we are always being 'rolled round in earth's diurnal course, / With rocks, and stones, and trees' (*PW*, II.216, 7–8).

Wordsworth uses no adjective to qualify the 'rocks and stones' in either poem. Nor will he choose between the two words. In the end, the world cannot be reduced by our limited terminology any more than it can be forced to contract into a single, loved person. Temporarily stones can be tidied into symbols of affection such as Margaret's cottage or Michael's sheep-fold, but the fluid weather of our world will dissolve them into a 'straggling heap' once more.

For Michael to base his entire life on such precarious symbols would be an irrational delusion. In as much as Michael loves Luke, he risks finding himself in a solitude which might 'overset the brain, or break the heart'. 'The weakness of humanity', which he shares with Margaret of *The Ruined Cottage*, brings him dangerously close to her final state, and at the end of *Michael*, too, Wordsworth sees the landscape as impressively marked with the ruins of human love. But Michael has the strength, derived from a different love, to pull back from the brink, rather than fall over into the illusion of vacuum.

The vision of the opening paragraph is never really abandoned by the poem. There is a kind of grandeur in finding oneself as a being who can never be truly alone, in recognizing that the kites flying overhead are as real as the few sheep one tends beneath, in accepting that the stones which can be ordered into a frail sheep-fold are ultimately inseparable from the eternal rocks. To live consciously in such a multifarious solitude is to be safe from the misery of loneliness. But to do so – as Michael's survival demonstrates – involves controlling, if not actually suppressing, the capacity to feel love for another person. To maintain his sense of purpose, to keep an ear for wind and weather, to still care for the land, Michael has to contain the intensity of his grief over Luke. Wordsworth constantly makes us question our lazier assumptions by compelling us to redefine our terms. In *The Ruined Cottage* the weakness of humanity is made to mean, not a callous lack of feeling, but a dangerous intensity of tenderness. So in *Michael* the strength of love is defined, not as the longevity of the father's tenderness for his son, but as the old man's stamina in remaining alive to the landscape's grandeur.

V

The opening paragraph, like the story for which it prepares us, contains another kind of ambivalence which is less obviously a controlled complexity. It is only because Wordsworth here writes with such instinctive honesty that the potential confusion is audible, and both its origin and its implications are intriguing.

The poem is at first more about reader and author than about a shepherd. It opens in an insistently vocative tone, deploying the words 'you' or 'yours' on six occasions in the first fifteen lines. Initially there is no audible respect for the farmers who live and work upon these hills. Instead the poem sounds confident only that the reader, a mere visitor, will be able to appreciate the 'utter solitude'.

Such an experience is conditional upon deviating from the more customary and sociable routes: 'If from the public way you turn your steps/Up the tumultous brook of Green-head Ghyll' (1–2). The reader is encouraged to approach the absence of all human associations as a positive advantage:

> But, courage! for around that boisterous brook
> The mountains have all opened out themselves,
> And made a hidden valley of their own.
> No habitation can be seen; (6–9)

The poet assumes that his audience shares the values which make no distinction between livestock and wild birds, between the stones with which farmers build, and the intractably natural rocks:

> they
> Who journey thither find themselves alone
> With a few sheep, with rocks and stones, and kites
> That overhead are sailing in the sky. (9–12)

The implication is that all are equally important aspects of the experience which rewards a determined pursuit of seclusion. The mountains opening out 'themselves' are precisely echoed by the travellers discovering 'themselves' to be open to this all-embracing vision. So humanity seems to have merged almost indistinguishably · with landscape.

Without warning, this tendency is reversed. No sooner has the audience faded into third-person travellers identified with the mountains, than the author steps forward to insist on his own presence. With disconcerting suddenness he focuses on 'a straggling heap of unhewn stones', and promises that 'to that simple object appertains a story' (17–19). Moreover this story is to have innately human interest in terms both of its subject, and of the author's autobiography:

> It was the first
> Of those domestic tales that spake to me
> Of shepherds, (21–3)

Momentarily, but crucially, we are bewildered.

Author and reader have, up to this point, colluded in attitudes which deliberately leave behind the merely 'domestic'. Their approach has seemed distinct from that of a professional farmer. Their glance at 'a few sheep' is posed in relaxedly imprecise terms.

They would no more dream of counting the animals than they would those incalculably free birds, 'sailing in the sky'. Both, to author and reader, appear like the rocks: equally stable parts of a natural world, givens which could only be misconstrued by human arithmetic and insulted by human possessiveness. They form a landscape as innately 'measureless to man' as that which Kubla Khan so rashly tried to contain.

But some farmer thinks of those few sheep as his. To him they belong in a flock on which he counts for his family's income. Sometimes he will literally count his sheep: in lambing time to calculate his flock's gains, and in a hard winter to assess his losses. The kites, by contrast, he will account as enemies. Such birds are perfectly capable of eating the eyes of a lamb which, though weakened by malnutrition or sickness, might otherwise have survived. A hill farmer cannot always afford the inclusive, undiscriminating vision of a poet.

Wordsworth is prepared for our suspicions. Before we can fully formulate a fear that he may simply not care enough about sheep farmers to notice such facts, he makes his embarrassingly honest confession:

> Shepherds, dwellers in the valleys, men
> Whom I already loved; – not verily
> For their own sakes, but for the fields and hills
> Where was their occupation and abode.
> And hence this Tale, while I was yet a Boy
> Careless of books, yet having felt the power
> Of Nature, by the gentle agency
> Of natural objects, led me on to feel
> For passions that were not my own, and think
> (At random and imperfectly indeed)
> On man, the heart of man, and human life.   (23–33)

Wordsworth can seldom have written so confusingly, but the clumsy candour with which such confusion is admitted makes him his own best critic.

Before the story can have a chance to gull us, its teller is self-consciously hesitant about its significance. Wordsworth attempts a distinction between interest in the shepherds 'For their own sakes', and 'for the fields and hills', but immediately allows it to collapse. The hills are glossed as the peculiar 'occupation and abode' of hill farmers. Since the landscape can thus be seen, not just as the natural world, but also as a place of work, we are confusingly led back to feelings which may be available only to those doing a particular job, and so to a concern with shepherds 'For their own sakes'. By the time Wordsworth recalls his response to 'natural objects', he has already revealed his interest in the 'straggling heap' of 'unhewn' masonry out of which, in the method builders call 'random stone', Cumbrian farmers contrive their essentially artificial enclosures. Wordsworth tries to assert that one concern leads logically to the other. He claims that it is 'the power/Of Nature' which leads him to care about what matters to people whose feelings may be different from his own. But the link between 'the gentle agency of natural objects' and curiosity about 'human life' is broken: Wordsworth interrupts himself with the parenthetical admission that his thinking here has been 'At random and imperfectly indeed'.

The first paragraph closes by raising one further issue which at first can seem irrelevant egotism, rather than a crucial doubt about the ensuing story. Wordsworth claims his strongest motive for telling the tale is a concern for 'youthful Poets, who among these hills / Will be my second self when I am gone' (38–9). We should not read this as merely a personal vanity about the poet's faring well in the hands of posterity. It evokes Wordsworth's humbly human wish that he can find a cheering analogy between the apparently contented farmers and himself. The second life with which an ageing shepherd can console himself in the prospect of his son inheriting the farm could help the poet to cheerfully accept his own mortality. The vanity, in the opposingly humble sense, of all such wishes is to be boldly considered in the story.

Michael may at one moment hope that his son's return to the land is as certain as that of the reliably recurring winds that blow across it: 'He shall possess it, free as is the wind/That passes over it' (246–7). Yet the shepherd more often remembers that winds can be ruthlessly variable, and that his livelihood depends on recognizing which wind is about to blow in direct opposition to his concerns:

> Hence had he learned the meaning of all winds,
> Of blasts of every tone; and oftentimes,
> When others heeded not, He heard the South
> Make subterraneous music, like the noise
> Of bagpipers on distant Highland hills.
> The Shepherd, at such warning, of his flock

> Bethought him, and he to himself would say,
> 'The winds are now devising work for me!'
> And, truly, at all times, the storm, that drives
> The traveller to a shelter, summoned him
> Up to the mountains: (48–58)

The poet himself must often have been amongst those others who 'heeded not' because they had no professional need to do so. Where Michael hears a clear warning, the well-travelled poet catches a merely musical echo of the Scottish Highlands. Certainly Wordsworth's memories of the Alps would suggest an undiscriminating delight in 'the tumult and the peace', an acceptance of 'winds thwarting winds' as a fusion of sounds. Michael, by contrast, needs to act before a storm can kill the weaker of those 'dumb animals whom he had saved / Had fed or sheltered' (71–2), so he must distinguish the threat of tumult from the promise of peace. Even the 'brook of Green-head Ghyll' which is twice described as 'tumultuous' by the poet, must seem more demandingly so to the shepherd (2, 322). According to another Lyrical Ballad, *The Idle Shepherd-Boys*, 'A Poet' should only need to be 'one who loves the brooks' (*PW*, I.241, 84), whereas a shepherd must sometimes see their waters as a 'black and frightful' threat to 'A thousand lambs . . . All newly born' who 'are on the rocks' at 'the river's stony marge' (66, 23–7). So it is an essentially 'unexpected' situation in which the poet himself finds a drowning lamb before the arrival of the young shepherds who were meant to be guarding the flock from just such a fate; as the last line complains, this is 'their trade' and not Wordsworth's (91–9).

If rescuing lambs is the job of a shepherd and not a poet, then rhetorical admiration for the landscape is more Wordsworth's work than Michael's. Wordsworth knows that there may be too much of the ventriloquist in his approach to Michael's speeches. He frankly admits, in a manuscript draft, how the shepherd would in fact react to the loftier claims made for him by the poem:

> No doubt if you in terms direct had ask'd
> Whether he lov'd the mountains, true it is
> That with blunt repetition of your words
> He might have stared at you, and said that they
> Were frightful to behold.   (*PW*, II.482, b 1–5)

But immediately after these wryly realistic lines, Wordsworth imagines that a poet, sufficiently gifted to 'talk of common things / In an unusual way', could manipulate the shepherd's response by 'questions apt'. Even then Michael himself would be persuaded merely to look, not talk, like a poet. One could guarantee only that:

> this untaught shepherd stood
> Before the man with whom he so convers'd
> And look'd at him as with a Poet's eye.
>
> *(PW, II.482, b 19–21)*

His commitment to the very farm itself would have to be taken on trust from facial expression:

> if you had asked if he
> For other pastures would exchange the same
> And dwell elsewhere, I will not say indeed
> What wonders might have been perform'd by bribes
> And by temptations, but you then had seen
> At once what Spirit of Love was in his heart.
>
> *(PW, II.482, b 23–8)*

Clearly Wordsworth, though wishing to find similarities between himself and the shepherd, recognizes that they would be embarrassingly hard to prove.

Wordsworth's admission that 'bribes' might well persuade Michael to move is far more damaging than its parenthetical position suggests. In the printed poem, Michael is to be admired for his healthy desire to farm at a profit. The landscape's 'book' which records 'So many incidents . . . Of hardship, skill or courage, joy or fear', is read by Michael as much from a small businessman's point of view as 'with a Poet's eye'. To the shepherd, the landscape is partly an accounting book, 'linking to such acts / The certainty of honorable gain' (65–73). So Michael might consider moving to lower and better land if he could afford the investment. We could not condemn him for this when we are required to respect him for doing his best by his family.

Michael, however, barely has a family. As another rejected manuscript passage spelt out perhaps too obviously, his abnormal situation may make him less challengingly like other hill farmers:

> he had less cause to love
> His native vale and patrimonial fields
> Or pleasure which is in the common earth

> Than others have, for Michael had liv'd on
> Childless until the time when he began
> To look towards the shutting in of life.   (PW, II. 483, 13–18)

Where the printed poem implies that, before Luke's birth, Michael does enjoy the landscape as 'the pleasure that there is in life itself', the emphasis has shifted from the 'earth' which other farmers can proudly own to 'The common air'; from land which they expect their sons to inherit to the landscape which a non-farming poet can appreciate. Since Michael's story begins in apparently permanent childlessness and ends in the virtual death of his only son, the plot forces the hero to abandon the traditional attitude of a hill farmer towards his farm's future. Thus the wish, so baldly revealed in the manuscripts, to make Michael less typical of his own kind and more like the poet could easily remain audible in the printed poem.

The poem's first paragraph clearly begs disturbing questions about our response to the ensuing story. Can there be any convincing similarities between a poet's and a hill farmer's attitudes? Is it as a soul sensitive to 'the power of Nature', and of 'utter solitude' that we should admire Michael? Or are we to see him as an important exemplum because the specialized effects of his work give him a rare system of values? Such a system might be quite different from that which allows author and reader occasionally to visit the place which Michael has inherited as home and livelihood. Is this to be a story about the inspiring beauty of 'fields and hills' where 'No habitation can be seen'? Or should we try to allocate the poem to a genre of essentially 'domestic tales', stories of men whose homes are working farms, and whose 'passions' may therefore be distinct from the poet's own?

VI

Faced by such alternatives, published criticism offers a choice of bewilderingly extreme emphases. On the one hand, there are those who stress *Michael*'s 'realism', to use David Perkins's term. He cites the poem as the clearest example of Wordsworth's ability to tackle subjects which 'have no intimate or important reference to his own personal history'.[5] Similarly Donald Wesling argues that Words-worth draws a firm distinction between his own major emotional commitment and those feelings which would matter most to a hill farmer: 'Wordsworth makes feeling as affection for property and family the peasant's deepest emotion, reserving imaginative feeling for himself.'[6] If so, would there not be an embarrassing distance between a poet so confidently claiming the title deeds to 'imaginative feeling' and a peasant so cruelly prevented from keeping both farm and family when his 'deepest emotion' makes either on its own valueless? John Danby, for instance, poses a shrewd question about 'The pleasure which there is in life itself', but then seems to deftly sidestep his own challenge: 'What here does "pleasure" mean in regard to "life" – the life that Michael knew, and Wordsworth knew, and we know? It is a magnificently simple and inclusive assertion. Wordsworth tends to use "pleasure" in a very final and hard-won sense.'[7] Surely this slides past the disconcerting possibility that 'the life that Michael knew' may be essentially different from Wordsworth's, and from the reader's.

Danby rightly praises Wordsworth's originality in rescuing shepherds from the fantasy of the pastoral tradition and insisting on the fact 'that they *worked*: and that they were members of a universe where work was of central importance'.[8] Yet the poet of 'Crossing the Alps' is 'halted without a struggle to break through' in a universe which does not have such work as its centre, and one recurring feature of the pastoral tradition is that the poet attempts to draw analogies between his own role and that of a shepherd, as Milton, for instance, does in *Lycidas*. Wordsworth gives fair warning at the end of *Michael*'s opening paragraph that – however much more sceptically – this poem too will be interested in that possibility.

So other readers do sense an overlap between Wordsworth's arguably blurred accounts of Michael's working life and of the poet's own. According to Hartman, Wordsworth

> establishes, in fact, a strange identity between himself and his main character. Both Michael and Wordsworth wish to save the land, the one for Luke, the other for the imagination. Michael desires Luke to inherit a land 'free as the Wind / That passes over it'; and Wordsworth tells Michael's story for the sake of 'youthful Poets, who *among these hills* / Will be my second self when I am gone'. The underlying concern, conscious in Wordsworth as shepherd-poet, is for the human imagination, which cannot be renewed unless it has a nature to blend with, not any nature, but *land* as free and old as the hills. . . . the land cannot retain its hold on Luke's

imagination. Can it, then, retain its hold through Wordsworth, who is restoring the covenant once more by wedding the mind of man and this goodly earth? The poet is Michael's true heir.[9]

This seems to me confused, but relevantly confused by what is actually present in the poem.

The truism that a hill farmer could not possibly conceive of a poet, who was not even a remote relative, as his 'true heir' matters more than Hartman implies. So does its converse: that Wordsworth himself would not actually wish to inherit the land and laborious life which Michael hopes to leave to Luke. Yet Hartman's emphases do underline the way that the poem's terms often dextrously balance between two quite different applications. We do sense that *'these hills'* and the *'land'* matter to Wordsworth both because of the peculiar significance they can only have for the hill farmer who owns one small part of them, and for an almost opposite reason: that Wordsworth longs to discover in Michael's life evidence that an undiscriminating delight in the total landscape and a love for one particular person can support each other.

Hartman is surely misinterpreting Michael's hope that he can keep the land 'free'. The context makes it clear that the land must belong to somebody. Michael is rejecting the plan 'to sell at once / A portion of his patrimonial fields' (223–4). He tells Isabel that

> if these fields of ours
> Should pass into a stranger's hand, I think
> That I could not lie quiet in my grave.   (230–2)

Michael opts instead for the bitter paradox that Luke, to save his own inheritance, must temporarily leave the land. Only then will it be certain that one day 'He shall possess it, free as is the wind / That passes over it' (246–7). Michael here clearly sees land as property to be possessed.

But though Hartman is wrong about what Michael means here, is he not curiously right about what Wordsworth means? Since this is the character's direct speech, Wordsworth is manipulating Michael into speaking not only for himself, but for the poet. Yet they clearly have different things to say. Michael is concerned with ownership as a palpable matter of selling or retaining title deeds. His whole point is how different Luke's experience of land which he owns can be from that of the traveller who merely passes through it. Yet Wordsworth provides Michael with a simile which better suits the casual tourist than the responsible owner-occupier. Michael cannot prevent strangers passing over his land any more than he can prevent the wind. But he still hopes to prevent a stranger owning it in a way that no wind, but only a rival human being, could attempt. Christopher Salvesen writes as if we all take it for granted that it is the landscape, and not particular kinds of work upon the land, which makes Michael significant:

> He is, after all, a man of special 'Wordsworthian' stature, and one who has recognised the power of landscape and mountain forms to impress themselves for the benefit of future good thinking and pure feeling.[10]

But surely he hardly ever sounds so much like a schoolmaster or priest, and does often sound quite like a shepherd. The future good to which he looks is frequently defined by reference to the specific nexus of field, flock and family. His 'unusual strength' impresses us as palpably physical rather than abstractly moral, and his energy is concentrated on preserving his family's rights to one relatively small stretch of land.

David Ferry too sees Michael's farm more as an emblem of the innocent natural world than an example of one particular means of earning a living:

> The farm in *Michael* is a place that seems almost out of time, secluded from the world and its affairs. While he lives there, the boy Luke is like a child of nature. But when he leaves the farm and goes far from his relation to eternal nature, he plays his family false. He does so *inevitably* because when he goes to the city he enters a corrupt, corrupting, and wholly human atmosphere. To live in the mortal world is *by definition* to be fickle.[11]

But surely Luke often strikes us as the son of an old farmer, rather than as 'a child of nature'. Like *The Brothers* and *The Last of the Flock*, *Michael* is more concerned with the innate precariousness of the farmer's relationship to land and family than with the external threat of an urban world. The agricultural environment itself, with its unlooked-for financial demands and its unpredictable weather, requires flexibility if not actual fickleness. The poem is not just about the 'relation to eternal nature', sought by Wordsworth himself. It is also about Michael's response to the vagaries of farming.

The tendency to treat Michael not as a shepherd but as an idealized self-portrait of Wordsworth reaches an extreme in John Beer's commentary. Here one might be forgiven for thinking that it is the autobiographical *Prelude*, and not a narrative poem, which is being quoted:

> had been alone
> Amid the heart of many thousand mists
> That came to him and left him on the heights.

The image of the cloud-wrapped man gives him a complex image for the progress of the adult man in a universe where he can never know the final truth: sometimes the cloud may open to reveal a landscape bathed in visionary light, sometimes it may enwrap him so completely as to threaten destruction. The dislocated sense of the phrase 'amid the heart' catches his insecurity finely.[12]

But whose insecurity? If these lines are about Michael as a real shepherd, then he could only be feeling insecure about his own physical safety, or anxious for his flock as the mists literally reduce visibility. He cannot fear that 'spots of time' where a man feels at the very centre of the world's pulsing life will be increasingly brief and rare as he grows further away from childhood. That is the elegiac poet's own role in *The Prelude*, which is indeed a portrait of the artist and not the story of Michael.

However, Wordsworth himself later used passages he had discarded from his writings for *Michael* in Book VIII of *The Prelude*.[13] They form part of a disastrous attempt to connect the poet's own response to the natural world with his vision of shepherds. Without the narrative discipline of *Michael*, the attempt fails both as art, and as argument. Book VIII is entitled 'Love of Nature Leading to Love of Man', but its clumsy verse soon destroys any credibility the thesis could have.

I cannot improve on Jonathan Wordsworth's demolition of this 'eulogy of the shepherd's way of life':

> Wordsworth's attempts to give it relevance are almost unbelievably lame:
>
> > My first human love,
> > As hath been mention'd, did incline to those
> > Whose occupations and concerns were most

Illustrated by Nature and adorn'd,
And shepherds were the men who pleas'd me first.

(MS Verse 20, The Prelude, VIII. 178–82)

Three 'spots of time' save the poetry from utter wretchedness, but impressive as the shepherd may be on his floating island amid the mist, or working his dog up the sun-lit mountainside, the descriptions hardly bear out the claim they were intended to illustrate:

For I already had been taught to *love*
My Fellow-beings, to such habits train'd
Among the woods and mountains. . . .

(VIII. 69–71 – Wordsworth's italics)

And there is a triumphant irrelevance about the conclusion to the famous simile of the 'Greenland Bears':

on rainy days
When I have angled up the lonely brooks
Mine eyes have glanced upon him, few steps off,
In size a Giant, stalking through the fog,
His sheep like Greenland Bears

. . .

Thus was Man
Ennobled outwardly before mine eyes,
And thus my heart at first was introduced
To an unconscious love and reverence
Of human nature. (VIII. 398–414)

The first claim is fair enough, the second hardly seems to follow. To complete the picture, half-way through the Book Wordsworth suddenly confides to Coleridge that he has been talking nonsense –

Yet do not deem, my Friend, though thus I speak
Of man as having taken in my mind
A place thus early which might almost seem
Preeminent, that it was really so. (VIII. 472–5)[14]

As Jonathan Wordsworth suggests, the poet's honesty here merely makes it 'unusually plain' that he 'has nothing to say'. One could add by way of contrast that the honesty of Wordsworth's best verse poses far more fruitful problems, derived from his determination to say so much.

Book VIII's dogmatic assertion that love of nature leads to love of man lacks the will to explore either concept in any detail. Fleeting glimpses of shepherds keep them at a safely blurred distance. There is no more pressure to verbalize the hill farmer's specialized relationship with his flock than there is to explore an Eskimo's attitude to polar bears. In *Michael*, on the other hand, the very plot imposes just such a pressure.

VII

Tied to the shifting implications of Michael's changing fortunes, the narrative admits that the right to associate the shepherd's attitudes with the poet's own must vary. After the opening paragraph's search for 'utter solitude' (13), we first meet Michael in lines which allow us to think of him as living alone: 'Upon the forest-side in Grasmere Vale / There dwelt a Shepherd, Michael was his name'. So begins the second paragraph's long description of Michael's way of life. That description makes no further reference to the homestead where he dwells, let alone to any family with whom he might share it. Instead we are told how often 'he had been alone'. Of course, Michael even here is not the distanced figure of Book VIII, since Wordsworth claims to know 'the shepherd's thoughts' about his fields and flock, and to understand his 'affections' for them (64, 75). Yet at first Michael is seen only in that terrain where his life would be visible to the tourists of the first paragraph. He works alone amongst 'Those fields, those hills' and though we are told that he makes an 'honourable gain', we have no sense that he means to support anybody but himself (73–4). A family, whose births and marriages and deaths might impose a more varying history, seems unlikely in the context of such a stable life: 'So lived he till his eightieth year was past' (61).

So the next verse paragraph has to begin conscious of the need to correct a false impression: 'his days had not been passed in singleness' (78). We do now hear about his wife, but Wordsworth does not reveal her name until another eighty lines have passed; and when Michael does at last address her as 'Isabel', he is beginning the speech which reveals his anguished decision to let his son leave (226). It is the existence of Luke which makes the poem in its third verse paragraph change direction as significantly as that fact alters Michael's life. Instead of the generalities offered earlier ('So many incidents . . . Of

hardship, skill or courage' (68–9)), we are now confronted by a
detailed moment typifying the intimate relationship between the
traditional hill farming team of a father and his son. They sit by their
fireside after supper working together at tasks which prove the
indivisibility of home and farm:

> perhaps to card
> Wool for the Housewife's spindle, or repair
> Some injury done to sickle, flail or scythe,
> Or other implement of house or field.   (106–9)

It is only when the poem enters Michael's cottage to describe his
family that we are obviously seeing more than those who walk
through the landscape of the first paragraph to seek 'utter solitude'
can see of a shepherd's life. Only here do we come close enough to
find the specific tools of a trade so obviously different from that of
writing poetry.

So long as solitude is thrust upon Michael by his lack of a son, he
can hardly afford to approach the fields which he inherited from his
own father with that concerned possessiveness which distinguishes
the owner of a part so clearly from a visitor to the whole. In his
extreme old age Michael himself returns to the kind of childlike
innocence so often celebrated in Wordsworth's verse. The adult's
ambitious, or anxious, concern with the future is softened by the
mercy of senile decay, and eventually 'By tendency of nature needs
must fail'.

But the birth of Luke awakens Michael to a more demanding view
of the land, and makes him in fact feel very much like any other hill
farmer. Appropriately it is in the ensuing paragraphs of the poem that
Wordsworth describes the shepherd so vividly in terms of his job and
thus evokes a way of life which is quite different from either the
author's or the reader's. Here are the lines about clipping which end
with Michael having to 'exercise his heart/With looks of fond cor-
rection' when the infant Luke:

> disturbed the sheep
> By catching at their legs, or with his shouts
> Scared them while they lay still beneath the shears   (159–76)

Here too are the lines in which Michael makes the child 'a perfect
shepherd's staff', and positions him 'At gate or gap, to stem or turn
the flock' (176–93).

Wordsworth is explicit about the impatience with which Michael is now looking to the future. Luke is given his job in the gathering 'prematurely' while he is, at best, still 'something between a hindrance and a help' (187–90). When Luke is only ten years old, he is taken every day up amongst 'the mountain blasts', and on 'to the heights'. His father's attitude to the land is now so different 'that the old Man's heart seemed born again' (194–203).

With Luke, Michael begins what seems to him to be a new life, but is in fact the traditional life of his forefathers. He now feels more passionately, and yet more vulnerably, alive. On the one hand he is more conscious of his delights: 'objects which the shepherd loved before / Were dearer now', and:

> from the boy there came
> Feelings and emanations – things which were
> Light to the sun and music to the wind;   (199–202)

On the other hand, Michael is more often concerned with the uncertain future: Luke is both 'his comfort and his daily hope' (206). When those hopes are defeated, Michael has once again to act without the normal sheep farmer's motivation. He has to find the will to do 'all kinds of labour' for what are now merely '*his* sheep', and for the land which is now no more than '*his* small inheritance' (458–9). Again he must respond 'to sun and cloud' and 'to the wind' (456–7), without any thought of an heir who could be 'Light to the sun and music to the wind'.

Like Michael himself building the sheep-fold, Wordsworth in writing the poem fluctuates as to how much significance the work can have to his own hopes. At worst, it reveals that, even for Michael, love of land and love for people can have nothing to do with each other. Then the sheep-fold represents only the sadly unfulfilled relationship between a father and a son. Wordsworth's own moments of pessimism allow him to write with full sympathy for such a view. Even when there is still reason to hope for Luke's return, Wordsworth can describe the building as an emblem only of love for Luke, and so separate from the farmer's 'daily work' that it has to be done in 'a leisure hour' (438–41). Understandably one critic describes Michael's 'building, or failing to build the sheep-fold' as 'merely symbolic', and having nothing to do with 'the human side of a bond with Nature'.[15]

But there are other moments when both Michael and his author feel a tentative hope that the sheep-fold can be made to stand, not for Luke in isolation but for an innate interlocking of land and family, a structure which would make the son's return so natural as to be almost inevitable. At such moments the sheep-fold does not seem 'merely symbolic'. It is literally 'the Fold of which / His flock had need', an integral part of Michael's 'daily work' for land and family, and in no way the sentimental hobby of 'a leisure hour'.

So we can return to Hartman's view that Wordsworth offers 'a strange identity between himself and his main character', and apply it with rather more precision. The claim that 'The poet is Michael's true heir' is too confident. The poem is, however, alive with Wordsworth's yearning to believe in an intimate relationship between his own feelings for landscape and Michael's for his land. The farmer's precarious hope that his flock and his son are innately destined to belong together is matched by Wordsworth's hope of discovering in himself the securely integrated values by which the farmer can now try to live. If Michael could build his sheep-fold, completing his emblem of the inseparability of farm and family, he would have convinced himself that Luke would return. If Wordsworth could offer such a conclusion as a credible ending to Michael's story, he would have convinced himself that, to hill farmers at least, there was no emotional conflict between 'the types and symbols of Eternity' and personal relationship. Then the only remaining doubt would be how far a hill farmer could be described as like the poet, rather than as someone whose job, if verbalized in detail, would make his situation seem too idiosyncratic for imitation.

Sometimes Michael is allowed to speak only in general terms: 'Our lot is a hard lot' (233). Wordsworth's own narrative can be as vague, recording merely that Michael 'Performed all kinds of labour for his sheep' (458). Delicacy may prevent Wordsworth even hinting at some of a hill farmer's chores: the castration of each year's crop of male lambs for instance, or the less savoury kinds of assistance that have to be given to diseased animals or to a ewe who is struggling to give birth. But this can explain neither the silence about other tasks – such as marking the sheep or hay-making or buying and selling stock – nor the absence of all reference to meat, which, with wool, must comprise the farm's major produce. Readers who rely for information solely on the poem might wonder what exactly Michael would do with the sheep-fold.

On the other hand, there is evidence of an intention sometimes to be far more informative. In the 1800 edition, Wordsworth appended a note to lines 333–4:

> It may be proper to inform some readers, that a sheepfold in these mountains is an unroofed building of stone walls, with different divisions. It is generally placed by the side of a brook, for the convenience of washing the sheep; but it is also useful as a shelter for them, and as a place to drive them into, to enable the shepherds conveniently to single out one or more for any particular purpose.

Wordsworth does sound dubious: 'It may be proper'. Some phrases presumably suggested too decisive a difference between the poet's most joyfully undiscriminating attitudes and those of the industrious farmer – 'different divisions', 'single out one or more for any particular purpose'. So this (anyway marginal) impression on the poem was removed, and later editions suppressed the note. Yet there remain substantial moments when Wordsworth does confidently choose to evoke the specialized work of a sheep farmer, as if Michael's industrious optimism can still be recognized as like the poet's own even when superficial differences are acknowledged.

Such a view seems to me to explain both why *Michael* is an oddly indecisive poem and why the inconsistencies that result do not detract from its power. Wordsworth's hesitation between allocating the sheep-fold to Michael's 'leisure hour' or to the literal 'need' of the flock is in sympathy with Michael's own doubts. Wordsworth's fluctuations between the confidently detailed evocation of clipping and the timidly generalized evasiveness of 'all kinds of labour for his sheep' do reflect uncertainty as to how close the poet can dare claim to be to the farmer. But they also loyally reflect the growth and decline of the vividness of Michael's work in his own mind.

At the end the only specific farming task which Wordsworth still dares to confront is the building of the sheep-fold. Like Michael, he compulsively returns to it. Like Michael, he equivocates between expressing a vestigial faith in the integrated values it was meant to represent and admitting helpless resignation to the meaninglessness of another stone being added. Like Michael, Wordsworth is more certain of what he wishes to be true than of whether it ever could be. The shepherd sometimes nerves himself to work on 'at the building of this sheep-fold', as if his groundless hope is as true a feeling as its defeat is a certain fact.

It is a stance which is often to be Wordsworth's own as a poet:

> But welcome fortitude, and patient cheer,
> And frequent sights of what is to be borne!
> Such sights, or worse, as are before me here –
> Not without hope we suffer and we mourn.
>
> (*Elegiac Stanzas*, PW, IV. 260, 57–60)

Michael strives to keep his side of the covenant, and thus repeatedly returns to the cruel fact that it has been rendered pointless. Wordsworth wants Michael's hopes to be fulfilled and to be conclusively proved relevant to his own situation. Defeated on both fronts, he records the triumph of Michael sometimes still refusing to admit defeat. Wordsworth does so with the forceful sympathy of a poet who was to go on struggling to build an optimistic symbolism long after the intuitions that inspired it were known to have gone, never to return.

While *Michael* was being written, Dorothy's name for the work was 'The Sheepfold', and so her Journal makes Wordsworth's efforts sound oddly like his hero's:

> William worked all the morning at the sheepfold, but in vain. [18 October 1800]; William worked . . . at the sheepfold [20 October]; William had been unsuccessful . . . at the sheepfold [21 October]; William composed without much success at the Sheepfold [22 October]; William had been working at the sheepfold [11 November].

In the final poem, which he completed on 9 December, Wordsworth is honest enough to allow the tale to tell against the thesis. The subtitle had promised 'A Pastoral Poem' but the traditional analogy between the poet and his shepherd-hero is never completed. The pronouns of 'I', 'me' and 'my', whose ten appearances had made the author's approach to Michael's valley seems so confident in the first verse paragraph, are never used in the last. Nor is there any mention of those 'youthful Poets' who were meant to find in this story the inspiration to become the present poet's 'second self' and build upon the foundations his work had laid 'among these hills'. Ironically it is only while Michael has still not gained what as a typical hill farmer he might most desire – a son to inherit flock, field and homestead – that his attitude to landscape has seemed close to that of the relaxedly unpossessive poet and reader who sought 'utter solitude' at the outset. The 'gentle agency / Of natural objects' which supposedly led the poet towards the 'passions' of 'human life' leads Michael in the end away from the ruins of the only impassioned human relationship he has had to endure. When the shepherd goes 'among the rocks', and still looks 'up to sun and cloud', he knows that he is being moved in a quite different direction from that which – on the many occasions when he never lifts a single stone – takes him to the sheep-fold. Michael, and the poem which respects his endurance, finally seem impressive because of a tough-mindedness which acknowledges that distinctions must be made.

Initially, perhaps, the upwards glimpse of 'kites / That overhead are sailing in the sky' may seem much the same as the downward glance at a 'straggling heap of unhewn stones'. The difference is at first one 'which you might pass by, / Might see and notice not'. Four hundred lines later the reader sees that indeed 'great changes have been wrought / In all the neighbourhood' (478–9), but 'neighbourhood' here is not some casual synonym for the natural landscape. It carefully introduces a distinction between forlorn alterations in the human scene and the secure movements of a larger cosmos. It was Michael's neighbours, supporting those hopes that people can neither fulfil nor wholly abandon, who named his home after a planet as if the place which a family had lovingly built could be as permanent as 'earth's diurnal round'. But the poem finally faces the bleak fact that

> The Cottage which was named the Evening Star
> Is gone – the ploughshare has been through the ground
> On which it stood;   (476–8)

On the other hand, this same last paragraph reminds us that we sometimes base our sense of security on far safer grounds: the earth itself whose resilient fertility can be tapped by the plough of 'a stranger's hand' (475–7); the surviving oak tree, which still 'is left / That grew beside their door' (479–80); the brook which has always been as 'tumultuous' as it was in the poem's first lines and will always be as 'boisterous' as it is in the last.

In 'Crossing the Alps' Wordsworth celebrates the moments when 'our home' seems to be the natural world and we feel a 'hope that can never die':

> in such visitings
> Of awful promise, when the light of sense

Goes out in flashes that have shewn to us
The invisible world, doth Greatness make abode.
There harbours whether we be young or old.
Our destiny, our nature, and our home
Is with infinitude, and only there;
With hope it is, hope that can never die,
Effort, and expectation, and desire,
And something evermore about to be.

(The Prelude, VI. 533–42)

But, like the streams with which it identifies, the vision of 'Crossing
the Alps' has not only the impact but also the limitations of a force
which moves in just one direction. The clarity of its language derives
from a lack of potentially embarrassing, yet potentially revealing,
curiosity. Such verse cannot embrace the possibility that 'effort, and
expectation, and desire' could mean something very different to a hill
farmer once he can begin working for his son's future.

By contrast, *Michael* has the occasional clumsiness, but also the
overall complexity, of verse which moves us by questioning its own
premises and ultimately admitting that its subject can, and perhaps
should, be seen in two quite different ways. The last lines mourn the
wasted tenderness of a man whose sheep-fold will now never stand in
its completed form, but they also celebrate the grandeur of a fluid
world whose energies will always be irrepressible:

<blockquote>
and the remains
Of the unfinished Sheep-fold may be seen
Beside the boisterous brook of Green-head Ghyll.   (480–2)
</blockquote>

The poem which begins by looking for synthesis invites us in the end
to see contrast.

THE EYE AMONG THE BLIND

I

Wordsworth's poetry, though so often about a defeated relationship between two people, usually concentrates on only one of them. As a narrative poem, *The Ruined Cottage* tells the story of Margaret. When Robert leaves, the poem does not digress to follow his fortunes; it remains with the wife he has abandoned. *Michael* too concentrates on one character's feelings. The account of Luke's separate life in the city is dismissively perfunctory, and even the response of one of his parents, Isabel, is (perhaps more culpably) almost ignored.

 But *The Idiot Boy*, in spite of its title, is not exclusively about Johnny. It is equally concerned with his mother, Betty. She and her son understand their world in such wholly different terms as to barely have a language in common. The poem thus offers two voices and makes no pretence that they can easily become one. Betty is cut off from dialogue with Johnny by his subnormality long before she allows him to ride off alone at night. At the end, even though its plot has by then reunited them, the poem's climax is the failure of dialogue between the doting mother's curiosity and her son's bland inability to even understand, let alone answer, her questions. While Betty fears that Johnny is lost for ever, she reminds us of Michael when his frustrated tenderness for his son seemed likely to 'overset the brain, or break the heart' (*PW*, II.93, 450). But, although we listen to Betty's harassed anticipation of such a bereavement, we also watch Johnny. He, far from being dead as his mother sometimes fears, is relaxedly alive to the grandeur of the countryside at night. So here Michael's other stance is recalled. Young Johnny offers a recognizable, if less consciously resolute, version of the old shepherd's continuing ability to feel at home in his landscape.

So *The Idiot Boy* does not need an obtrusively ambivalent narrator like *The Ruined Cottage*'s Pedlar who, stimulated by dialogue with the Poet, can articulate opposed ways of looking at the scene of Margaret's life. Nor does *The Idiot Boy* have to push its characters to a latently tragic crisis like that which forces Michael himself to equivocate between values which are, for him, interlocking 'links of love' (*PW*, II.92, 401). The dualism of *The Idiot Boy* is straightforwardly expressed by the simultaneous, and yet startlingly different, experiences of the two characters whose stories are told.

Wordsworth himself tells their tales, in an amused tone of voice. Sometimes he even sounds comfortably donnish as he ridicules literary fads and teases his contemporary readers about their taste for the violent and the supernatural. But often his wryly sympathetic attitude to Betty leads him to adopt a style close to her own idiomatic chatter. He abandons the flexible patterns of blank verse which can rise to such poignant climaxes in *The Ruined Cottage* and *Michael*. Instead *The Idiot Boy* rattles along in firmly rhyming stanzas and imitates the popular ballads of Betty's own oral tradition.

Although the comic plot hinges on the absurdities of Betty's love for her son, Wordsworth provides her with both direct speech and telling gesture with which to invite a more tender response to her tenderness. It is the essence of Johnny's role both in her life and in the poem that he, by contrast, is incapable of normal speech. But his actions, or more often his successes in avoiding action, speak for themselves, and his one triumphantly muddled attempt at direct speech in the final stanza allows his resistance to language to have virtually the last word. Johnny's comfortably inarticulate stasis is thus very different from the tacit despair that prevents Margaret from repairing her cottage or Michael from building his sheepfold.

So each of the two great blank verse narrative poems has far more in common with the other than with *The Idiot Boy*, even though the latter was written in March 1798, after the completion of *The Ruined Cottage* and before the composition in 1800 of *Michael*. Moreover *The Idiot Boy* is a crucial document in understanding a later poem, the *Immortality Ode*, which was not completed until 1804. A strictly chronological approach can suggest that the poems are mere stages in the development of some ponderously linear argument. They are not. Throughout his 'Great Decade' of creativity, Wordsworth's open-minded curiosity about human life is such that the conclusion reached in one work is too thoughtfully open-ended to supply an assumption which the beginning of the next can take for granted. So I have decided to deal with *The Idiot Boy* and the *Ode* here. It seems sensible to approach them after an account of the mutually illuminating *Ruined Cottage* and *Michael*, and immediately before my investigation of Wordsworth's 'Solitaries', characters whose baffling independence is so clearly anticipated by the Idiot Boy himself.

II

The Idiot Boy opens with a mock-epic arming of its hero. Susan Gale, a neighbour, is ill, and Betty has persuaded herself that Johnny, in spite of his mental deficiences, is competent enough to ride off on the family pony to fetch the doctor. Betty thus becomes an absurd, and yet oddly touching, example of the pathetic fallacies created by love. She wants her son to have the fun of running an errand. She wants to give him the responsibility, and the achievements, allowed to children who have developed normally. But Johnny is not normal. Sending him to act out her fantasy, Betty soon recognizes that she may be putting him at risk. Both her wish to allow him the adventure, and her fear of letting him go, signal her affection. Mary Jacobus, though she sees it as more central than I do, shrewdly identifies the paradox:

> it is love that inspires the contradictory emotions which make up Wordsworth's narrative. 'The Idiot Boy' turns on the conflict between maternal pride, on the one hand, and maternal anxiety, on the other. Sending her son to fetch the doctor gratifies Betty's pride in 'Johnny's wit and Johnny's glory' (l. 136). But it also conflicts with her deepest instinct, concern for his safety and well-being –

> > There's not a mother, no not one,
> > But when she hears what you have done,
> > Oh! Betty she'll be in a fright.   (24–6)

The narrator's participation – his adoption of Betty's language and tone – allows us to see what is at stake. This is a real emergency for Betty herself ('What must be done? what will betide?' (l.41), even if it is not the kind of drama the ballad-reader expects.[1]

But love's confusions are not just pathetic in the poem. They are often ridiculous, even grotesque. Jacobus herself notices that *The Idiot Boy* 'presents love almost as a form of unbalance',[2] and J. F. Danby observes that Wordsworth, as 'the satirist of feeling', exposes 'an essential . . . idiocy in emotion itself'.

Danby argues that 'a comedy of the passions' can be recognized by glancing at the plot since it is Betty's excessive 'concern for Susan' which 'makes her send Johnny off on the errand':

> Fatuously she sees her idiot son as public hero. When he does not return, fear for his safety brings her back to the facts, and dispels neighbourly concern . . . the pattern is repeated in Susan, too. Her mysterious illness vanishes as she frets more and more about the others. Finally she is cured of imaginary illness by real emotional distress. The idiocy of passion can precipitate its puppets into irrational misery or unpredictable joy. It all depends, but the dependence is not on the actors in the story as prudent agents. Man, as mere man of feeling, sits on a crazy seesaw.[3]

Yet the 'man of feeling', when reading *The Idiot Boy*, responds not only to Betty's passion of love. He also identifies with her son's emotive delight at riding through the nocturnal landscape. The real seesaw of the poem thus carries even more than Danby suggests. At one extreme there is indeed the fluctuating misery and joy of Betty, the harassing fears and hopes of a life in which only human relationship carries any weight. But the reader is required to watch this being repeatedly balanced by another extreme: Johnny's undiscriminating joy in himself, his pony and the world.

The plot literally separates mother and son so that these two extremes can be explored without the poem seeming to labour the distinction. As Betty prepares to say farewell to Johnny, Wordsworth is able to maintain his comic tone and yet clearly reveal their separate experiences. With his own affectionate thoroughness, he records the repetitions of Betty's fussing:

> And Betty o'er and o'er has told
> The boy who is her best delight,
> Both what to follow, what to shun,
> What do, and what to leave undone,
> How to turn left, and how to right.

> And Betty's most especial charge,
> Was, 'Johnny! Johnny! mind that you
> Come home again, nor stop at all, –
> Come home again, whate'er befall,
> My Johnny, do, I pray you, do.'   (51–60)

Wordsworth's ear for the precise tones of the speaking voice allows him to imitate loyally Betty's anxious bossiness. Those repeated vocatives, for instance, make audible both her need to make Johnny concentrate and her exasperated fear that he is incapable of doing so. In the poem's first use of direct speech, Betty articulates a priority which excludes all mention of the journey's supposed purpose – the fetching of the doctor. At the very moment of sending Johnny off, all Betty can speak to is her overriding need to have him safe at home.

The very next lines turn to Johnny himself, whose inability to use words is at the centre of his happy idiocy. We are at first told that Johnny answers to his mother's pleas for reassurance. But this only ensures that we are alert when the claim is, almost immediately, shown to be false:

> To this did Johnny answer make,
> Both with his head and with his hand,
> And proudly shook the bridle too;
> And then! his words were not a few,
> Which Betty well could understand.
>
> And now that Johnny is just going,
> Though Betty's in a mighty flurry,
> She gently pats the pony's side,
> On which her Idiot Boy must ride,
> And seems no longer in a hurry.
>
> But when the Pony moved his legs
> Oh! then for the poor Idiot Boy!
> For joy he cannot hold the bridle,
> For joy his head and heels are idle,
> He's idle all for very joy.   (62–76)

Johnny, far from seeming properly aware of the use of the reins ('How turn to left, and how to right'), merely shakes the bridle as yet another expression of cheerfulness to add to those he makes 'with his head and with his hand'.

No wonder his mother ends up gently patting the pony's side, expressing, as Paul Sheats remarks, 'her dependence on the saner of the two travellers.'⁴ Johnny seems to have 'the deep power of joy' with which to relaxedly 'see into the life of things' (*Tintern Abbey*, *PW*, II. 260, 48–9). His mind thus lacks the practical sense of direction by which to recognize the use of things like reins for reaching some anticipated destination. His world cannot be approached in such terms. Wordsworth has already protested:

> Good Betty, put him down again;
> His lips with joy they burr at you;
> But, Betty! what has he to do
> With stirrup, saddle, or with rein? (13–16)

Whether he shakes the bridle or lets it drop, he only expresses the same happiness.

Its inexpressibility in words is hinted in Wordsworth's helpless reiterations of the one word, 'joy'. Whether Johnny burrs and babbles his parody of language or subsides into being as 'still and mute' as the moon, his comprehensive delight proves him incapable of understanding his mother's anxiety. Wordsworth identifies with Betty's optimistic fantasy that, for her part, she can interpret Johnny's words and gestures, but the boy's movements in fact tend towards a stasis which can communicate contentment and nothing else. Usually he remains as incommunicado, and as motionless, as the holly branch he holds. This is supposed to be used as a riding crop with which to motivate and direct the pony. But in the event:

> while the Pony moves his legs,
> In Johnny's left hand you may see
> The green bough motionless and dead:
> The Moon that shines above his head
> Is not more still and mute than he. (77–81)

Wordsworth is not trapped by his rhyme scheme into offering 'you may see' as padding. The phrase is like the drawing aside of a curtain to expose a pictured stability. Johnny's tranquillity is exhibited as unexcelled even by the loftiest lights of the universe he makes his own. Like the protagonist of *The Pedlar*, who 'saw one life, and felt that it was joy' (217), Johnny, always and everywhere, feels at home. The Pedlar cannot understand the anxious love which at parting burdens his father 'with a heart / Forboding evil' (237–8). Similarly,

Johnny can find no meaning in his mother's repeated insistence that
he 'Come home again'. Johnny is a mental nomad. His sense of
belonging moves with him as surely as the moon.

Betty, by contrast, needs to believe he will return. She needs to
know not just that he is happy but that he will be safe. So, with
determined inconsistency, she persuades herself that both his silence
and his gibberish are reassuring:

> Proud of herself, and proud of him,
> She sees him in his travelling trim,
> How quietly her Johnny goes.
>
> The silence of her Idiot Boy,
> What hopes it sends to Betty's heart!
> He's at the guide-post – he turns right;
> She watches till he's out of sight,
> And Betty will not then depart.
>
> Burr, burr – now Johnny's lips they burr,
> As loud as any mill, or near it;
> Meek as a lamb, the Pony moves,
> And Johnny makes the noise he loves
> And Betty listens, glad to hear it.   (89–101)

Betty is 'Proud of herself, and proud of him' because his silence,
unlike his burring, allows him to seem as competent as any other child
earnestly setting off to perform an adult's task. But even Betty senses
something awesome about his silence, an inaccessibility which is at
once pathetic and impressive. It is Betty's own whisper which is
echoed in the solemn hush of 'How quietly her Johnny goes'.

The similes, 'loud as any mill', 'Meek as a lamb', are simple enough
in their references to Betty's own rustic environment to sound like
her own. But they hint also at experiences from which she may feel
excluded. Johnny's involvement with the forces of the natural world
is as intimate as that of a waterwheel; one is reminded of Wordsworth
himself recording in *The Prelude*: 'My mind did at this spectacle turn
round / As with the might of waters' (vii. 615–16). The rushing torrents, which for Betty will represent only danger, strike Johnny as
the delightful sources of his own energy. Similarly, his comfortable
identification with the horse is extended by comparison with the
lamb to imply a sense of belonging with all animals. Those character-

istics which distinguish horses as more intelligent, or more useful, than other beasts are unknown to Johnny.

So mother and son separate into extreme versions of their different worlds. She hurries off to what is later developed as a comedy of garrulous conversation with her neighbour, while Johnny 'makes the noise he loves' not in words but in music. He moves, as serenely as the moon, into a symphony of natural sounds where his own mumblings can chime and chime again:

> Away she hies to Susan Gale:
> Her Messenger's in merry tune;
> The owlets hoot, the owlets curr,
> And Johnny's lips they burr, burr, burr,
> As on he goes beneath the moon.   (102–6)

Betty cheers herself in defiance of all logic. It is not the slightest use to a messenger to be as tuneful as the owls. On the contrary, it is absolutely essential that he should be more articulate. But Betty has to turn facts inside out to make them fit her inconsistent feelings.

Johnny, like his pony, has none of Betty's fluctuating emotions:

> His steed and he right well agree;
> For of this Pony there's a rumour,
> That should he lose his eyes and ears,
> And should he live a thousand years,
> He never will be out of humour.

> But then he is a horse that thinks!
> And when he thinks, his pace is slack;
> Now, though he knows poor Johnny well,
> Yet, for his life, he cannot tell
> What he has got upon his back.

> So through the moonlight lanes they go,
> And far into the moonlight dale,   (107–18)

The boy is close enough to the animal to be virtually interchangeable. His backwardness retains the 'glad animal movements' of Wordsworth's 'boyish days' which are mourned in *Tintern Abbey* (*PW*, II.261, 73–4). If Johnny and his pony think at all, it is only to recognize their absurd ignorance of what each is supposed to do with the other. Such thoughts will never put them 'out of humour', but

only slacken any slight sense of urgency Betty might have been able
to convey. They cannot register the world with her fretfully alert
'eyes and ears'. As in 'Crossing the Alps', it is the 'dull and heavy
slackening' of such faculties which allows child and pony into the
freewheeling world of 'The unfettered clouds, and region of the
Heavens,/Tumult and peace, the darkness and the light'. Boy and
beast fade away, less and less distinguishable from each other, just as
the moonlight seems to soothe away all distinction between the lane
they should be following and the surrounding dale. Their blissful
ignorance of time passing makes them as placid as immortals for
whom even 'a thousand years' is neither here nor there.

But to Betty, as Johnny fails to return, time seems to pass all too
noticeably:

> 'As sure as there's a moon in heaven,'
> Cries Betty, 'he'll be back again;
> They'll both be here – 'tis almost ten –
> Both will be here before eleven.'

> Poor Susan moans, poor Susan groans;
> The clock gives warning for eleven;
> 'Tis on the stroke – 'He must be near,'
> Quoth Betty, 'and will soon be here,
> As sure as there's a moon in heaven.'

> The clock is on the stroke of twelve,
> And Johnny is not yet in sight:
> – The Moon's in heaven, as Betty sees,
> But Betty is not quite at ease;
> And Susan has a dreadful night.

> And Betty, half an hour ago,
> On Johnny vile reflections cast:
> 'A little idle sauntering Thing!'
> With other names, an endless string;
> But now that time is gone and past.   (142–61)

There is some entertainingly shrewd observation of psychology
here: the hypochondriacal Susan having to compete more and more
noisily for attention, and the voluble Betty trying to distract herself
from fear by indulging in crossness. Yet beneath the neatly amusing

narrative, Wordsworth challenges the reader to accept more profound paradoxes.

Betty's repeated colloquialism about the moon evokes the opposite of what she intends. The vulnerability of Johnny is precisely that he behaves as if he were an invulnerable part of the natural world, as secure on earth as is the 'Moon in heaven'. Betty consciously recognizes this as a dangerous delusion, yet her similes secretly conspire with Johnny to believe it.

Moreover Betty's choice of invective instinctively reveals what is at once infuriating, and yet endearing, about Johnny. Naming him an 'idle sauntering Thing', she recalls his ecstatic trance at feeling the horse begin to move beneath him: 'For joy his head and heels are idle, / He's idle all for very joy.' (75–6). No mother, remembering her son enjoying such spectacular happiness as that, can sound convincingly cross.

III

For Wordsworth 'idle' is hardly ever an idle term. It implies not so much a fantasizing evasion of work as a properly passive acceptance of the facts. In *To My Sister* the summons to idleness is a repeated rejection of the falsifying world of language: 'bring no book: for this one day / We'll give to idleness.' (*PW*, IV. 59, 15–16, 39–40). Wordsworth's own 'sense of joy' there, like Johnny's in *The Idiot Boy*, is a release from our usual, arbitrary sense of time:

> No joyless forms shall regulate
> Our living calendar:
> We from to-day, my Friend, will date
> The opening of the year.
>
> Love, now a universal birth,
> From heart to heart is stealing,
> From earth to man, from man to earth:
> – It is the hour of feeling.   (*PW*, IV. 60, 17–24)

Betty measures out her hours in terms of mounting anxiety. But Wordsworth in *To My Sister* hopes to build out of one moment a lasting commitment to the 'silent laws' which keep Johnny in tune with his world:

> One moment now may give us more
> Than years of toiling reason:
> Our minds shall drink at every pore
> The spirit of the season.
>
> Some silent laws our hearts will make,
> Which they shall long obey:
> We for the year to come may take
> Our temper from to-day.   (*PW*, IV. 60, 25–32)

This often charming lyric has many admirers but seems to me ultimately shallow in ways which reveal precisely why *The Idiot Boy*,
for all its jokiness, can seem so profound.

The lyric is fairly complacent about the terms it deploys. 'Love' of
one person for another ('heart to heart') is blandly assumed to be
much the same as the delight we feel in a reciprocal relationship with
the environment ('From earth to man, from man to earth'). *The
Idiot Boy*, by contrast, shows that these can be diametrically opposed
emotions. Since Betty's anxiety and Johnny's serenity are simultaneous, the reader witnesses quite different experiences during the
same 'hour of feeling'. The two ways of feeling expose each other as
arguably idiotic, and yet as too much like our own to be patronized.
To My Sister perhaps admits that its aspiration towards more consistent emotions can only be a fantasy but fails to ask whether its
fulfilment would be such an unmitigated blessing. Poet and reader
are invited to pretend that they despise books and value only those
laws which remain 'silent'.

The Idiot Boy respects not only Johnny's silence but his mother's
all too articulate worries. It thus requires the reader to be less
self-indulgently single-minded than either of them. It invites us to
respect our own humanity as capable of far more disparate emotions
than we usually claim, and yet, because of this, capable of identifying with not one but two idiots. Lacking a sense of humour, *To My
Sister* can make its indistinguishable characters sound appallingly
twee:

> Edward will come with you; – and pray,
> Put on with speed your woodland dress;
> And bring no book: for this one day
> We'll give to idleness.   (13–16)

The Idiot Boy can both laugh at Betty's exasperation over her 'idle, sauntering Thing' and take seriously Johnny's implicit claim that life is about being 'idle all for very joy'.[5]

To My Sister, in its feebler moments, may seem culpably unimaginative in its failure really to use words, but *The Idiot Boy* is quite consciously weighing the value of being imaginative. On the one hand, because Johnny cannot imagine some of the dangers inherent in his midnight ride, he cannot consciously evade them. Yet on the other hand, grown-ups pay a heavy cost in happiness for being so much more imaginative about the risks involved. Susan and Betty infect each other with increasingly alarmist notions: 'That Johnny may perhaps be drowned, / Or lost, perhaps, and never found' (179–80). When Betty's anxiety compels her to leave Susan and begin a search, she hopefully imagines Johnny in all she sees:

> In high and low, above, below,
> In great and small, in round and square,
> In tree and tower was Johnny seen,
> In bush and brake, in black and green;
> 'Twas Johnny, Johnny, everywhere.   (207–11)

She does not conceive of the whole world as one life by recognizing that its myriad life-forms interconnect. Instead she creates the simple fantasy that the cosmos is no more than the one person she hopes to find. Wordsworth in 'Crossing the Alps' saw in 'first, and last, and midst, and without end' the 'symbols of Eternity' through which to escape his fretful need to search. But Betty 'In high and low, above, below' sees only the harassingly mortal child she seeks.

In Betty's dottily unrealistic parody of pantheism, the world has changed its centre so as to keep pace with her own altered feelings. Margaret in *The Ruined Cottage*, in her more hopeless search, offers a bleaker clarity about the real source of change:

> About the fields I wander, knowing this
> Only that what I seek I cannot find.
> And so I waste my time: *for I am changed*,   (350–2)

But in her own comic idiom, Betty's wild imaginings sometimes do echo *The Ruined Cottage*: there Margaret's more pathetic optimism also ensures that 'evermore her eye / Was busy in the distance, shaping things / Which made her heart beat quick' (455–7). Both women seem unable to relax into the mental 'indolence' which one *Prelude* manuscript recommends:

> A most wise passiveness in which the heart
> Lies open and is well content to feel
> As nature feels and to receive her shapes
> As she has made them   (*The Prelude*, p. 566)

Like Johnny in his 'idleness', such minds:

>   rest upon their oars
> Float down the mighty stream of tendency
> In the calm mood of holy indolence   (ibid.)

It is an 'indolence / Compared to which our best activity / Is oftimes deadly bane'. Betty's busily active intelligence might, on some future occasion, pull Johnny back in time from floating into an unnecessarily early death, but meanwhile her mental energy is itself 'deadly' in its obliteration of present life. Almost as much as Margaret, she is too distracted by the merely hypothetical to notice her actual surroundings.

Straining to hear one absent human voice, Betty becomes deaf to a harmony that is, for Wordsworth, audibly present in the immediate landscape:

> She listens, but she cannot hear
> The foot of horse, the voice of man;
> The streams with softest sound are flowing,
> The grass you almost hear it growing,
> You hear it now, if e'er you can.
>
> The owlets through the long blue night
> Are shouting to each other still:
> Fond lovers! yet not quite hob nob,
> They lengthen out the tremulous sob,
> That echoes far from hill to hill.
>
> Poor Betty now has lost all hope,
> Her thoughts are bent on deadly sin,
> A green-grown pond she just has past,
> And from the brink she hurries fast,
> Lest she should drown herself therein.   (282–96)

The chilling extremes of despair which drive Margaret virtually to commit suicide become comic exaggeration in *The Idiot Boy*. We need have no real fears for Betty. Her bossy practicality works much better on herself than it does on Johnny, and she will always hasten to put a sensible distance between herself and temptation. The chapel jargon of 'deadly sin' may seem absurdly hyperbolic in its condemnation of her fleeting thoughts. Yet the comedy carries much the same implications as Margaret's more convincingly simple confession of 'waste' and of having 'done much wrong' to herself. Betty's obsessive love for Johnny does reject the available world and turn it into something of a wasteland. She does wrong herself in her harassed disregard for the landscape's soothing music – its streams and grass and owls.

For Betty the landscape either does not exist or is transformed by her imagination into symbols of her own panic. The living universe is fragmented into often zany ways of dying:

> Oh saints! what is become of him?
> Perhaps he's climbed into an oak,
> Where he will stay till he is dead;   (222–4)

To what could just about be called natural hazards like oak trees and 'the wandering gipsy-folk', Betty adds magical dangers. She torments herself with the idea that Johnny has been kidnapped by goblins: 'Or in the castle he's pursuing / Among the ghosts his own undoing' (229–30). Wordsworth has no difficulty in finding a language for Betty's distress. With the help of folklore, he can make her credibly garrulous about all that can be conceived as threatening the child she loves.

But when he turns to describe Johnny's very different experience, Wordsworth indulges in a couple of angry stanzas and rails at the muses for betraying him (337–46). The joke is not without point. Betty's unhappy imaginativeness is innately verbal. She only knows what to fear because she tells herself about it. But Johnny, who has of course been perfectly safe and happy throughout, seems to have no more need of language than is felt by his placid pony.

Certainly Johnny is incapable of ever telling anyone what he has been doing. So Wordsworth can only hypothesize, borrowing Betty's fantastic imagery of ghosts and reversing its implications:

> Perhaps he's turned himself about,
> His face unto his horse's tail,
> And, still and mute, in wonder lost,
> All silent as a horseman-ghost,
> He travels slowly down the vale.   (322–6)

Johnny is too innately backward to have acquired that defensive sense of dignity which would confine most of us to sitting the right way round on a horse. But his ignorant freedom from such rules grants him what looks like a deeper dignity. Wordsworth will not misrepresent Johnny by confining him within our logics or our language. The emphasis on his wordlessness ('still', 'mute', 'silent') suggests that he cannot be understood in our terms. Normal language is too shallow to match the profundity of his subnormal experience. But Johnny can show his rejection of our logics by reversing them. Where Betty sees ghosts as threats to the one person she loves, Johnny's sense of life beyond death – if he did trouble himself with any sense – might exalt himself into a horseman-ghost.

Wordsworth, in trying to guess how Johnny sees himself, knows he is misrepresenting the case. Johnny does not see himself. He sees 'in wonder lost' a world from which he feels no such separation. His lack of self-consciousness means also that he cannot really see his mother. He is incapable of recognizing the peculiarly imaginative love which she feels. His happiness proves him to be wholly unaware of the anxiety he is causing her. His serenity and her worries both derive from his inability to approach the world as a hostile environment.

Significantly Wordsworth specifies that Betty's major fear is the risk inherent in a waterfall. In 'Crossing the Alps', waterfalls had functioned unambiguously to validate Johnny's kind of vision. Here Betty's very different outlook is permitted equal force. As a loving mother, she fears her fearless son will be drowned while 'playing with the waterfall' (231). Susan first puts the thought into her head by suggesting that the likeliest of 'sad mischances' is 'That Johnny may perhaps be drowned;' (178–9). Betty herself is soon afraid that he may have abandoned the relative security of his seat on the pony: 'To hunt the moon within the brook, / And never will be heard of more' (215–16). The joking narrator's own hypothesis suggests less obviously alarming methods by which the child may be trying to raid the sky: Johnny could be riding higher into the hills: 'To lay his hand upon a star, / And in his pocket bring it home' (320–1). But even Wordsworth's hypothesis has Johnny riding past 'cliffs and peaks so high' as to sound far from safe. It therefore hardly challenges the reasonableness of Betty's notion that Johnny may have gone moon-hunting in an even more dangerous element. She is frightened of Johnny's capacity to treat the world as one huge, and unquestionably safe, toy. It is his attitude, as much as the torrent's innate danger, which makes 'playing with the waterfall' sound so hazardous.

IV

Johnny is indeed finally discovered perilously 'near the waterfall, / Which thunders down with headlong force' (347–8). This discovery of Johnny safe and well is made by narrator and reader before Betty herself finds him. The delay is crucial. It allows us to contemplate Johnny as he is, and has been, before his hysterical mother disturbs the scene. Furthermore, once our own curiosity has been satisfied, we are later free to concentrate entirely on Betty when she is let in on the secret.

For the undisturbed Johnny, the waterfall's tumult is no more alarming than the moonlight's peace:

> Who's yon, that, near the waterfall,
> Which thunders down with headlong force,
> Beneath the moon, yet shining fair,
> As careless as if nothing were,
> Sits upright on a feeding horse? (347–51)

He seems to be in the dozy state enjoyed by Wordsworth himself in *Strange Fits of Passion* (see pp. 48–9). Johnny's journey has presumably been stopped at a point of the horse's choosing since it is a good place to graze. Johnny, like the profitably baffled traveller of 'Crossing the Alps', allows himself to be 'Halted, without a struggle to break through'. He is as carefree 'as if nothing were' because, for him, neither his own vulnerability nor his mother's anxiety exist. Yet behaving 'as if nothing were' may properly acknowledge the fact that 'everything is': that waterfall and moonlight are interdependent aspects of the same scene. Johnny's comfortably confused sense of 'first, and last, and midst, and without end' combines all sights equally into 'the working of one mind'. His supposedly defective mentality cannot sense its own separateness. It cannot isolate him in his own fretful ego.

Johnny frees himself by freeing his world from the self-assertive demands that others make:

> Unto his horse – there feeding free,
> He seems, I think, the rein to give;

> Of moon or stars he takes no heed;
> Of such we in romances read:
> – 'Tis Johnny! Johnny! as I live.   (352–6)

Two fantasies are equally discredited here. The first is Betty's pan-
icky idea that Johnny may go hunting the moon in the brook. The
second is the narrator's humorously epic hypothesis that Johnny
reaches for a star to put in his pocket.

Both are dismissed, superficially because they reflect shallow literature, more seriously because they impose on Johnny our own dotty
delusions of grandeur. Johnny inhabits the real grandeur of nature.
So he does not dream of being sufficiently separate from the world to
make raids upon it. He could, of course, have been drowned or fallen
over a cliff. But Betty and the narrator were quite wrong to think he
would have done so in pursuit of their kinds of fantasy. Indeed
Johnny's relaxed acceptance of fact entrusts him to the eminently
reliable pony. So long as he leaves the reins alone, it is extremely
unlikely that he will be led by the pony into a waterfall or over a cliff.
Dumb animals are not as imprudent as aggressively articulate human
beings who are bent on proving something about themselves.

It is a very different reading of these lines which allows even J. F.
Danby's admiring account of the poem to perhaps under-estimate
Johnny's significance. Danby takes the boy to be 'as shut out from
the various harmony' of the natural world:

> as inevitably as he is excluded from the confusions of the human
> order. Where the Idiot is concerned, Wordsworth is a realist:

> > Of moon or stars he takes no heed;
> > Of such we in romances read.[6]

But in fact Johnny is not shut out from the landscape. He is admitted
precisely because he does not take heed of it, or heed for himself, in
the divisive way that we do. It is Johnny who is the realist. He has no
restless fantasies about extracting what he wants from the cosmos.
For him, fishing for the moon or pocketing a star are not just absurd
hyperboles: they are literally unthinkable.

Johnny feels the factual world too intimately to stand back and
rearrange it into poetical fictions. Authors need a reader who can
contribute at least a modicum of creative imagination with which to
bring literature to life. But Johnny, who can hardly speak, obviously
cannot read and is equipped with no such creative imagination. Nor

is he burdened with the destructive one which can pick out of an integrated landscape the one danger spot of the waterfall and keep a vigilant eye on it as a potential enemy.

The next stanza offers us an illuminating contrast. Betty appears, still helplessly searching a world whose only sound she imagines to be hostile:

> She hardly can sustain her fears;
> The roaring waterfall she hears,
> And cannot find her Idiot Boy.   (359–61)

The delay thus allows us to contemplate our own foolishness by observing Betty's. We have been told in time that the terror of the waterfall is a mistake. We can recognize the wastefulness of her fragmented vision. Wordsworth, in 'Crossing the Alps', integrated 'the features of the same face' to both see and hear 'the stationary blasts of waterfalls'. But Betty is blind to everything except her own fears, deaf to everything except the sounds of danger in the 'roaring' water. She feels nothing except her frustrated need of 'Him whom she loves, her Idiot Boy' (366).

This simple fact of Betty's love for Johnny is to be reiterated more than once in the description of their final reunion. To her he is essentially the same as a normal child would have been: her own son whom she is bound to love. Yet, at the moment of discovery, her gestures admit the abnormal interdependence of boy and pony, and the extent to which love of her son's idiotic passivity must embrace the animal on whom his life depends. When she spots them, her overwhelming sense of relief explodes with at least equal force upon the pony and the child:

> She darts, as with a torrent's force,
> She almost has o'erturned the Horse,
> And fast she holds her Idiot Boy.   (374–6)

Her manic delight dances around an almost centaur-like confusion of pony and person:

> And now she's at the Pony's tail,
> And now is at the Pony's head, –
> On that side now, and now on this;
> And, almost stifled with her bliss,
> A few sad tears does Betty shed.

> She kisses o'er and o'er again
> Him whom she loves, her Idiot Boy;
> She's happy here, is happy there,
> She is uneasy everywhere,
> Her limbs are all alive with joy.   (382–91)

This almost seismic ecstasy brings her, in every sense, as close as she can ever be to her son.

Yet those earlier lines about Johnny himself, which are echoed here, had evoked a very different joy:

> For joy he cannot hold the bridle,
> For joy his head and heels are idle,
> He's idle all for very joy.   (74–6)

His massive placidity allows him to be 'idle all'. But his mother's ubiquitous excitement only makes her 'uneasy everywhere'. Johnny enjoys himself and his pony with an open-handed relaxation: 'he cannot hold the bridle'. But Betty's joy at finding child and animal safe has the tight-armed tension of a wrestler's hug, and threatens to throw pony and rider to the gound as 'fast she holds her Idiot Boy'.

The child's happiness is unchanging. His 'joy' is observed three times in as many lines, and its secure stasis expresses nothing but itself: 'The Moon that shines above his head / Is not more still and mute than he' (80–1). His delight is not to be measured by any memories of more distressed moments like those signalled by 'a few sad tears'.

His mother, by contrast, exposes her emotions as distinctly as Margaret allowing her cottage to collapse or Michael struggling to build his sheep-fold. In her own magnificently undignified way, Betty too has a wholly communicative sign language. When she has glimpsed Johnny:

> She looks again – her arms are up –
> She screams – she cannot move for joy;
> She darts, as with a torrent's force,   (372–4)

Betty needs no condescending author to define her emotions by comparisons which are beyond her. Betty's earlier imaginings of Johnny being drowned in a waterfall make the simile of the 'torrent's force' triumphantly her own. She literally bodies forth a need to hold on to Johnny which has proved equal in strength to the most forceful danger she can imagine.

Johnny, like his pony, has an almost invisible contentment, a pleasure in the world too passive to be demonstrably impassioned. Betty, on the other hand, feels a pleasure which is inextricably entangled with her passionately energetic fear for the boy's safety. So she is soon demonstrating once again her mistrust of the world:

> She pats the Pony, where or when
> She knows not, happy Betty Foy!
> The little Pony glad may be,
> But he is milder far than she,
> You hardly can perceive his joy.

> 'Oh! Johnny, never mind the Doctor;
> You've done your best, and that is all':
> She took the reins, when this was said,
> And gently turned the Pony's head
> From the loud waterfall.   (392–401)

Betty speaks to her son as if he were a normal child, likely to remember that he was meant to be fetching the doctor, likely to feel ashamed of failing, and therefore likely to want and understand her verbal reassurance.

But Betty's direct speech here is bordered on both sides by gestures which concede that Johnny may understand as little as his horse. Like the pony she pats, he has some dim awareness of being cosily back in Betty's favour. Like the pony, he allows her to take the reins and lead them away from what she alone finds alarming. The pony is supposedly 'a horse that thinks', and the Idiot supposedly an errand runner. But such suppositions are affectionate fantasies. Neither animal nor boy can ever in reality be led to understand 'the loud waterfall' in Betty's terms.

So Wordsworth forces us to approach Johnny also on the boy's own terms. Johnny's attitude is innately different from that of an adult, and he is doomed, or privileged, to remain different for ever. His majestically unconcerned mind is incapable of maturing. He is not the *Immortality Ode*'s 'growing boy', around whom 'Shades of the prison-house begin to close' (*PW*, IV. 279, 67–8). Johnny will remain ignorantly enlightened. To the incommunicable openness of his mind, the magic of moon and sun will always reach. He cannot become the self-consciously detached 'Man' who 'perceives it die away / And fade into the light of common day' (*Immortality Ode*,

76–7). Even at the very end of *The Idiot Boy*, Johnny audibly retains the fertile muddle of his mind. He celebrates the novelty of cockerels who have whimsically modulated their song into a startlingly unfamiliar nocturne, and the brilliance with which the sun has turned itself into a mysteriously cold moon:

> 'The cocks did crow to-whoo, to-whoo,
> And the sun did shine so cold!'
> – Thus answered Johnny in his glory,
> And that was all his travel's story.   (450–3)

Betty, in a sense, still has not found Johnny. He eludes her in a private language within which he can remain 'in wonder lost' (324).

But before exploring the full implications of endless interchange in this, *The Idiot Boy*'s last and best joke, we can usefully turn to the *Immortality Ode*. The *Ode* confronts the soberingly irreversible changes that eventually overtake the normal child. Here the rest of us, unlike Johnny, are pushed irresistibly towards a bleakly emptied world where 'nothing can bring back the hour / Of splendour in the grass, of glory in the flower' (178–9). Johnny remains securely spellbound 'in his glory', confidently asserting as facts the intimate incongruities of his dream-like vision. But his adult readers, when considering their own more transitory responses, are disturbingly exposed to the questions of the *Ode*:

> Whither is fled the visionary gleam?
> Where is it now, the glory and the dream?   (56–7)

V

Wordsworth begins the *Immortality Ode* by remembering the time when he was still young enough to feel what Johnny will always feel:

> There was a time when meadow, grove and stream,
> The earth, and every common sight,
>   To me did seem
>   Apparelled in celestial light,
> The glory and the freshness of a dream.
> It is not now as it hath been of yore; –
>   Turn whereso'er I may,
>   By night or day,
> The things which I have seen I now can see no more.   (1–9)

The delicious novelty discovered by the Idiot Boy on his journey through an unfamiliarly nocturnal landscape is invisible to the experienced adult. Wherever the poet travels, regardless of whether it is night or day, he sees only his own diminished vision.

Of course the *Ode*, like so much of Wordsworth's poetry, is not only a resigned elegy. It vehemently tries to resurrect Johnny's kind of excited awe in the very act of mourning its loss. Though Wordsworth's verse is often about our lazy ignorance of 'every common sight', it is also, as Coleridge said, an attempt 'to give the charm of novelty to things of every day' and to remove 'the lethargy of custom' which interposes a 'film of familiarity' between our eyes and 'the wonders of the world before us'. Coleridge's own italics stress that the essential quality of Wordsworth's vision is that it is *'fresh'*.[7] But whatever its achievement, the subject of Wordsworth's poetry is frequently the staleness of his own vision.

For Johnny the moon may have the vivacity of daylight enjoying a whimsical metamorphosis. But for Wordsworth in the *Immortality Ode*, the moon is just another equally lifeless image in a list whose beauty must be conceded as an aesthetic fact. The child tacitly acknowledges a reflection of his own gay gravity in moonlight which 'is not more still and mute than he' (80–1). The respectful adult of the *Ode* tries to verbalize how much he sees to admire, and succeeds only in exposing how little he feels; for him the moon is a remote and envied visionary, inaccessibly lost amongst undeniable, and yet unemotive, facts:

> The Rainbow comes and goes,
> And lovely is the Rose,
> The Moon doth with delight
> Look round her when the heavens are bare;
> Waters on a starry night
> Are beautiful and fair;
> The sunshine is a glorious birth;
> But yet I know, where'er I go
> That there hath past away a glory from the earth.　　(10–18)

Such a world has the drabness of an aesthete's shopping list. Wordsworth labours to reconstruct its vividness by verbalizing its distinct delights. But in effect his weary voice fragments it into meaninglessly unrelated statements, and damns it with the faint praise of tautology: 'beautiful and fair'.

In the third stanza the poet longs to escape his deadening human language: to join the 'joyous song' of birds and the natural rhythms to which 'young lambs bound' and 'every beast' seems to 'keep holiday'. But Johnny's identification with his pony is a child's privilege. The adult Wordsworth can only make a frenetic attempt to recover it vicariously, and demand to be surrounded by an experience which is no longer his: 'Thou Child of Joy,/Shout round me, let me hear thy shouts, thou happy Shepherd-boy!' (34–5). Wordsworth wants somebody to drown out the words with which adults talk themselves out of happiness. Johnny, with his ecstatic burring, would do. But a normal shepherd-boy can supply sufficiently incoherent sounds while he is still very young.

Initially normal children do seem able to enjoy a world which they cannot describe. In terms of our adult vocabulary they are often deaf and dumb, but the deficiency may allow them to relish the entertaining truth of things which have not yet been blurred into words. So the *Ode* addresses itself to the phenomenon of a child's mind in a tone mixing envy with admiration:

> thou Eye among the blind,
> That, deaf and silent, read'st the eternal deep,
> Haunted for ever by the eternal mind, –
> Mighty Prophet, Seer blest!
> On whom those truths do rest,
> Which we are toiling all our lives to find,
> In darkness lost, the darkness of the grave,
> Thou, over whom thy Immortality
> Broods like the Day,   (112–20)

The most portentous phrases here – 'Mighty Prophet, Seer blest' – admittedly demonstrate more of language's innate clumsiness than Wordsworth probably intended. An adult vocabulary may lure us into 'toiling' for truths which silence would freely give, but it does not compel us to talk to our children as if they were Old Testament pundits. However, in the paradoxical process on which Wordsworth is embarked, such lapses are perhaps inevitable. He means to free us from our bland assumptions about the ordinariness of children's thoughts. His demystification thus seeks to actually reveal the existence of mystery. It asks us to bend our minds to the possibility that children – perhaps because their speech can still sound so ignorant – manage to know a great deal more than adults.

Most of the stanza, in fact, voices an incisive and yet disconcertingly credible challenge which has its precise applications to *The Idiot Boy*. That story may partly be about the simple fact that children are more prone than adults to wander until they are literally 'In darkness lost'. But it is largely about the less obvious benightedness of his mother. Betty, who to this extent at least is a typical adult, works on the deluded assumption that those who have not found their way back to other people should be feeling lost. Her own attitudes ensure that she cannot be enlightened. If she toils all her life to protect her essentially mortal child, she will fill her head with the very 'darkness of the grave' which she means to outwit. Her love, in spite of its energetic searches, can discover no absolute peace of mind. What she would accept as wholly reassuring truths are not to be found in a world which is, thanks to her definition, dangerous.

But truths for a child are not facts to be sought restlessly. They are things. His relationship with them is so inextricably immediate that their reality seems to 'rest' on him, as surely as his security leans on them. To an absorbed child, the night need not be a dangerous darkness where he nervously waits to be found by other people. It can be like the day: a time of such recurrently fresh amusements that his experience seems timeless. Johnny, for instance, can seem as ready as his pony to 'live a thousand years' without being put 'out of humour'. But even a thousand is finite, an adult's revealingly inadequate expression for the inexpressible mood in which a child cannot conceive of his days being numbered. Such 'Immortality / Broods like the Day' over Johnny that even sunlight and cock-crow seem permanent fixtures, however deliciously they may disguise themselves.

Children are often as thoughtless as the *Ode*'s terms suggest. They can be 'deaf' to their parents' anxious advice and to the sound of danger in a waterfall. They are usually 'silent' about a world which they cannot yet understand by reducing it to its component parts. In the language of discriminating taste by which an adult tries to identify beauty, a child is illiterate. Yet this incapacity may allow children to 'read' the coherent joy encoded deep within the world. Adults, distracted by their environment's superficially fragmented ingredients, may discover far less. For Johnny at least, hill and dale, moon and sun, pony and person are as fluidly interdependent as the 'eternal deep'. He recognizes their complementary roles as 'the types and symbols of Eternity'. So an apparently absent-minded child may see much more than the adults who fretfully look out for his safety. He may well be an 'Eye among the blind'.

The *Ode* wrestles with the problem that the informed lucidities it admires in children must be expressed as ignorant confusions in terms of an adult's language:

> those obstinate questionings
> Of sense and outward things,
> Fallings from us, vanishings;
> Blank misgivings of a Creature
> Moving about in worlds not realised,   (142–6)

Yet it is those earliest worlds of feeling, so unamenable to logic and to language, on which, even in our maturity, we still largely depend:

> those first affections,
> Those shadowy recollections,
> Which, be they what they may,
> Are yet the fountain light of all our day,
> Are yet a master light of all our seeing;
> Uphold us, cherish, and have power to make
> Our noisy years seem moments in the being
> Of eternal silence: truths that wake,
> To perish never;
> Which neither listlessness, nor mad endeavour,
> Nor Man, nor Boy,
> Nor all that is at enmity with joy,
> Can utterly abolish or destroy!   (149–61)

During the 'noisy years' of our maturity, we wastefully verbalize our mortality by explaining life as a linear movement of time. Yet we still can have instinctual recollections of those imperishable truths which only an unbroken silence could properly respect.

What we thus occasionally recover is partly a profound common sense. We still sometimes glimpse the dazzlingly simple facts by which we survive: the 'fountain light', which is the source of all our energies and dominates our vision, is to some extent the literal sun whose magnificent mysteriousness is acknowledged by Johnny. In spite of the fears voiced by Betty and the narrator, Johnny is incapable of the 'mad endeavour' which might distract him from enjoying such knowledge: he will not seek the fragmented truths available to an explorer of the stream. But the *Ode* sees the rest of us becoming increasingly 'at enmity' with our world, and doing so from a relatively early stage. It is not just 'Man' but 'Boy' who can develop a destructive stance towards 'those first affections'.

In the *Ode* Wordsworth posits the myth of pre-existence in which even the earliest feelings of the newborn baby are echoes of some prior dimension. Such a dimension could involve no relationship between mortal human beings. Yet elsewhere Wordsworth often feels that the primal emotions involve not only an admiration for things, but also an affection for people. He can write that 'from the first' we have feelings both 'of grandeur and of tenderness', that 'There doth our life begin' (*The Prelude*, p. 571, 1–6). In the earliest stage of human life, the baby enjoys an unselfconsciously intimate contact with its surroundings which is almost indistinguishable from the parent who seems to be their unquestioned centre. The pre-verbal discovery with lips and hands of the mother's breast is like a training ground for understanding that larger world on which the baby is equally dependent for life. So Wordsworth's autobiography in *The Prelude* reaches back for:

> that first time
> In which a Babe, by intercourse of touch,
> I held mute dialogues with my Mother's heart.   (II. 282–4)

At this stage 'the infant sensibility, / Great birthright of our Being' is 'Augmented and sustained' by a human relationship which has nothing to do with words (II. 285–7).

So *The Prelude* can present the baby's love for his mother, and his admiration for the world, as a single affectionate exploration in which the two are an almost inseparable 'Presence':

> blest the Babe,
> Nurs'd in his Mother's arms, the Babe who sleeps
> Upon his Mother's breast, who, when his soul
> Claims manifest kindred with an earthly soul,
> Doth gather passion from his Mother's eye!
> Such feelings pass into his torpid life
> Like an awakening breeze, and hence his mind
> Even in the first trial of its powers
> Is prompt and watchful, eager to combine
> In one appearance, all the elements
> And parts of the same object, else detach'd
> And loth to coalesce. Thus, day by day,

> Subjected to the discipline of love,
> His organs and recipient faculties
> Are quicken'd, are more vigorous, his mind spreads,
> Tenacious of the forms which it receives.
> In one beloved Presence, nay and more,
> In that most apprehensive habitude
> And those sensations which have been deriv'd
> From this beloved Presence, there exists
> A virtue which irradiates and exalts
> All objects through all intercourse of sense.   (II. 239–60)

Thus 'the intercourse of touch', learnt by 'mute dialogues' with the mother's form, spreads naturally into the more general 'intercourse of sense' with 'All objects'. The mind, undistracted by any imagining of the absent, gains a tenacious hold on what, in parent and environment, can combine and coalesce into 'one beloved Presence'.

This is clearly echoed by the 'presence that disturbs' the adult of *Tintern Abbey* 'with the joy / Of elevated thoughts' when he recaptures:

> a sense sublime
> Of something far more deeply interfused,
> Whose dwelling is the light of setting suns,
> And the round ocean and the living air,
> And the blue sky, and in the mind of man:
> A motion and a spirit, that impels
> All thinking things, all objects of all thought,
>   (*PW*, II. 261–2, 94–100)

But the fleeting intuition of the mature poet lacks the palpable security of the baby who literally drinks knowledge at his mother's breast. Breastfeeding preserves the child's sense of interfused dependence on the world as physically as if he were still in the womb and still nourished by the transfusions of an umbilical cord:

> No outcast he, bewilder'd and depress'd;
> Along his infant veins are interfus'd
> The gravitation and the filial bond
> Of nature, that connect him with the world.
> Emphatically such a Being lives,
> An inmate of this *active* universe;
>   (*The Prelude*, II. 261–6, Wordsworth's italics)

At first, even after he has been born, the baby can see neither his mother nor his environment as separate from himself. His demanding energy brings them to life as surely as they sustain his existence:

> From nature largely he receives; nor so
> Is satisfied, but largely gives again
>
> . . .
>
> his mind,
> Even as an agent of the one great mind,
> Creates, creator and receiver both,
> Working but in alliance with the works
> Which it beholds. – Such, verily, is the first
> Poetic spirit of our human life;
> By uniform controul of after years
> In most abated or suppress'd, (II. 267–77)

The process of perception for the baby is as mutually creative as the interchanged smiles with which he learns to 'gather passion from his Mother's eye'.

If human relationship could confine itself to silent smiles, our commitment to each other and to our world might remain harmoniously indistinguishable. But the language we learn to talk makes 'infantile' a derogatory term, and provides a script with which to make the world unreal. It is unsurprising that *The Prelude*'s portrait of division between mother and child is set in a theatre (VII. 365–406). The mother, on whose cheeks 'the tints were false,/A painted bloom', Wordsworth has hastened to forget, and 'scarcely at this time' can remember her at all (371–3, 391–4). She has faded amongst the squalid chatter of her adult companions whose 'oaths, indecent speech, and ribaldry/Were rife' (389–90). But the child was still at the last poignant stage, when he was only just beginning 'to deal about/Articulate prattle', and could still be held on to as an image of innocent insight:

> But I behold
> The lovely Boy as I beheld him then,
> Among the wretched and the falsely gay,
> Like one of those who walk'd with hair unsinged
> Amid the fiery furnace. He hath since
> Appear'd to me oft-times as if embalm'd
> By Nature; through some special privilege,

> Stopp'd at the growth he had; destin'd to live,
> To be, to have been, come and go, a Child
> And nothing more, no partner in the years
> That bear us forward to distress and guilt,
> Pain and abasement,   (VII. 394–405)

Wordsworth's paradox is painfully clear. This young eye amongst the blind must himself be able to turn a blind eye. He must ignore much that interests his mother and other adults. His self-sufficient joy must be inattentive not only to lewd theatre but also to the kind of verse in which Wordsworth envies him. The silence of joy is incompatible with learning a language which, as well as permitting adults to be 'falsely gay', also allows one person to be the supportive 'partner' of another as they face their common mortal destiny of 'distress and guilt'. To stay permanently alive to the natural world, the child must be 'embalm'd' into a premature death. Wordsworth's wish is for the impossible. Only the mentally defective Johnny can be 'Stopp'd at the growth he had' and yet survive. As a fact which *The Idiot Boy* celebrates with the child himself and yet regrets for Betty's sake, Johnny must be accepted as always going to be 'a Child / And nothing more'.

Unlike Johnny, the normal child is under pressure to grow up. The point is made more than once in Wordsworth's contributions to *Lyrical Ballads*. In the dialogue of *We Are Seven*, the poet fails to bully a child into adopting an adult vocabulary. The little girl stubbornly refuses to count her family as irretrievably diminished by the loss of the dead brother and sister whom she still loves (*PW*, I. 236). But *Anecdote for Fathers* does succeed in fulfilling Wordsworth's bleak subtitle: 'Shewing how the art of lying may be taught'. Here a father, driven by his adult sense of linear time, compares his family's present home unfavourably with their past. He discriminates between his 'former pleasures' and the place where he is at present voicing his mature awareness of 'pain' (*PW*, I. 241, 9–20). He presses his young son to verbalize a similar comparison:

> 'Now tell me, had you rather be,'
> I said, and took him by the arm,
> 'On Kilve's smooth shore, by the green sea,
> Or here at Liswyn farm?'   (29–32)

The gesture, which seems close to a bully's arm-twisting, gives physical force to the father's infliction of language, and the child is

eventually wrenched out of the silence in which he has been blandly
accepting his present surroundings. He fields the demanded answer,
claiming to prefer Kilve (33–6). But he does so too casually for his
father who 'still . . . held him by the arm' (34). The boy has replied 'In
careless mood', sounding to that extent still as uncorrupted as Johnny. So the father knows he has so far lured his son only to the margins
of his own restlessly verbal world. He insists that the child splits
experience into finer distinctions. Specifying some of the advantages
of Liswyn, he 'three times' demands: 'Why, Edward, tell me why?'
(47–8). The child has 'blushed with shame' to discover that he cannot
give his father a reason (42–6), so he finally surrenders. He is reduced
to desperately finding something he can claim to dislike in his present
environment (49–60).

The boy in *Anecdote for Fathers* is only 'five years old' (1).
According to the *Ode*, a six-year-old has already embarked on
potentially disastrous self-education. As the child grows more fluent
in language, he tends to grow more rigid in response. His games
anticipate the polarized emotions of adult life: he 'frames his song' to
each new 'fragment from his dream of human life', rehearsing his
future roles in 'A wedding or a festival/A mourning or a funeral'
(86–95). He learns to 'fit his tongue/To dialogues of business, love,
or strife' (98–9). As soon as he grows bored with pretending to be
already in one kind of adult situation, 'The little Actor cons another
part' (100–3). Increasingly distracted from the realities that surround
him, the child behaves 'As if his whole vocation/Were endless imitation' (107–8).

Wordsworth watches helplessly as the child's imagination runs to
meet its own destruction:

> Thou little Child, yet glorious in the might
> Of heaven-born freedom on thy being's height,
> Why with such earnest pains dost thou provoke
> The years to bring the inevitable yoke,
> Thus blindly with thy blessedness at strife?
> Full soon thy Soul shall have its earthly weight,
> Heavy as frost, and deep almost as life!   (122–8)

Ignorant of the blessedness of their peculiar vision, children are
impatient to discard it. Their behaviour is as 'blindly' destructive of
their own joy as the 'listlessness' or 'mad endeavour' of the grown-
ups they imitate.

Children gradually burden themselves with what *Tintern Abbey* calls 'the heavy and the weary weight/Of all this unintelligible world' (*PW*, II.260, 39–40). But they are able to do so only by adopting the adult terminology in which we demand that it should be understood. In a fine sonnet, Wordsworth voices the inane slogans of maturity with which we exhaust our capacity for feeling by babbling to each other:

> late and soon,
> Getting and spending, we lay waste our powers:
> Little we see in Nature that is ours;
> We have given our hearts away, a sordid boon!
> This Sea that bares her bosom to the moon;
> The winds that will be howling at all hours,
> And are up-gathered now like sleeping flowers;
> For this, for everything, we are out of tune;
>
> (*PW*, III.18, 1–8)

Those fretful chimes of adult language – 'late and soon,/Getting and spending' – deafen us. We cannot hear the larger harmony, whose unharassed sense of time embraces 'all hours' and whose relationships have the unstinting openness of the sea baring itself to the sky.

According to *Tintern Abbey* we talk ourselves out of this symphony and into a discordant chaos of 'evil tongues,/Rash judgements . . . greetings where no kindness is', and 'all/The dreary intercourse of life'. The 'sad music of humanity', at its most vocal, thus has 'ample power/To chasten and subdue'. At its bleakest, perhaps, it is concentrated into 'the din/Of town and cities' heard 'in lonely rooms' (*PW*, II.260–2, 128–31, 91–3, 25–6).

But the *Ode* itself suggests that the verbal music of our humanity need not always sound so sterile. Language equips the adult to express his feelings at 'A wedding or a festival', as well as at 'A mourning or a funeral' (94–5). It allows not only sham social gestures but also greetings where there *is* kindness. It admits us not just to competitive conversations about getting and spending but also to exchanges of tenderness: 'To dialogues of business, *love*, or strife' (99, my italics). Similarly the child of *Anecdote for Fathers* is not only persuaded to discover deficiencies in a landscape that had before seemed wholly satisfying; he is also alerted to a previously unsuspected vulnerability in an adult. His father is, in the end, understood to need a sympathy which his son cannot provide until he too has shared the experience of loss. The children of *The Ruined Cottage* more obstinately refuse to see life as anything other than a game. So, greeting their father's manic gestures with unvarying smiles, they cannot begin to communicate with his suffering. They can neither speak nor understand the compassionate language with which one of their parents can pity the other.

It is a language which compels adults at least to try to express more than Johnny's silent and single-minded vision. Wordsworth acknowledges in the *Ode*'s final stanza a concern for others which has given him some of Betty's vigilance: 'an eye/That hath kept watch o'er man's mortality' (198–9). His feelings may sometimes seem to have diminished in intensity, but they have audibly expanded in range. Wordsworth can sometimes still 'feel', in his 'heart of hearts', the 'might' connecting 'Fountains, Meadows, Hills, and Groves'. But he is no longer able to live single-mindedly in a stable world dominated by their 'more habitual sway' (187–92). To be maturely alive is to identify not only with the glory of children enjoying their apparent immortality, but also with the fears of parents, anxiously aware that the person one loves can be injured or even killed:

> Thanks to the human heart by which we live,
> Thanks to its tenderness, its joys, and fears,
> To me the meanest flower that blows can give
> Thoughts that do often lie too deep for tears.   (201–4)

The *Immortality Ode* thus closes on thoughts which flourish in a natural landscape and which – if they frequently seem 'too deep for tears' – are presumably often beyond the reach of words. Yet Wordsworth even here tries to articulate more than the thoughts of a child. The poet's gratitude embraces the penultimate stanza's 'thoughts that spring/Out of human suffering' (183–4). At times a grown man may feel again as securely rooted to the earth as he did in childhood. But it is not only because of those moments that Wordsworth is so moved by 'the meanest flower'. It is also because of moments when human beings feel they belong, not with flowers, but with each other. At such times we try, by word and gesture, to share an often fearful tenderness about which the natural world seems dumbly ignorant.

Wordsworth may long that *The Prelude*'s child in the theatre could be like a flower: 'destined to live,/To be, to have been, come and go . . . no partner in the years/That bear us forward' (VII.401–4).

Indeed the imagery with which the boy is described seeks to establish the similarity: he is 'A rosy Babe' (367), and 'in face a cottage rose,/Just three parts blown' (379–80). But such images admit that they can only have a temporary appropriateness. The human chatter of the theatre to which his mother has taken him cannot long remain ignored. Like the 'little Actor' of the *Ode*, he will learn 'dialogues of business, love, or strife'. He will discover the social world of 'A wedding or a festival, A mourning or a funeral', and recognize it as the proper theatre for much that his 'human heart' is compelled to enact (94–9). Nature will not give him 'some special privilege' to remain in the joy she grants to 'the meanest flower that blows'. He cannot escape his destiny as our partner.

The *Ode*'s final image thus belongs partly 'In that sweet mood when pleasant thoughts/Bring sad thoughts to the mind' of *Lines Written in Early Spring* (PW, IV. 58, 3–4). There the pleasure of recognizing 'that every flower/Enjoys the air it breathes' leads the poet 'to lament/What man has made of man' (11–12, 23–4). Through the *Ode*'s 'dialogues' of 'love, or strife', we discover in each other intensities of personal emotion which often force us into shared exile from the world 'Of splendour in the grass, of glory in the flower' (179). Yet through the language of 'the human heart' we alone learn to acknowledge the preciousness of all transitory appearances, to cherish not only the inarticulate innocence of a child at the theatre but also 'the meanest flower that blows'.

VI

So *The Idiot Boy*, in remaining relatively inarticulate, may be deprived. Certainly those who love him are deprived of full relationship. From their point of view, his mind can indeed seem frustratingly defective. It gives him no means of communicating his feelings, no way of sharing his experiences with another person. Johnny's lack of language may save him from self-conscious loneliness, but it drives his mother further into hers. When 'Johnny makes the noise he loves', he uses no words: 'Burr, burr – now Johnny's lips they burr/As loud as any mill' (97–8). His mother 'listens, glad to hear it' because she loves him and all that he does. But she cannot understand it. When 'Johnny burrs and laughs aloud', one cannot tell 'whether in cunning or in joy' (377–9). The inarticulate child may seem satisfyingly close to the 'truths' of 'Immortality', but he is bafflingly distant from other people. His wordless burring, though loyal to his own experience, cannot convey it to those who love him.

So *The Idiot Boy* ends with the doting mother asking the impossible:

> For while they all were travelling home,
> Cried Betty, 'Tell us, Johnny, do,
> Where all this long night you have been,
> What you have heard, what you have seen:
> And, Johnny, mind you tell us true.'
>
> Now Johnny all night long had heard
> The owls in tuneful concert strive;
> No doubt too he the moon had seen;
> For in the moonlight he had been
> From eight o'clock till five.
>
> And thus, to Betty's question, he
> Made answer, like a traveller bold,
> (His very words I give to you,)
> 'The cocks did crow to-whoo, to-whoo,
> And the sun did shine so cold!'
> – Thus answered Johnny in his glory,
> And that was all his travel's story.   (436–52)

Johnny's tangled diction captures the world's intricate unity. Where the mature poet of the *Ode* and *Tintern Abbey* has to generalize about this 'sense sublime / Of something far more deeply interfused' (*PW*, II. 262, 95–6), *The Idiot Boy* can be specific. He can offer a precise example of a 'common sight' revealing itself as 'Apparelled in celestial light' (*Immortality Ode, PW*, IV. 279, 2–4).

At the very end of his tale, Johnny will still not be distracted away from the facts of his experience. He cannot be taught the 'art of lying' which the intelligent child of *The Prelude* is, with the development of 'articulate prattle' until a vocabulary in which to be 'falsely gay' has grown to devalue the true joy of silent idleness (VII. 369, 396). Johnny's gibberish still articulates 'the first / Poetic spirit of our human life'. In him, it will not be 'abated or suppress'd' by 'uniform controul of after years' as *The Prelude* says it will be 'In most' (II. 275–8). He will not abuse his insight by the inaccuracies of normal usage. He will speak only of what it means to live in those felt realities which are so dimly echoed by the Ode's generalized elegy about 'The glory and the freshness of a dream'. He remains 'in his glory'. Johnny's answer, limited in vocabulary and limitless in appreciation, defines the singularity of his vision. It is an answer for all seasons. Nothing in the course of the poem has altered his outlook. For the rest of his life, the strangely static life of the subnormal, it will survive.

But his triumph is his mother's tragi-comedy. Unlike the normal child she might have had, Johnny willl never learn to speak her language. Betty's love has some needs which her son's contented burring cannot answer. She has an optimistically biased ear for any sound of progress in 'The Boy, who is her best delight' (53), but Johnny still gives her little excuse for hope. To Betty, 'all his travel's story' must sound frustratingly slight. To the eavesdropping reader, it can – in the light of revelations like that of 'Crossing the Alps' – sound gloriously adequate. To Wordsworth, who once said that Johnny's words had been 'the foundation' of the whole poem,[8] they have the value of at once saying everything about grandeur, and nothing about tenderness. The zany incisiveness of Johnny's speech connects him to the world as surely as it isolates him from his mother. So at the poem's close the reader is stranded between envy of a happily self-contained child and sympathy for an often unhappily affectionate parent.

Wordsworth himself has succeeded in only partially growing up. He commutes with uneasy fascination between two worlds, striving to do justice to two intriguingly opposed visions. One can still seem close to Johnny's. Wordsworth envies and respects the boy's intuitive ear for the harmonies that surround us (the 'tuneful concert' of the owls, for instance) and his instinctual faith that the natural world is his to enjoy as if it were a home he inhabits: 'For in the moonlight he had been'. But Wordsworth also identifies with Betty's harassed exclusion from all this. He understands that, until a missing child is found, there is not much that we can be expected to 'see in Nature that is ours'. At such a time fretful thoughts of 'late and soon' are bound to make us unappreciative of hooting owls, ensuring – however temporarily – that 'For this, for everything, we are out of tune'.

Johnny may seem impressively free of the often ridiculous fears that contort his mother. But Wordsworth is also impressed by those very anxieties, however laughably undignified he knows they can seem. In a letter defending the poem, he writes: 'I have indeed often looked upon the conduct of fathers and mothers of the lower classes of society towards Idiots as the great triumph of the human heart. It is there that we see the strength, disinterestedness and grandeur of love.' Betty has the strength to love a creature incapable of recognizing, let alone returning, the intensity of her love. She loves a mind so feeble that it cannot glimpse danger even in a waterfall. So she condemns herself in the short term to inevitable worry and in the long term to likely grief. In such folly Wordsworth discovers a tenderness impressive enough to stand for 'the great triumph of the human heart'. Indeed he calls it a 'grandeur': the very word that he normally reserves for all that Betty sacrifices. Betty's love confines her to a fretful life in an illusory world, but its stature is inseparable from its frequently absurd blindness.

Yet this voice, at once amused and touched, is but one of the poem's voices. The other is also recaptured in the accurate ambivalence of that same letter:

> I have often applied to Idiots, in my own mind, that sublime expression of Scripture that 'their life is hidden with God'. They are worshipped, probably from a feeling of this sort, in several parts of the East. Among the Alps where they are numerous they are considered, I believe, a blessing to the family to which they belong.[9]

'Crossing the Alps' might make us expect Wordsworth to believe that region to be especially blessed with Idiot Boys, children who would see 'the stationary blasts of waterfalls' not as a worrying threat to their vulnerably separated selves, but as a richly entertaining aspect of the game that is their universal home. As it happens, we know that Wordsworth had read of the disproportionate number of subnormals in the Swiss mountain communities,[10] and Sir William Empson assures me that it was a scientific fact, explicable in terms of the mineral content of their drinking water. But, of course, wherever somebody like Johnny lived, he would be an 'Eye among the blind'. Any scenery would reveal to him the inclusive grandeur of the universe to which he belongs. Any community might see his behaviour as almost supernaturally enigmatic, a life 'hidden with God'. Similarly no Alpine beauty spot would be potent enough to distract Betty from her urgent sense of that one child's preciousness and fragility. Seeing so much that children, perhaps rashly, fail to notice, a parent cannot always escape the responsibility of being, in a very different way, an 'Eye among the blind'.

Wordsworth's best poetry is too thoughtful to be dogmatic. He is often our English Socrates, answering us with the wisdom only of a lucidly confessed ignorance, and informing us only of how little we can know about our world, ourselves and each other. The intensity of his intuitions validates two quite different kinds of feeling. His verse struggles with the problems of compelling us to attend to one without seeming to undervalue the other. But his challengingly split subject matter demands expression for, as he told one friend in a letter, 'we have no thought (save thoughts of pain) but as far as we have love and admiration'.[11]

So the *Ode* ends with the mature gaze of 'an eye/That hath kept watch o'er man's mortality' (198–9), even though it frequently fulfils the contrary promise of its full title, and does evoke 'Intimations of Immortality from Recollections of Early Childhood'. Similarly, *The Idiot Boy* fluctuates between following Betty's increasingly frantic sense of hours ticked away and focusing instead on Johnny's serene ignorance of the clock. Wordsworth's vision thus implicitly admits that, in glimpsing one of our conflicting feelings, it may be momentarily turning a blind eye to the other. But in exploring such difficult terrain, we cannot afford to patronize his tentative insights. On ground where the rest of us seem often to stumble about in unrelieved blindness, we should perhaps elect the confessedly one-eyed man king.

5

THE EYE OF NATURE

EARLIER SOLITARIES: 'OLD MAN TRAVELLING:
ANIMAL TRANQUILLITY AND DECAY',
'THE OLD CUMBERLAND BEGGAR' AND THE
'DISCHARG'D SOLDIER'
OF 'THE PRELUDE', IV. 363–504

I

The Solitaries demand a poetry which, without being any less moving, is more tentative than that of *The Idiot Boy*. In that poem the endearingly ordinary mother and her quite extraordinary son may baffle each other but they do not baffle us. We are told clearly enough, while they blunder through their wildly optimistic attempts to find a common language, that their experiences are in fact hopelessly different. Guided by a confidently humorous storyteller, we can meet each of his characters with an appropriately distinct response. We will find no such guidance in the verse which explores Wordsworth's own hesitation as to how he should approach the Solitaries. A meeting with any of these disconcertingly ambiguous strangers may invite the tactful sympathy which we bring to someone who is obviously worse off than ourselves, or it may require us to pay respectful attention to one of those elders who really are our betters. The poetry is decisively lucid only in its resolve to make both impressions equally impressive.

At moments the Solitaries are, like Betty, explicitly human. Their appearance, though daunting, still appeals to us for recognition, daring us to look further and see that even the most peculiar-looking people are indeed people and must suffer from feelings like our own. Most of the Solitaries are very old and all are visibly deformed; so they bring to the problem of pain a blunter physicality. While Betty, and even Margaret of *The Ruined Cottage*, seem partly to think themselves into distress, the Solitaries look as if they have been forced to dwell in a discomfort as inescapable as their own ageing bones.

Yet their advancing years sometimes seem to be paradoxically carrying them back to a second childhood which is comparable to, but intriguingly different from, Johnny's. After a round-trip through experience, the return of grown men to simplicity raises possibilities beyond those of an idiot boy's stationary innocence. Wordsworth can look to them for a consciously achieved wisdom, even if their response to this, as to so much else, tends to be an enigmatic silence. He can also seek in the placidity of such old men not a lost past but a looming future. Since idiot boys are born, not made, the poet need not fear (or hope) that he could turn into Johnny. However, the young poet could – would presumably wish to – reach his own old age. Behind those opaquely wizened faces may lie the promise of a peace beyond any risk of fading back into common understanding, or the threat of a blank senility from which no traveller returns.

So the problem of approach for Wordsworth is twofold. Before he can decide what they represent, he must determine how far common humanity demands that he recognize them as individuals with their own particular needs. They may be men who move us to understand their problems in concrete detail. Or they may have already exalted – or reduced – themselves to the stability of abstract nouns. The Leech-gatherer, for instance, is described nine times as a 'Man', but the title of his poem asserts that he is also 'Resolution and Independence'. *The Prelude*'s blind beggar, mundanely 'propp'd against a Wall' in a London street, seems ready 'to explain / The story of the Man'. Yet he finally belongs in 'another world' as 'a type / Or emblem of the utmost that we know' (VII. 612–22). Wordsworth remembers introducing the Discharg'd Soldier to a friend with the firm statement that 'here is a Man'. Even so the verse is able to discover in the soldier a series of abstract qualities: 'A desolation, a simplicity / That seem'd akin to solitude' (*The Prelude*, IV. 484, 418–19). 'The Old Cumberland Beggar' sounds committedly specific until we remember that Wordsworth generalized the title by placing it first beneath a group heading: 'Poems Referring to the Period of Old Age'. However, it is for the shortest of those poems that Wordsworth constructs the most elaborate label, one which meticulously spells out the challenge posed by all the Solitaries. Its original full title is *Old Man Travelling: Animal Tranquillity and Decay*. This announces not only an individual, deliberately moving person but also a pair of latently opposed abstractions which hover side by side in their own unresolved ambiguity.

The title's warning seems only fair: the poem is partly about a man making a difficult journey to reach the person he loves, but it is also about a peacefulness which could decline into bovine stupidity. The work is so arrestingly incisive that I can quote it in full:

> The little hedge-row birds,
> That peck along the road, regard him not.
> He travels on, and in his face, his step,
> His gait, is one expression; every limb,
> His look and bending figure, all bespeak
> A man who does not move with pain, but moves
> With thought. – He is insensibly subdued
> To settled quiet: he is one by whom
> All effort seems forgotten, one to whom
> Long patience hath such mild composure given,
> That patience now doth seem a thing, of which
> He hath no need. He is by nature led
> To peace so perfect, that the young behold
> With envy what the Old Man hardly feels.
> – I asked him whither he was bound, and what
> The object of his journey; he replied
> 'Sir! I am going many miles to take
> A last leave of my son, a mariner,
> Who from a sea-fight has been brought to Falmouth,
> And there is dying in an hospital.'
>
> (*PW*, IV. 247, *app. crit.*, text of *Lyrical Ballads*, 1798)

Two startlingly different statements are being made here: the cautious description which is so thoughtfully developed by the observer and the Old Man's own, almost clumsily factual, account of himself. Our problem is whether these can possibly add up to a single unified statement by the poet.

There are of course hints of paradox even before the Old Man speaks. Apparently 'subdued / To settled quiet', he still 'moves', and he 'does not move with pain' as an animal might 'but moves / With thought' as only a human being can. The 'birds, / That peck along the road' may treat him like some indigenous wild creature of their own landscape, but he chooses to use that road for its peculiarly human purpose and 'travels on'. However, in spite of these ambiguities, the first fourteen lines mainly emphasize how impassive the man seems to be. They are, after all, an observer's summary of externals and justify the subtitle, *A Sketch*, which the poem carried until the edition of 1845. At this stage he is apparently silent, and it is only appearances ('face . . . step . . . gait . . . limb . . . look . . . figure') that can 'bespeak' the inner emotions – if any – that he feels.

Wordsworth's verbal sketching here does not build up a detailed portrait of personality. The description is in fact essentially reductive, constantly redefining its own terminology until words which innately tend to assert character are forced to deny it. The unchanging 'expression' is not something which the old man adopts; it simply 'is', and in fact functions so unexpressively that it is no clearer 'in his face' than in his 'every limb'. The phrase which yokes 'His look and bending figure' makes his glance as unwittingly informative as his humped back. Since what these 'bespeak' seems to be a 'settled quiet', they are credited with the power of speech as if to suggest that the man himself might be found dumbly wanting. Similarly 'effort' is present to remind us of a human stance which he seems to have 'forgotten', and 'patience' is almost pedantically qualified until it disappears as 'a thing, of which / He hath no need'. Even this cumulative contradiction in terms apparently still leaves the Old Man looking as if he has more inner consciousness than the verse will concede: we are told that he 'hardly feels' even what little we might 'behold' in him.

The grammar too is carefully aimed to discredit any activity he might claim. The supposed subject of 'The Sketch' is not allowed to be the subject of its first sentence. He must concede that role to diminutive rivals. 'The little hedge-row birds', who are allowed to govern the opening verbs, dismissively negate the one that introduces him: they 'regard him not'. Instead of thinking, he 'moves / With thought': thought accompanies him somewhat as his shadow might do, an uninvited fellow-traveller. Similarly he has been 'by nature led', so his situation is not one he has found for himself. The margin of the manuscript shows Wordsworth originally planning to say that the old man was merely 'resigned to quietness', but the poem reduces him more decisively to a passive object by making him 'insensibly subdued / To settled quiet'. Even the personal pronoun which should define him as a creature characterized by conscious wishes can introduce an unqualified self-denial: 'He hath no need'.

The poem's last four lines are therefore clearly intended as a surprise, whether we judge the shock to be stimulating and informative or just meaninglessly jarring. The observer of this apparently 'settled quiet' suddenly asks it to answer as a person with a purpose. The old man is questioned, not only about his destination, but also about his reasons for wanting to get there. The new assumptions implied by these questions turn out to be surprisingly justified. This is indeed no tranquil animal but a man ready to speak, and to speak frankly about his own individual priorities. His words define a tragedy which is peculiarly human. The 'hedge-row birds', mindlessly pecking their food, can articulate nothing about either lasting parental love or the war whose savage costliness such love can measure. The mere fact of dialogue itself demonstrates that the observer, and the old man who had seemed to him so alien, are in fact members of the same strange species.

Wordsworth's 'Advertisement' to the 1798 *Lyrical Ballads* (where this poem first appeared) had anticipated a reader who might find the verse disconcertingly odd, one who would have 'to struggle with feelings of strangeness and awkwardness'. He challenged such readers to acknowledge that the poems were in fact about 'human passions, human characters, and human incidents' (*PW*, II. 383). This emphasis on the peculiarly human, on what all men in the last resort have in common with each other, is repeated in the 1800 Preface. The aim is to trace 'what is really important to men', 'the primary laws of our nature', 'the essential passions of the heart', 'those elementary feelings', 'the great and simple affections of our nature' (*PW*, II. 384–8). The Old Man's speech assumes a shared understanding that the love of a father for his son is a primary law of human nature, that the desire to take leave of those one cares for before the final separation of death is an essential instinct of the human heart. Once the observer hears the facts, he will understand why even such an Old Man feels compelled to attempt a journey of 'many miles'. The strangely 'settled quiet' of animal tranquillity seems to have been replaced by the familiar restlessness of human suffering.

Is the poem then hopelessly inconsistent? One defence might be that it warns us not to make glib assumptions. The first fourteen lines would then be a necessarily false start before truth is enforced in the last six. On such an interpretation, the observer and the reader are initially misled by what appears to be an alien, if impressive, object. Later we are embarrassed to find that we had been patronizing what we supposed we were admiring, and had been intriguing ourselves with a specimen when we were in fact confronted by a person. The shock of this revelation ambushes us into admitting our common humanity. We thus recognize 'the great and simple affections of our nature', which we had previously missed through being too much 'spectators ab extra'. This last phrase is Coleridge's in an attack on Wordsworth for 'utter non-sympathy' with his characters, approaching them without the imaginative insight to see beneath externals.[1] The charge has been repeated often enough. David Perkins, for instance, argues that Wordsworth, who portrays 'natural objects' in a 'vivid, concrete and detailed' way, tends to present human beings as 'mere, stark abstractions'.[2] But some of Wordsworth's own verse seems fully conscious of the price paid by such a tendency. Perhaps Tranquillity and Decay are meant to be seen as falsifyingly stark abstracts: they may obscure a figure whose speech will insist in a concrete and detailed way that he is an 'Old Man Travelling'.

Certainly in one of the *Poems on the Naming of Places*, Wordsworth explicitly anatomizes the dangers of superficial assessment. In 'Point Rash Judgement' he records how he and his companions initially misjudged a figure sighted at a distance:

> Through a thin veil of glittering haze was seen
> Before us, on a point of jutting land,
> The tall and upright figure of a Man
> Attired in peasant's garb, who stood alone,
> Angling beside the margin of the lake.   (PW, II. 117, 45–9)

They assume that he fishes merely for fun. He seems to be indulging in a hobby when he could be working in the harvest to earn the money he will need when winter comes, so they pompously reduce him to an exemplum of the 'Improvident and reckless'. (50–5). A closer look reveals that what they took to be a sign of self-indulgent tranquillity in fact images a fellow human being struggling to survive:

> we approached
> Close to the spot where with his rod and line
> He stood alone; wherat he turned his head
> To greet us – and we saw a Man worn down
> By sickness, gaunt and lean, with sunken cheeks
> And wasted limbs, his legs so long and lean
> That for my single self I looked at them,
> Forgetful of the body they sustained. –
> Too weak to labour in the harvest field,

The man was using his best skill to gain
A pittance from the dead unfeeling lake
That knew not of his wants.   (55–66)

The repetition of the fact that he 'stood alone' (48, 57) provides a
fixed point by which we can measure how far the observing Wordsworth has to travel from first impression to belated insight. The
illusion of a placidly self-sufficient solitude is left far behind as we
approach a man who struggles to sustain himself in poignant isolation.

Another verbal echo – 'the dead . . lake' – imposes a further
dimension. Wordsworth had earlier in the poem described how he
and his friends happily strolled along, relishing a natural landscape
which evoked interdependent life: the breeze which would otherwise
be 'invisible' came alive to their sight in movements of a dande-
lion seed which it blew along the surface of the 'dead calm lake'
(11–25). But now the lake can no longer suggest the serenity of death
but only its callousness. The 'dead unfeeling lake' of line 65 knows
nothing of the poor man's wants. Wordsworth comes to see that he
too, in being comfortably 'calm', had been ignorantly 'unfeeling'.
Distracted by the beauty of that landscape, he had failed to recognize
the humanity of the figure by the lake, had failed to 'temper . . .
thoughts with charity' (70–3). So his altered view of the fisherman
rattles his confidence in both the natural world and himself:

The happy idleness of that sweet morn,
With all its lovely images, was changed
To serious musing and to self-reproach.   (67–9)

For the Idiot Boy to be 'idle all for very joy' may be harmless enough,
but the adult Wordsworth was in danger of self-consciously enjoying
an 'idleness' which allowed him to priggishly condemn it in others. A
pleasure in 'lovely images' on this occasion made him so stupidly
blind to a fellow human being that, like 'the dead unfeeling lake', he
'knew not of his wants'.

On one reading, *Old Man Travelling* too may be a literary booby-
trap. However, 'Point Rash Judgement' is so clearly didactic because
it only has the one, rather laboured, point to make. There can be no
prizes for guessing that the proper response to a starving fisherman is
at the very least to wish him tight lines and a full belly, and at best
to give him food ourselves. Obviously it would be despicable to

imagine that he may not feel as painfully hungry as a passing group of sensitive intellectuals would if they had to face malnutrition. In a just society, hunger would be eliminated and death by starvation prevented. Yet, as *Old Man Travelling* suggests, death from some cause, however delayed, will remain inevitable. So how necessary or desirable is it that the living should mourn the dead? Michael, for instance, finds that the loss of even the most beloved son need not 'overset the brain or break the heart' and can be made, at the very least, 'endurable' (*PW*, II.93, 449–50). The discomfort of the fisherman's poverty is exposed as an ugly certainty, but the sense of loss in *Old Man Travelling* emerges only as a threatening possibility. Just how vividly does he anticipate the bereavement he is about to suffer, and how intensely will he feel it? Our knowledge of human nature may supply 'those elementary feelings' that are likely to torment a man watching his son die, but they are not explicit in the poem. The first fourteen lines have hinted that the old man may have been released from 'the primary laws of our nature', and that possibility is not decisively removed even by his words at the end. The content of his speech may reveal cause for grief but its tone is not impassioned. The bluntly specific details of 'to Falmouth' and 'in an hospital' make his statement not only more realistic, but also less obviously emotive.

Would a lack of emotion make the old man seem pathetically disabled by 'Decay'? Or would it suggest that he was capable of a peace we should 'behold / With envy'? Do we want him to be a fully sensitive human being if that will merely allow him to register pain? Should we not prefer him to be so 'insensibly subdued' that our first impression is confirmed and we can reassure ourselves that he 'does not move with pain'? Should we admire the grandeur of tranquillity glimpsed in the first fourteen lines, or feel that it represents a decline into some animal-like station beneath the 'great and simple affections of our nature'? The strangeness in those lines makes us almost relieved to reach the suggestion that the man is driven by something as familiar as a tragic tenderness for his son. Yet our own tenderness as sympathetic readers might make us want to protect him from it. We may fear that grief over his son's death could break his already 'bending figure' and cause his own death. But we may also sense that those who cannot grieve are, in an important sense, dead already. In what is tantalizingly the only sentence Geoffrey Hartman offers on the poem, he suggests that 'two kinds of death are juxtaposed'. As

well as 'the premature cutting-off' represented by the son, there is the
father 'being insensibly and slowly subdued to nature'.³ The implication seems to be that, provided the old man is not awakened to grief,
he will soon, like Lucy, be 'Rolled round in earth's diurnal course,/
With rocks, and stones, and trees' (*PW*, II. 216, 7–8). He too would
then pose the problem of whether such a state represents a triumphant reunion with the animated universe or a defeated dwindling
into an inanimate object, 'a thing that could not feel' (*PW*, II. 216, 3).
'But persons are not things', insisted Coleridge, rebuking economists
who treated people as commodities. He stated a 'sacred principle'
that 'a person can never become a thing, nor be treated as such
without wrong'.⁴ With this the Wordsworth who wrote the confession of 'Point Rash Judgement' might blushingly agree.

Yet in *The Prelude* to be treated as 'a thing' can be almost flatter-
ing. As a boy it was in moments of privileged communion that
Wordsworth 'conversed/With things that really are' (II. 412–13).
One such conversation is interrupted by the bald fact of a child's
death in a transition as violent as that in *Old Man Travelling*:

> There was a Boy, ye knew him well, ye Cliffs
> And Islands of Winander! many a time
> At evening, when the stars had just begun
> To move along the edges of the hills,
> Rising or setting, would he stand alone
> Beneath the trees, or by the glimmering Lake,
> And there, with fingers interwoven, both hands
> Press'd closely, palm to palm, and to his mouth
> Uplifted, he, as through an instrument,
> Blew mimic hootings to the silent owls
> That they might answer him. – And they would shout
> Across the wat'ry Vale, and shout again,
> Responsive to his call, with quivering peals,
> And long halloos, and screams, and echoes loud
> Redoubled and redoubled; concourse wild
> Of mirth and jocund din! And when it chanced
> That pauses of deep silence mock'd his skill,
> Then sometimes in that silence, while he hung
> Listening, a gentle shock of mild surprize
> Has carried far into his heart the voice
> Of mountain torrents; or the visible scene

Would enter unawares into his mind
With all its solemn imagery, its rocks,
Its woods, and that uncertain Heaven, received
Into the bosom of the steady lake.

     This Boy was taken from his Mates, and died
In childhood, ere he was full ten years old.
Fair are the woods, and beauteous is the spot,
The Vale where he was born; the Churchyard hangs
Upon a Slope above the Village School,
And there, along that bank, when I have pass'd
At evening, I believe that oftentimes
A full half-hour together I have stood
Mute – looking at the Grave in which he lies.

                          (*The Prelude*, v. 389–422)

The explicitly 'mute' gaze with which this passage finally contemplates the grave seems to make audible that silence which follows the Old Man's announcement of death, an announcement to which the observer who has questioned him can add nothing.

Wordsworth's modern commentators, however, far from being stunned into silence by 'There was a Boy', have been embarrassed into voluble attempts to explain it away. An early manuscript of the opening paragraph uses the first rather than the third person, and thus provides scholars with an explicitly autobiographical version of the owl-hooting. They have deployed it to suggest that the second paragraph infiltrates a fraud which the reader should simply skip. Its omission allows them to identify with the boy's happy acceptance of the 'solemn imagery' of 'the visible scene', while comfortably ignoring what seemed to the poet equally relevant: the discomforting certainty that all such boys do themselves become invisible. They must sooner (like this child) or later (like the Old Man's son and eventually the Old Man himself) vanish beneath the far more chilling solemnity of a graveyard. They may then be raised to that other tantalizingly 'uncertain Heaven' of Christian cosmology, but they are still lost to human sight. This boy is admittedly 'taken from his Mates' at what those who sentimentalize nature call an 'unnaturally' early age. But a luckier child lives on only to gradually disappear as he is transformed into an unrecognizably grown adult. How many of us can feel that in talking about our childhood we are not remembering

THE EYE OF NATURE

selves who are no longer alive? The grammar of nostalgia often declines from the living present ('I am a Man') to a dead past ('There was a Boy').

The juxtaposition forces us to face a still more crucial thought: each child can never know whether the things which 'enter unawares' into his own mind form an identically 'visible scene' in the minds of his schoolfellows. Wordsworth's own note to the poem does recall that all his friends enjoyed imitating owls, but he could still only guess how far 'the voice of mountain torrents' at such moments was carried into their hearts. *The Prelude*, like all literature, of course assumes that the author's feelings can be shared with unknown readers, let alone personal friends. Yet Wordsworth's concern is with peculiarly private experiences of gain and intensely personal feelings of loss. In the light of this, his hesitation as to whether the opening paragraph can be a third-person or only a first-person account seems to me intelligently curious about the truth and his final decision, not what F. W. Bateson, for instance, calls it: 'an attempt to pass fiction off as fact'.⁵ Nor can I agree with Bateson when he dismisses the second paragraph as a best ignored, 'sentimental conclusion' which was 'concocted to tie up the loose ends' when Wordsworth wanted to publish 'There was a Boy' as a self-contained poem in *Lyrical Ballads*.⁶ The addition of the second paragraph is in fact what compels the reader to admit the 'loose ends' of human response. The retention of the elegiac close when Wordsworth made the sequence part of *The Prelude* proves that its juxtaposition of two different kinds of poetry still seemed to him to reflect two different ways of feeling which should reckon with each other.

The phobia which drives critics scurrying away from the second paragraph of 'There was a Boy' is equally perceptible in discussion of *Old Man Travelling*. There the issue is whether one would rather read the full original version or the later texts which cut the last six lines. One of its earliest readers – Dr Burney in the *Monthly Review* for June 1799 – admired the description as 'Finely drawn' but rejected 'the termination'. Wordsworth, undeterred, printed the poem in full up to and including the edition of 1805. However, in 1815 he cut all of the last six lines. Such retreats from ambivalence were common enough as Wordsworth's poetic nerve gradually failed, but the eager approval of modern critics is surprising. John Jones, for instance, is confident that 'the last six lines were a mistake, and he saved the poem by omitting them . . . they do violence to the nature of the old man'. For Jones the old man is 'a study of integration' and 'does not need to do or say anything – he is'.[7] But this seems to me too easy an answer to the questions so strenuously begged by the poem. If the old man has wholly decayed into an animal-like insensibility, he perhaps merely *is* 'Tranquillity'. But in as much as he still 'moves / With thought' and 'travels on', he may well 'need to do' and indeed 'say' things if he is to express his true nature. Surely the poem is too conscious of uneasy paradox to offer 'a study of integration'.

John Beer attempts a broader view:

> If the reader resists the bathos, the poem gains a new dimension from the original ending, which transforms the opening picture. . . . The old man's travelling form at first affects one like the sight of a moving force in nature, a river or a planet, passing on its predestined way according to nature's own peaceful laws. . . . But as soon as he speaks, he reveals the operation of another law in the universe, a magnetic pull between life and life, which turns his travelling into an epic journey; his desire to see his dying son is one of nature's sublimities.[8]

Such elegantly constructive criticism may build too many bridges across a gulf whose intractability the poem means to expose. The consistency of John Beer's rhetoric makes the first fourteen lines (where the Old Man is supposedly a 'moving force in nature') sound remarkably like the last lines (where the news from a Falmouth hospital somehow still evokes 'one of nature's sublimities'). If at first he seems to gravitate 'according to nature's own peaceful laws' like 'a river or a planet', how can we see 'another dimension' when we learn that he is responding to 'the magnetic pull of life and life'? In fact, the Old Man is moved towards Falmouth as his own essentially idiosyncratic centre of gravity. Its sole pulling power is the imminent death of just one 'mariner' amongst the sea-fight's presumably numerous casualties. The attraction of his own son, even in death, is so potent that all life available nearer home cannot hold him back, nor can any life he meets *en route* distract him off course.

His bleak acceptance of the fact that his son really is dying utterly rejects any pathetic fallacy: he does not fantasize some grandly 'general law of the universe' which might stoop to pity a loss so subjectively defined and – relative to the total ecosystem – so small. Sometimes 'nature's own peaceful laws' can seem ruthlessly impar-

tial: they sentence to death even those whom we love most. Yet
rebelling against such a universe can make us feel like lonely outlaws
everywhere. The private loyalties of love may demand futile gestures
of defiance against forces which are indeed universally powerful. The
Old Man may unwittingly be making such a gesture in his logically
profitless plod towards the Falmouth hospital. Certainly he is likely
to return having gained only the feeling that his world is a poorer
place. The shock of his own words, so uncompromisingly prosaic, so
stubbornly tied to mundane specifics, insists that there are in fact
many miles between the sublime of nature's vivacious indifference
and the often ridiculous needs of our finally morbid human relationships.

If we do eventually find the Old Man's journey touching and even
heroic, we still do so in the knowledge that he travels against the
trend of the very world through which he passes, and that our
sympathetic respect is, in a crucial sense, unnatural. The questions
which invite him to travel back into our world of personal relationships and particular places also drive him into an imaginary exile,
distracting him from that larger tranquillity into whose endlessly
fertile earth all our concerns and curiosities must finally decay. The
verse, whose uncomfortably stretched range of tone thus points to
both grandeur and tenderness, is demanding of the reader, and our
temptation to tidy it down into a more comfortable consistency is
bound to be strong. Yet in doing so we sell ourselves short, and
reduce the range of:

> the very world which is the world
> Of all of us – the place where in the end,
> We find our happiness, or not at all!
>
> (*The Prelude*, x. 726–8)

II

The portrait of *Old Man Travelling* must seem to many readers quite
odd enough. Yet in *The Old Cumberland Beggar* Wordsworth
pushes the case to even greater extremes. The former may seem so
frail that birds think it safe to ignore him, but the Beggar is so decrepit
that he is helpless when they try to steal his food:

> He sat, and ate his food in solitude:
> And ever, scattered from his palsied hand,

> That, still attempting to prevent the waste,
> Was baffled still, the crumbs in little showers
> Fell on the ground; and the small mountain birds,
> Not venturing yet to peck their destined meal,
> Approached within the length of half his staff.
>
> (*PW*, IV.234, 15–21)

Old Man Travelling's bare description merely mentions his 'bending figure', but *The Old Cumberland Beggar* examines an almost brutally detailed deformity: the Beggar's back is so bent that it cripples even his ability to see where he is going:

> Instead of common and habitual sight
> Of fields with rural works, of hill and dale,
> And the blue sky, one little span of earth
> Is all his prospect. Thus, from day to day
> Bow-bent, his eyes for ever on the ground,
> He plies his weary journey; seeing still,
> And seldom knowing that he sees, some straw,
> Some scattered leaf, or marks which, in one track,
> The nails of cart or chariot-wheel have left
> Impressed on the white road, – in the same line,
> At distance still the same. Poor Traveller!
> His staff trails with him; scarcely do his feet
> Disturb the summer dust; he is so still
> In look and motion, that the cottage curs
> Ere he has passed the door, will turn away,
> Weary of barking at him.   (48–63)

Coleridge's complaint that Wordsworth was only capable of 'feeling *for*, but never *with*' his characters is proved false by such a passage.[9] The thoroughness of identification here in fact narrows Wordsworth's focus to an almost microscopic view of the Beggar's own abnormally limited world: a world of other people's trivial losses – 'some straw'; a world of nature's random discards – 'some scattered leaf'; a world whose dimensions are as remorselessly unchangeable as a coach's wheelbase – 'in the same line, / At distance still the same'. The Beggar's predetermined route seems to give him no more choice than the 'staff' which lifelessly 'trails with him'. He hardly seems to know that he is at least physically humanoid: his lowered vision of himself sees only a pair of feet, shuffling so feebly that they scarcely 'Disturb the summer dust'.

His tantalizingly slow progress eventually makes the exasperated dogs 'turn away, / Weary of barking at him'. Their impatience points by contrast to the extraordinary stamina of patience which the Beggar himself needs. It is a stamina which those who would see his experience clearly – and amongst these are Wordsworth's hard-pressed readers – must learn to share. Those dogs, at first ignorantly aggressive and then baffled into apathy, do not really see the Beggar. Nor do the birds for whom he represents no more than the prospect of a 'destined meal'. The other species thus emphasize the author's – and hopefully the reader's – peculiarly human response. Imagining how little the Beggar sees, we are to imagine too all that he must be missing in 'hill and dale, / And the blue sky', those visual beauties which only people seem to appreciate. Our compassion reaches out, in the almost vocative phrase 'Poor Traveller!', to one who we can guess must find his journey 'weary'. Wordsworth twice states that 'He travels on, a solitary Man' (24, 44), adding to the line's second appearance: 'His age has no companion'. The repetition may risk boring the reader into a dog-like empty-headedness, but it bravely asserts an endurance which the human mind can find impressive and a loneliness which the human heart can pity. Identification may be difficult but not impossible for creatures who, by definition, can imaginatively anticipate and thus reach the time when their own 'age has no companion'.

As an almost grotesquely obvious image of human frailty, the Beggar seems bound to stimulate, perhaps even create, the tenderness from which he benefits:

> He travels on, a solitary Man,
> So helpless in appearance, that for him
> The sauntering Horseman throws not with a slack
> And careless hand his alms upon the ground,
> But stops, – that he may safely lodge the coin
> Within the old Man's hat; nor quits him so,
> But still, when he has given his horse the rein,
> Watches the aged Beggar with a look
> Sidelong, and half-reverted.   (24–32)

Birds and dogs and summer dust may be undisturbed, but the sauntering horseman is suddenly halted just as the strolling Wordsworth in 'Point Rash Judgement' found his 'happy idleness' instantly 'changed / To serious musing' (*PW*, ii. 117, 67–70). The 'primary laws of our nature' compel a reaction in the horseman which is appropriately revealed by the peculiarly human signals of facial expression – 'a look / Sidelong, and half-reverted'. The Beggar matters to Wordsworth partly because of this ability to inspire the 'simple affections of our nature', to cause what *Tintern Abbey* calls:

> that best portion of a good man's life,
> His little, nameless, unremembered, acts
> Of kindness and of love.   (*PW*, II. 260, 33–5)

As the Beggar revisits each house on his cyclical journey he 'keeps alive / The kindly mood' (91–2) and:

> Where'er the aged Beggar takes his rounds,
> The mild necessity of use compels
> To acts of love;   (98–100)

Outsider though he seems, he in fact binds together the community in the knowledge 'That we have all of us one human heart' (153). Such a message runs risks of sounding flaccidly sentimental, and it must be admitted that most readers could wish the poem to be shorter. But even where the poem is most concerned with the Beggar as a source of tenderness, it is stiffened by a curiosity as to whether compassion is the defining trait of the species, the crucial distinction between men and animals. Its best verse does actively investigate, rather than merely assert, 'the primary laws of our nature'.

But all this of course is only one side of the poem. The same passage about the Beggar's vision of the road can be seen as pointing not only to an essentially human being who inspires sympathy, but also to a nearly inanimate object which we approach with awe. Christopher Salversen writes:

> This curious 'closed' vision, coupled with his endless motion onwards (which yet, 'he is so still / In look and motion', is barely apparent), makes him a kind of thing of the earth; he seems almost identified with the earth itself. And for this reason he is someone out of human time; he goes on, inevitably, like the road on which he travels. . . . he might be taken to represent a way of seeing which is not concerned with the outer world of human activity or even of natural scenery – he presents a state of 'wise passiveness', of tranquillity in time and the 'quiet eye' of inward vision, which Wordsworth, of the 'sensuous' eye, of the backward-looking in

memory, and the forward-looking desire in work, could not hope to achieve.[10]

Certainly the Beggar's vision lacks much of what is normally associated with human sight. He seems unable to choose where to direct his eyes. They accompany him at a set angle as unvarying as the pattern formed by the wheels of the cart:

> On the ground
> His eyes are turned, and, as he moves along,
> *They* move along the ground; (45–7)

Nor can he make much sense of the little he does see: He has 'a fixed and serious look / Of idle computation' (11–12), and this equivocal statement seems to resolve itself negatively when he is described as 'seeing still, / And seldom knowing that he sees' (53–4).

The partial blindness is supported by a degree, at least, of deafness. He often hears neither the 'rattling wheels' of a coach nor its driver's warning shouts so that the coach has to leave the road to get round him (37–43). A gulf of silence seems to separate him from other people, none of whom are said to speak to him in all the descriptions of his receiving alms. Unlike the father of *Old Man Travelling*, the isolated beggar is asked no questions and makes no statements in a poem of almost 200 lines. A manuscript version had gone so far as to say that 'His very name' is 'forgotten among those / By whom he lives', and the printed poem preserves this sense that it is the villagers themselves who have abstracted an individual person into a symbolic image:

> the villagers in him
> Behold a record which together binds
> Past deeds and offices of charity, (87–90)

It is they who focus on him as an object. Wordsworth may begin the poem by stating that he himself 'saw' the beggar, but it is the horseman who so compulsively 'Watches' him (31). The toll-gate woman 'sees' him (34). In fact 'all behold in him / A silent monitor' (123). They seem to recognize in his grotesque shape not only a pathetic parody of their own nature, but also something fascinatingly alien. He inspires them to act humanely, but he is watched partly because his own humanity seems on the point of disappearing. He is poised at the gripping moment of the conjurer's 'Now you see it, now you don't.' He may even now be circling down towards the wholly inanimate state of Lucy:

> No motion has she now, no force;
>   She neither hears nor sees,
> Rolled round in earth's diurnal course
>   With rocks, and stones, and trees.   (*PW*, ii. 216, 5–8)

Certainly, the closing paragraph of the poem insists that he must finally belong 'in that vast solitude to which / The tide of things has borne him' (163–4).

However, the poem's close also spells out the potential callousness of our asking the Beggar to go on with his rounds. At first, the verse finds it easy enough to sneer at so-called humanitarians who wish to tidy him away into some sheltering workhouse. Yet Wordsworth soon forces us to remember just how rough is the weather of that world to which we want to keep him exposed:

> – Then let him pass, a blessing on his head!
> And, long as he can wander, let him breathe
> The freshness of the valleys; let his blood
> Struggle with frosty air and winter snows;
> And let the chartered wind that sweeps the heath
> Beat his grey locks against his withered face.   (171–6)

Many readers understandably find these lines daunting. Cleanth Brooks calls them 'shockingly candid' and asks how anyone can justify 'letting an old man walk the roads in all weathers'.[11] Jonathan Wordsworth, accepting the challenge, replies:

> In Wordsworthian terms, the beggar does not suffer. His life may or may not seem attractive to modern readers, but the wind that sweeps the heath is 'chartered' because it too is breathing a blessing on the old man's head. Wordsworth no more wishes suffering on him than he wishes it on his sister – 'let the misty mountain-winds be free / To blow against thee' – at the end of *Tintern Abbey*.[12]

This seems to me only one of the two answers offered by the poem to its own strange question: can the Beggar himself really find a 'struggle' between his 'blood' and 'frosty air' an attractive prospect?

We cannot assume that the Beggar consciously enjoys the integrated world of *Tintern Abbey*'s more optimistic passages. There is a difference of tone between the serenities of:

> Therefore let the moon
> Shine on thee in thy solitary walk;
> And let the misty mountain-winds be free
> To blow against thee: (*Tintern Abbey*, 134–7)

and the turbulence of a 'Struggle with frosty air and winter snows'. In one Wordsworth speaks softly but directly to his sister, inviting her to offer her own invitation to the natural world. In the other he is addressing politicians and telling them not to interfere with a beggar whose own wishes are not consulted and must remain opaque. Dorothy will be free to choose the occasion and the direction when she takes her 'solitary walk'. If in this she resembles anyone in *The Old Cumberland Beggar*, it is the poet's own persona – 'I saw an aged Beggar in my walk' (1). But the Beggar himself is to plod endlessly around one preordained route 'in that vast solitude to which / The tide of things has borne him' (163–4). Dorothy is a healthy young woman, still enjoying, according to the immediately ensuing lines, the 'wild ecstacies' of youth which can only 'in after years' be 'matured / Into a sober pleasure' (*Tintern Abbey*, 138–40). The Beggar is a decrepit old man. His face is 'withered' and the locks which the wind beats into it are 'grey'. Moreover Dorothy is invited to look up to 'steep woods and lofty cliffs' and value them as reminders of a pleasure shared by people who love each other (157–9). The Beggar can see nothing 'of hill and dale' and 'His age has no companion' (45–51).

However, the world glimpsed in other passages of *Tintern Abbey* may well lurk behind the weather to which Wordsworth exposes the Beggar. The problem is how to apply the relevant lines. As a poignantly enfeebled and yet still recognizable man, the Beggar may strike the lowest audible note in 'the still, sad music of humanity' (*Tintern Abbey*, 91). The poem would then be forcing us to expand 'the great and simple affections of our nature' to embrace even the oddest fellow-being in our 'unremembered acts / Of kindness and of love' (*Tintern Abbey*, 34–5). Or we may be guided by *Tintern Abbey* to discover in the Beggar a very different figure who, like Wordsworth himself, can be 'laid asleep / In body and become a living soul' (*Tintern Abbey*, 45–6). The old man's failing eyesight and hearing may cut him off from 'all the mighty world / Of eye, and ear' enjoyed by Wordsworth and Dorothy (*Tintern Abbey*, 106–7). Alternatively his diminished vision may allow him to inhabit permanently that

universe which Wordsworth can only fleetingly visit at moments
when:

> with an eye made quiet by the power
> Of harmony, and the deep power of joy,
> We see into the life of things.   (*Tintern Abbey*, 47–9)

The physical decline which distances the Beggar from other people
does seem to have brought him symbolically, as well as literally,
closer to the earth: he cannot share the ordinary detached pleasure
that most people derive from 'sight / . . . of hill and dale / And the blue
sky' (48–50), but his very inability to look up at the hills prevents him
separating the world into hills as sights and himself as observer. It
allows him to dwell more palpably amongst them, 'Surrounded by
those wild unpeopled hills' (14). Similarly his inability to see 'the blue
sky' may give him a stronger

> sense sublime
> Of something far more deeply interfused,
> Whose dwelling is the light of setting suns,
> And the round ocean and the living air,
> And the blue sky, and in the mind of man:
> (*Tintern Abbey*, 95–9)

The 'bow-bent' Beggar cannot easily look at the sun even when it
weakens at the end of the day. But he can belong with it even in its
noontime brilliance by inhabiting the living air which it colours. It is
explicitly 'In the sun' that he eats his meal (12).

Sunlight becomes the major element in the non-human world of
hills and birds and trees presented in the closing lines of the poem.
The difficulty for both Wordsworth and the reader is just how to
place the old man within the landscape. We ask ourselves what
relationship is proper, or even possible, between him and the natural
universe he inhabits:

> Let him be free of mountain solitudes;
> And have around him, whether heard or not,
> The pleasant melody of woodland birds.
> Few are his pleasures: if his eyes have now
> Been doomed so long to settle upon earth
> That not without some effort they behold
> The countenance of the horizontal sun,

Rising or setting, let the light at least
Find a free entrance to their languid orbs,
And let him, *where* and *when* he will, sit down
Beneath the trees, or on a grassy bank
Of highway side, and with the little birds
Share his chance-gathered meal; and finally,
As in the eye of Nature he has lived,
So in the eye of Nature let him die! (183–97)

With tough-minded precision Wordsworth insists on both the odd-ity and the importance of what he is saying. The Beggar must be left alone in his present environment even if he himself can no longer notice the relationships which it offers. The melody of birds – recognized as a 'pleasant' harmony by author and readers – must surround him even if he cannot hear it. The birds must continue to share his food even though we recall from the first paragraph that 'his palsied hand' will go on 'attempting to prevent the waste' (16–17). He must remain as he was at the beginning of the poem 'In the sun' (12), and yet it would be an effort for him to look at it even in its lowest positions at dawn and sunset. He must continue as a virtually blind figure whose 'languid orbs' cannot return the gaze of 'the eye of Nature' beneath which he has lived. But Wordsworth is careful to stress by repetition that he exists not beneath but '*in* the eye of Nature'. This suggests that losing his individual ability to see as a person has made him a portion of some larger vision.

The dual implications of this extraordinary idea are faced with defiant frankness in the last line where the poem leaves him to 'die'. As a person exposed to the elements, he will, in a simple, physical sense, perish. Alternatively as a being already released from the limiting laws of human nature, he may even now be living with the hills and birds and trees as one small portion of the eternal land-scape's vision of itself. In that case he has already in his role as a peculiarly human and separate consciousness prematurely expired. The 'So' which links the last two lines would then suggest not an arguable appropriateness but an inevitable causal link: 'As in the eye of Nature he has lived, / So in the eye of Nature let him die!' The very extent to which he has been living so close to the earth may already be allowing those qualities which identify him as human to die away. If so, the politicians have only a limited power. They may be able to meddle with his physical life, prolonging it for a few years in the

workhouse, but may be too late to resurrect a human consciousness –
whether we define this as a sense of self, or a need to feel love, or an
awareness of visible beauty in the world about him, or indeed
a capacity for intense pain. As in *Old Man Travelling*, it is not
just that we do not know how far the Beggar can ever be alive
again to such things; we also do not know whether we wish him
to be.

A resuscitation which brings him back to our world may be no
affectionate kiss of life. It may merely reimpose what *Tintern Abbey*
calls 'the heavy and the weary weight/Of all this unintelligible
world' (39–40). Reopening his eyes to 'all that we behold/From this
green earth' (*Tintern Abbey*, 104–5) might also drag him back from a
blessedly deprived vision in which there are

> neither evil tongues,
> Rash judgements, nor the sneers of selfish men,
> Nor greetings where no kindness is, nor all
> The dreary intercourse of daily life,
>
> (*Tintern Abbey*, 128–31)

How likely is it that he will find in our world of relationships and
intense emotions enough joy to compensate for reawakened suffering, enough love to console him in the return of loneliness? Is the
primary law of our nature an instinct for tenderness? Or does the
Beggar's surrender of individuality express an even stronger instinct
to merge with the earth which sustains us?

From such questions the poem refuses to retreat into any falsely
simple answer. Yet structurally it is able to achieve a unified conclusion without sacrificing the duality of its stance. The Beggar, even if
we approach him simply as a fellow human being, is now very old
and the workhouse is a far from promising alternative to his present
way of life. We cannot be sanguine about the ability of such a man to
face happily the radical change to institutionalized existence. Alternatively, in as much as we do acknowledge his grandeur in being at
home in a universe from which we feel so alienated, we are likely to
keep a respectful distance, staring at a mystery with which it would
be impertinent to interfere. So both the values posed by the verse
allow us to support Wordsworth's final plea. We may care about him
as someone who could be defensively conscious of his own personal
dignity, or we may admire him as a now indistinguishable component of that revelation through which all things, *except* vulnerably

self-conscious personalities, are made equally visible. Pathetic or enviable, he clearly belongs 'in the eye of Nature'.

III

The poet who observes the Old Cumberland Beggar says little about his own feelings, but the autobiographical *Prelude* includes a strange meeting where Wordsworth's own experience is as striking as that of the Solitary whom he confronts. At first the poet here seems in a remarkably appropriate mood to understand how much somebody else may simply wish to be left alone. He has himself chosen to walk at night because the roads are then deserted enough to offer 'deeper quietness / Than pathless solitudes' (*The Prelude*, IV. 367–8). He can even describe his own frame of mind in the very terms which introduce *Old Man Travelling* – he too is at present 'Tranquil' (376) and relaxed into 'A consciousness of *animal* delight' (397, my italics). Instead of that energetically 'meddling intellect' which 'Mis-shapes the beauteous forms of things' (*PW*, IV. 57, 26–7), the poet's 'exhausted mind' is sufficiently 'worn out' by this time of night to be 'Quiescent' (380–1) and open itself to the immediate scenery:

> Thus did I steal along that silent road,
> My body from the stillness drinking in
> A restoration like the calm of sleep
> But sweeter far. Above, before, behind,
> Around me, all was peace and solitude,
> I look'd not round, nor did the solitude
> Speak to my eye; but it was heard and felt.
> O happy state! what beauteous pictures now
> Rose in harmonious imagery – they rose
> As from some distant region of my soul
> And came along like dreams; yet such as left
> Obscurely mingled with their passing forms
> A consciousness of animal delight,
> A self-possession felt in every pause
> And every gentle movement of my frame.   (385–99)

The verse has an aptly soothing beat so that the repetitions of 'solitude' and 'rose' suggest the rhymes of a lullaby. But we must stay awake to their carefully wrought implications. The poet's own mood is only '*like* the calm of sleep'. Far from being unconscious, he enjoys a heightened consciousness, delighting in all that the workaday mind cannot know and that the literally dreaming mind cannot value.

Darkness gives the landscape a shadowed unity, composing its 'beauteous pictures' into 'harmonious imagery'. They themselves actively rise instead of being passively observed, yet their origin seems as intimately the poet's own as his dreams. They move towards him ('came along'), but the sequence of 'their passing forms' is revealed by his physical movement along the road. Feeling possessed by his surroundings ('Above, before, behind,/Around'), the poet feels in fact self-possessed, recognizing the rhythms of the earth as securely patterned to the syncopations of his own heart and lungs and legs. He does not look *out* at the scenery with the eye of an aesthete; he feels it '*in* every pause/And every gentle movement of my frame', so that his own vision is 'Obscurely mingled' with the 'eye of Nature'.

He is thus 'dispos'd to sympathy' (380), but the context makes it clear that sympathy here means intimacy with: 'such near objects as from time to time,/Perforce intruded on the listless sense' (378–9). He is in sympathy with things. He is not necessarily disposed to feel compassion for a fellow human being in need. Yet he is about to be confronted by a figure who may be just that. The stranger whom he suddenly sees is slumped against a milestone and apparently resigned to remaining there indefinitely. His stasis could of course be an optimistic image suggesting that a man can grow so 'Tranquil' that he comes to dwell permanently in that 'happy state' which the young poet can only visit in rare and fleeting moods. On the other hand, this strangely placid character may need to be alerted to the danger of staying where he is if his emaciated body is not eventually to perish of exposure.

The poet's initial reaction is literally evasive:

> While thus I wander'd, step by step led on,
> It chanc'd a sudden turning of the road
> Presented to my view an uncouth shape
> So near, that, slipping back into the shade
> Of a thick hawthorn, I could mark him well,
> Myself unseen.   (400–5)

Far from advancing to recognize a fellow human being, Wordsworth cowers away like a Peeping Tom. He needs to compare this 'uncouth shape' with his knowledge of other men before he can decide whether he is just faced by a rather extraordinary person or by something more alarmingly alien:

> He was of stature tall,
> A foot above man's common measure tall,
> Stiff in his form, and upright, lank and lean,
> A man more meagre, as it seem'd to me,
> Was never seen abroad by night or day.
> His arms were long, and bare his hands; his mouth
> Shew'd ghastly in the moonlight; from behind
> A milestone propp'd him, and his figure seem'd
> Half-sitting, and half-standing. I could mark
> That he was clad in military garb,
> Though faded, yet entire. He was alone,
> Had no attendant, neither Dog, nor Staff,
> Nor knapsack; in his very dress appear'd
> A desolation, a simplicity
> That seem'd akin to solitude. Long time
> Did I peruse him with a mingled sense
> Of fear and sorrow.   (405–21)

John Jones notes some of the ambiguities of this apparition:

> He is in the world, yet placed 'half-sitting, and half-standing', between the worlds. . . . Thus when, after sustained concrete description, Wordsworth turns to three of his favourite abstractions – 'desolation', 'simplicity', 'solitude' – they are ready to work very hard for him.[13]

Certainly the Soldier – like the Old Man and the Cumberland Beggar – does suggest two quite different ideas that are 'akin to solitude': the 'desolation' of the lonely and the 'simplicity' of the self-sufficient. Yet the latter, in the present context, is bound to be significantly more muted. Even if it is a comfortably independent 'solitude' which the Soldier enjoys, it cannot seem so impressively rare to a poet who, on this occasion, has already twice been able to use the term in describing his own mood. The interruption of that mood creates explicitly mixed emotions, and the poetry's 'mingled sense' balances against 'sorrow' not admiration but 'fear'.

Wordsworth is struck first by his own exposed position. The sight totally blocks off what this book of *The Prelude* has earlier called the 'quiet stream of self-forgetfulness' (294). Suddenly remembering who and where he is, Wordsworth sees how vulnerable he might seem to what could be a robber or a ghost. To stand alone can mean to lack allies and Wordsworth is consciously thrown back on his own defences. He gropes for reassurance by reminding himself that the roofs of the nearby village are still 'visible among the scatter'd trees / Scarce distant from the spot an arrow's flight' (427–8); but the image hardly makes the poet sound convinced that his own inevitably slower flight from bush to safety would pass unchallenged.

The poet's sudden panic derives largely from the very darkness which had earlier convinced him that 'all was peace and solitude'. When the Old Cumberland Beggar is discovered 'in the Sun', he is at least clearly visible, but the Soldier 'in the moonlight' compels a provisional response to inadequate evidence. This opening description twice uses the word 'seem'd' as well as 'shew'd' and 'appear'd'. Wordsworth even details a specific misapprehension caused by the darkness. He says at line 416 that the Soldier has no stick, and only after another fifty lines does he reveal that there in fact was 'a Traveller's staff' which had at first been 'unobserv'd'. He can only 'suppose' that earlier it had dropped out of the Soldier's 'slack hand / And lain till now neglected in the grass' (461–3). Thus the reader is made to stumble through the original experience at the floundering poet's side, at first ignorantly keeping this mysterious apparition at a safe distance and only later discovering the mundane details which might encourage a more sympathetic approach.

The Soldier is made even more frightening by bizarre noises. This too is new. The Old Man Travelling is finally given a straightforwardly articulate voice. The Old Cumberland Beggar is allowed to maintain a dignified silence throughout. The Soldier, by contrast, is burdened with disconcerting sounds which seem involuntary:

> From his lips, meanwhile,
> There issued murmuring sounds, as if of pain
> Or of uneasy thought; yet still his form
> Kept the same steadiness; and at his feet
> His shadow lay, and mov'd not.   (421–5)

> I wish'd to see him move; but he remain'd
> Fix'd to his place, and still from time to time
> Sent forth a murmuring voice of dead complaint,
> Groans scarcely audible.   (429–32)

This grotesque parody of communication is highly disturbing. What could have been a clear appeal for sympathy is present and yet 'scarcely audible' as such. The sounds may voice 'pain' but they could mean 'uneasy thought': perhaps even an uneasy conscience. If so, a past which makes him so uncomfortable hardly guarantees that he has now become safe company in such a deserted spot. The 'complaint' instead of evoking distressed life seems 'dead': ghost-like sounds from a mouth that explicitly looks 'ghastly'. The idea that the Soldier may not be fully alive is reinforced by his being absolutely stationary. Any movement at all might slightly reassure Wordsworth, who looks even to the man's shadow for some sign of life. It is indeed with a movement that the Soldier does at last make a recognizably human signal.

Significantly this revelation only occurs after Wordsworth has made his own move and 'hail'd him'. Wordsworth has to suppress his 'heart's specious cowardice' and act with a faith that any creature with a humanoid body must be human (432–6). Only when the poet has come out of hiding can the Soldier come to life:

> Slowly from his resting-place
> He rose, and with a lean and wasted arm
> In measur'd gesture lifted to his head,
> Return'd my salutation.   (436–9)

The return for Wordsworth's trust has the force of a resurrection.

The ensuing conversation allows what had seem'd an 'uncouth shape' to explain himself as a man with an almost boringly ordinary tale to tell. Having served abroad, he has been paid off and is making his way back to his home village. Like any soldier he is able to offer tales of 'hardship, battle, or the pestilence' (471). But none of these experiences are so remarkable that the poet thinks them worth recording. Wordsworth decides mundanely enough that he must be found 'food / And lodging for the night' (458–9) and leads him to a friend's house where this is successfully arranged. Repetition later stresses that shelter is sought just for 'This night' (486). So Wordsworth is offering nothing like the life sentence which the workhouse threatens to impose on the Old Cumberland Beggar. The Soldier, 'travelling to his native home' (449), can be introduced at the cottage as a wayfarer who has been only temporarily, and unwillingly, halted: '"here is a Man / By sickness overcome . . . he is faint and tired"' (484–7).

Before leaving, Wordsworth speaks as if the Soldier now seems abnormal only in his reluctance to make perfectly normal needs clear:

> I entreated that henceforth
> He would not linger in the public ways
> But ask for timely furtherance and help
> Such as his state requir'd.   (489–92)

The Soldier, however, is not to be so easily bossed:

> At this reproof,
> With the same ghastly mildness in his look
> He said 'my trust is in the God of Heaven
> And in the eye of him that passes me.'   (492–5)

This is the only piece of direct speech which the poetry grants him. He uses it, after a conventional piety, to insist that it is not up to him to make his vulnerability more obvious. He firmly reimposes that responsibility on the poet and any other stranger who might meet him. It is up to them to overcome 'the heart's specious cowardice' and suppress that fear of the unknown which so often serves as a rationale for callousness. His weird appearance and peculiar mumbling cannot excuse anyone whose imagination is too idle or too timid to see beyond them.

The Soldier is not being pointlessly coy. An obvious request 'for timely furtherance and help' would force the men apart into clear roles of the helped and the helper. They might then imagine a greater difference between their situations than could really exist when two equally mortal creatures stand together in the same place, at the same moment, beneath the same 'eye of Nature'. Certainly when the Soldier at the very end does seem to lose some of his diffidence, an explicit thankfulness points also to separation from the man who is being thanked:

> in a voice that seem'd
> To speak with a reviving interest
> Till then unfelt, he thank'd me; I return'd
> The blessing of the poor unhappy Man;
> And so we parted. Back I cast a look,
> And linger'd near the door a little space;
> Then sought with quiet heart my distant home. (498–504)

The Soldier's 'reviving interest' allows him to notice an innately divisive fact: what he can no longer provide for himself has been easily supplied by a complete stranger. The poet looks back on what has now become a 'poor unhappy Man' and forward to his own relatively comfortable prospects as explicitly 'distant' from the Soldier.

To some extent the men are bound to feel 'parted' by the expression of gratitude. It speaks to a poignantly real gulf between the vigour of youth and the feebleness of age, between the healthy and the sick, between the famished and the fed. The point is made by one of the *Lyrical Ballads* where Simon Lee, a 'poor old Man', is in desperately conscious need of help from a Wordsworth who is lucky enough to be still young and healthy (*PW*, iv.64, 87). Simon needs 'To unearth the root of an old tree' if he is to force his 'scrap of land' into providing even starvation rations for himself and his wife. This land had been 'from the heath/Enclosed when he was stronger' (45–6), but now the wilderness enjoys an easy victory over his grotesquely aged body:

> And he is lean and he is sick;
> His body, dwindled and awry,
> Rests upon ankles swoln and thick;
> His legs are thin and dry.   (33–6)

The clumsiness of Wordsworth's language here bravely confronts Simon's inelegant tragedy which is no more, and no less, than the ugly fact of physical helplessness.

The natural process of decay has weakened the old man far more than even the 'stump of rotten wood' which he strives to dislodge. Yet to Wordsworth, still casually possessed of youthful strength, the task is almost ridiculously easy and Simon's huge gratitude pathetically disproportionate:

> I struck, and with a single blow
> The tangled root I severed,
> At which the poor old Man so long
> And vainly had endeavoured.
>
> The tears into his eyes were brought,
> And thanks and praises seemed to run
> So fast out of his heart, I thought
> They never would have done.

> – I've heard of hearts unkind, kind deeds
> With coldness still returning;
> Alas! the gratitude of men
> Hath oftener left me mourning.   (85–96)

Wordsworth's miserable impatience for Simon to 'have done' with
his thanks signals discomfort at an exposed gulf. From the old man's
point of view, tearful gratitude is wholly appropriate to such an
enormous gain, but from Wordsworth's own angle, it is utterly
excessive because he has given so little from such vast reserves of time
and muscle power. He feels bereaved because Simon's thanks take
away the illusion of common ground. The heath over which Wordsworth strolls so comfortably is to Simon, in his increasingly unequal
struggle to survive, an exhausting rival. Its deeply rooted challenge
threatens defeat. Physical existence which for the young man is the
easy exercise of power in strong arms is for Simon a painful and
humiliating stumble on deformed legs.

The poet's vision of the landscape must narrow, in sympathy with
the plight of Simon and his wife, to a question which is bitterly
rhetorical: 'But what to them avails the land / Which he can till no
longer' (47–8). The meeting leads to unqualified 'mourning' because
Simon's own attitude has none of the ambiguity of the Old Man
Travelling and the other Solitaries. Simon's tears make it all too
clear that he himself feels his situation to be as desperate as it looks
to the young poet.

The Prelude's Soldier also allows himself to be moved by bor-
rowed energy, at least physically. The crucial question is how far, and
how profitably, does he feel moved in his own mind by Wordsworth's well-meant prodding? The answer remains as intriguingly
enigmatic in his case as it is embarrassingly loud in Simon's. The
young Wordsworth of *The Prelude* may momentarily glance back at
a figure whose thanks have made him sound decisively a 'poor
unhappy Man', but the Soldier himself may still see his situation as
far from pathetic.

Both men, before their meeting, seem possessed of a certain grandeur which is then audibly diminished as they get in each other's
way. Wordsworth's own mood of 'peace and solitude' is demolished
with almost comic abruptness when he stumbles across the 'uncouth
shape'. By contrast, the Soldier's return to self-consciousness is more
gradual and may never be complete. At first, ignorant of Words-

worth's presence, he does not so much talk to himself as babble in an
inarticulate stream of consciousness which makes him sound literally
like a river. His 'murmuring sounds' recall the poet's earlier description of 'the brook / That murmur'd' through his own thoughts when
he too felt that he was the only human figure in that landscape:

> the road's wat'ry surface, to the ridge
> Of that sharp rising, glitter'd in the moon
> And seemed before my eyes another stream
> Creeping with silent lapse to join the brook
> That murmured in the valley.   (372–6)

With his back to the milestone, the Soldier may also see that road not
as a measured route to peculiarly human destinations, but as just
'another stream' in a fluid world whose power 'to join' can embrace
his own 'stream of self-forgetfulness'. When first sighted he is explicitly not a 'Man Travelling' and thus seems less dynamic than even
the hero of *Animal Tranquillity and Decay* or the Cumberland
Beggar of whom it is twice recorded that 'He travels on'. 'Half-
sitting, and half-standing', the Soldier may be frozen not in the act of
setting off once more but at the moment of settling back for ever.
Certainly his weird ability to hold the pose for that 'Long time' while
Wordsworth thinks it prudent only to 'peruse' him suggests a tenacious sense of place: he could prove more unshakeably at home here
than a poet who has so easily been exiled into timorous curiosity.
When directly approached he is admittedly willing to rise and greet
his visitors. But the 'measur'd gesture' with which he touches his hat
could suggest thrift with energies already so dwindled that they must
soon be non-existent, and he will not speak until he has 'resum'd /
His station as before' (439–40).

Even when the poet's practical concern has prompted the Soldier
into giving some account of himself, he sounds explicitly 'unmov'd'
by the story of his own life. He tells it: 'with a quiet uncomplaining
voice, / A stately air of mild indifference,' (442–4). While he still
thought himself alone, he may have had no conscious memories of
his difficult past, or indeed any wearying anticipation of the journey
that lies ahead. It is the meeting which compels him to describe himself as moving through time, and he sounds almost bored by the task:

> solemn and sublime
> He might have seem'd, but that in all he said
> There was a strange half-absence, and a tone

> Of weakness and indifference, as of one
> Remembering the importance of his theme
> But feeling it no longer. (473–8)

Perhaps he is still distracted by what *The Prelude* has earlier called 'sounds that are / The ghostly language of the ancient earth'. Listening to these, the human soul can feel a similar haziness, and

> Remembering how she felt, but what she felt
> Remembering not, retains an obscure sense
> Of possible sublimity. (II. 335–7)

If Wordsworth's intrusion can only drag the Soldier back to 'a half-absence' from the human world, then arithmetic suggests that he still has at least half a mind to stay where he is, remaining absent-minded about an individual whose uncomfortable biography of 'hardship, battle, or the pestilence' he is asked to recall as his own.

Signs of a strange insensibility still bewilder the poet even when the Soldier agrees to walk with him to the cottage. He is to be introduced there as 'a Man / By sickness overcome', and yet he is visibly able to move 'without pain' (466). Indeed Wordsworth's 'ill-suppress'd astonishment' is at the mere fact that such a 'tall / And ghastly figure' can manage – or perhaps will deign – to move at all (467–8). The Soldier still speaks 'With the same ghastly mildness in his look' when the topic is precisely whether a man should feel bound to save himself from his own fecklessness by becoming sufficiently animated to summon help (493). His parting gesture – touching 'his hat again / With his lean hand' – hints that little may have changed since he first set eyes on Wordsworth and then promptly sat back against his milestone. Admittedly we are told that his final thanks are offered:

> in a voice that seem'd
> To speak with a reviving interest,
> Till then unfelt, (498–500)

Yet even this ends by reminding us how unprecedented is this indication of feeling, and it may be significant that it is shown only when the Soldier knows that the poet's assistance or interference is now finished. The Soldier's own sense of security, though gradually diminished in the eyes of his at first insecure and then compassionate beholder, may in fact survive the encounter: it may still be, like his uniform, 'Though faded, yet entire'.

If so, the closer that the poet comes to caring about the apparent distress of a 'poor unhappy Man', the further he in fact moves away from the Soldier's real experience. The context ensures that, whatever a common-sense humanitarianism might usually demand, we do not view the poet's well-meant move as inevitable. His 'exhausted mind' has so recently been relishing its own 'listless sense / Quiescent' that he might have felt no interest in disturbing the Soldier's. Such moods are unlikely to energize the helping hand or even allow the eye to notice someone who may need it: 'I look'd not round, nor did the solitude / Speak to my eye; but it was heard and felt' (390–1). To the poet of such sensations the inattentive 'mildness' of the Soldier's 'look' might have suggested only that he too was in that 'happy state' where the natural world's 'beauteous pictures' are not an exhibition to be distantly perused but a drama as intimately internal as one's 'dreams', as organically one's own as 'every pause / And every gentle movement' of one's breath (392–9). Nor does the poet's own 'consciousness of animal delight' suggest that he is bound to interpret the Soldier's mumblings as a complaint at human pain rather than a murmuring contribution to the scene's 'harmonious imagery' (397, 394). If Wordsworth had assumed that the Soldier was merely relaxing, like himself, into the eye of nature, he could have passed by on the other side and the two men need never have troubled each other. In fact the sudden shock of stumbling upon a human figure where it had seemed that 'all was peace and solitude' jolts the poet into feeling his own individuality as alarmingly distinct from those less vulnerable things with which he has been identifying. Once scared into watching out for his own safety, he can eventually be led to see the Soldier too with the *Immortality Ode*'s 'eye' which is prepared to keep 'watch o'er man's mortality' (*PW*, IV. 285, 199). But so long as he still feels 'obscurely mingled' with the permanence beneath those 'passing forms' of a nature that itself can never pass away (396), he is unlikely to feel pity either for himself or for anyone else.

Yet the older Wordsworth claimed in the title of Book VIII that *The Prelude* demonstrated 'Love of Nature leading to', and not away from, 'Love of Man'. So he was predictably unhappy with the direction taken by the episode of the 'Discharg'd Soldier'. He cut from the 1850 text the description which revealed how totally the young poet feels at one with his surroundings before they are invaded by the threat of the Soldier. Most commentators simply ignore the

omission. Those who do not seem to find it inexplicable. Helen
Darbishire, for instance, thinks that the preliminary self-portrait
which Wordsworth later suppressed is 'strictly relevant to his purpose': 'The sudden vision of the old soldier, still, uncouth majestic,
rising up as from another world, gets much of its sublime effect from
the contrast with the mood that preludes it . . . . Why then did he
strike the passage out?'[14] Surely the terms here suggest an answer to
their own puzzled question. The Soldier can be seen as 'uncouth'
(first dangerously coarse, then vulnerably clumsy), and at such moments he does seem a contrast to the poet's own earlier mood in
which his 'every gentle movement' had felt smoothly in tune with the
earth. However, the description's other tendency which is indeed to
make the Soldier seem 'majestic' and even 'sublime' leads us to see
him as very definitely not 'from another world'. He then impresses
us precisely because he still seems absorbed in that very same world
of dignified 'peace and solitude' which the poet himself had initially
been enjoying. Before they are distracted by discovering each other's
existence, both men may feel sublimely identified with the same
'harmonious imagery' of a nocturnal landscape which they unwittingly share. While both still register the 'beauteous pictures' which
seem to arise 'like dreams' from each man's own soul, they may in
fact have far more in common than when they turn to face each other.
So the description of the Soldier, far from offering a decisive 'contrast
with the mood that preludes it', in fact contains echoes which suggest
a disconcerting similarity.

If we value those natural laws which the Soldier may have been
learning to love, we cannot rejoice as he is led away to what is indeed
'another world': the world of consciously sought shelter and laboriously built homes, the eventually always 'ruined' world of Margaret
and Robert's *Ruined Cottage*, the ever-dwindling world of Simon
Lee's smallholding. If, on the other hand, we value the feelings which
grow in such homes and which have taught the young Wordsworth
at least to try to save a stranger from pain, then we would obviously
be ill-advised to hope that either man could be led towards such
feelings by 'Love of Nature'. It is this contrast between the destinations of 'Love of Nature' and 'Love of Man' which the older Wordsworth needed to soften. Without the introductory account of the joy
which lies behind the poet's own 'listless' appearance, the sacrifice
both men may be making in giving and receiving kindness is a less
disturbing possibility. It is of the essence of the problem posed by the

poetry that we cannot be sure whether the Soldier's own definition of his exposed situation is 'sublime' acceptance or 'uncouth' discomfort. Wordsworth can only say: 'solemn and sublime / He might have seem'd but', and the 'but' matters. Here too we are offered no more than 'an obscure sense of possible sublimity'. There are many qualities which the Soldier 'might have seem'd' to possess; there are none which seem absolutely certain.

The difficulty of guessing at another man's experience points not only to pathetic limitation but also to awe-inspiring potential:

> how awful is the might of Souls
> And what they do within themselves
>
> . . .
>
> in the main
> It lies far hidden from the reach of words.
> Points have we all within our souls
> Where all stand single; this I feel
> And make breathings for incommunicable powers.
>
> (*The Prelude*, III. 178–88)

The most sympathetic eye, though it can find food and shelter, cannot know how each man may feel in the eye of nature. Full respect for a stranger perhaps acknowledges how much about him lies beyond the reach of even the friendliest questions and must remain 'hidden'. Yet the first-hand account Wordsworth gives of his own mood prior to the meeting skilfully allows us to glimpse, behind the ensuing dialogue, that otherwise incommunicable world where all do indeed stand single. So, as the poet leaves his own solitude to summon the murmuring Soldier back within 'the reach of words', we sense possible loss as well as gain. Both men may be closing their ears to what *The Excursion* calls:

> Authentic tidings of invisible things;
> Of ebb and flow and everduring power
> And central peace subsisting at the heart
> Of endless agitation.   (IV. 1144–7)

THE MIND'S EYE

LATER SOLITARIES: 'RESOLUTION AND INDEPENDENCE' AND THE 'BLIND LONDON BEGGAR' OF 'THE PRELUDE'

I

About ten days before he began to write *Resolution and Independence*, Wordsworth recited to Dorothy a strikingly irresolute poem he had composed about his own solitude. Here the poet at first sees his isolation as a wholly positive escape from the timorous verbalizations of the human mind. To be alone is to join the hushed peacefulness of inanimate objects that have no words to utter:

> These Chairs they have no words to utter,
> No fire is in the grate to stir or flutter,
> The ceiling and floor are mute as a stone,
> My chamber is hush'd and still,
>   And I am alone,
>   Happy and alone.
>
> Oh who would be afraid of life,
> The passion and the sorrow and the strife,
>   When he may be
>   Shelter'd so easily?
> May lie in peace on his bed
> Happy as they who are dead.   (*PW*, IV. 365)

But the nakedness of the death-wish here, the emphasis on silence and its obvious exclusion of human relationship apparently seemed too alarming. Only 'Half an hour afterwards' according to the manuscript, Wordsworth wrote another stanza. This attempts to reverbalize the experience so as to disassociate it explicitly from its chilling associations with death and loneliness:

I have thoughts that are fed by the sun.
　The things which I see
　Are welcome to me,
　Welcome every one:
I do not wish to lie　　.
　Dead, dead,
Dead without any company;
　Here alone on my bed,
With thoughts that are fed by the Sun,
And hopes that are welcome every one,
　Happy am I.   (*PW*, IV. 365–6)

The repetitions here may seem to protest a little too much, but the denial, if not convincing, is clear. The mind now welcomes back the ordinary human consciousness of time with 'hopes' about the future. The rejection of eternal quietism seems absolute.

　But of course to accept the need of human company is to admit that, if being 'Happy' depends on remaining 'Here alone', such happiness cannot last. To think about the future is to admit that some time one may again be 'afraid of life, / The passion and the sorrow and the strife'. Crying out at the horror of being 'Dead without any company', the poet defines his own nature as quite different from that of things which 'have no words to utter'. So the poem lurches into a last stanza which makes a pathetic appeal for the impossible. Wordsworth yearns to feel endlessly surrounded by 'Life', and yet to be as sheltered from disturbing feelings as he would be in 'Death':

O Life, there is about thee
A deep delicious peace,
I would not be without thee,
　Stay, oh stay!
Yet be thou ever as now,
Sweetness and breath with the quiet of death,
Be but thou ever as now,
　Peace, peace, peace,   (*PW*, IV. 366)

The repetitions now bring the plea very close to admitting its own hopelessness. Wordsworth insists on a more conscious and intense desire to feel alive than can be expressed by his inhuman surroundings which remain 'mute as a stone'. Yet he struggles to reduce the language of this desire to a virtually inarticulate 'quiet'. The reiteration of 'Peace, peace, peace' allows speech to dwindle until it is indeed little more than 'breath'.

This fantasy that one could somehow be dead to sorrow but alive to one's need of other people was still sufficiently compulsive a week later to be bizarrely acted out. Dorothy records in her Journal that on 29 April 1802 Wordsworth pretended to be dead and yet alive to what she emphasizes as a peculiarly *'peaceful'* life about him:

> William lay, and I lay, in the trench under the fence – he with his eyes shut, and listening to the waterfalls and the Birds. There was no one waterfall above another – it was a sound of waters in the air – the voice of the air. William heard me breathing and rustling now and then, but we both lay still, and unseen by one another; he thought that it would be as sweet thus to lie so in the grave, to hear the *peaceful* sounds of the earth, and just to know that our dear friends were near.

This game allows precisely for a combination of 'breath with the quiet of death', for a kind of company in as much as Wordsworth hears his sister breathing, and yet for a kind of oblivion to other people's existence so long as he keeps his eyes shut. But it is make-believe. The same journal entry ends with their returning from their walk to confrontations which force a choice: 'Met old Mr. S at the door – Mrs. S poorly' and Dorothy herself having to go to bed early feeling 'sick and ill'. Whether Wordsworth responded with sympathy or remained in a death-like trance is not recorded. Presumably, once neighbour and sister had taken to their beds for such negative reasons, he did not feel that he could be 'Shelter'd so easily' by simply going off to 'lie in peace' on his own bed. He would have had to choose between seeming attentive when such 'dear friends were near' and shutting his eyes so that he could again concentrate on the 'peaceful sounds of the earth'.

Some of this ambiguous experience lingered. Writing *Resolution and Independence* three days later, he describes 'the air' as 'filled with pleasant noise of waters' (*PW*, II. 235, 7), echoing the journal's 'sound of waters in the air – the voice of the air', and the cheering 'thoughts that are fed by the sun' clearly inform the later poem's celebration of 'All things that love the sun' (8). Yet *Resolution and Independence* also continues the curiosity about death. On the one hand, it explores Wordsworth's fear that he too must end as one of the 'mighty Poets in their misery dead' after an old age which will intensify his sense of

'Cold, pain and labour, and all fleshly ills' (115–16). On the other hand, death still makes its bleak appeal as perhaps the only credible escape route from a consciousness which tortures itself with 'fears and fancies', 'Dim sadness – and blind thoughts' (27–8). The doubts of 'I have thoughts that are fed by the sun' and of the short-lived fantasy in the trench 'that it would be as sweet thus to lie so in the grave' are visible in the hesitant description of the Leech-gatherer as 'not all alive nor dead,/Nor all asleep' (64–5). In *Resolution and Independence* there is still indecision as to whether isolation must belong in a list of sorrows – 'Solitude, pain of heart, distress and poverty' (35) – or can be defined as the central quality of an inspiring figure who moves 'alone and silently' (131) to suggest that peace of mind is available to man.

The poet who looks to the Leech-gatherer for guidance is importantly a man and not a boy. Wordsworth's admittedly debatable view is that only adults suffer much from the fear of death and that children usually take for granted that they will live for ever. In *The Prelude* Wordsworth strives to distinguish between his mature mind's conscious delight in the sunshine as a guarantee that he is still, for the time being, fully alive and the more instinctual response he enjoyed in the explicitly 'thoughtless hour' of childhood:

> Thus daily were my sympathies enlarged,
> And thus the common range of visible things
> Grew dear to me: already I began
> To love the sun, a Boy I lov'd the sun,
> Not as I since have lov'd him, as a pledge
> And surety of our earthly life, a light
> Which while we view we feel we are alive;
> But, for this cause, that I had seen him lay
> His beauty on the morning hills, had seen
> The western mountain touch his setting orb,
> In many a thoughtless hour, when, from excess
> Of happiness, my blood appear'd to flow
> With its own pleasure, and I breath'd with joy.
> *(The Prelude*, ii. 181–93)

The adult consciously looks for 'a pledge/And surety' because he thinks of existence as precarious. In the later lyric it is because the 'thoughts that are fed by the sun' are indeed thoughts and not unthinking sensations that they are so audibly attempts to counter the fear of being 'Dead without any company'. The child's response is more physical. He sees the palpability with which the mountains touch the setting sun as if reciprocating the embrace with which he lays 'His beauty' on them at dawn. The child's blood pulses with 'its own pleasure'. Its independent 'flow' is no more subject to mental manipulation than are the circulating movements of the sun by which his body is warmed. The air which is 'breath'd with joy' is still enjoyed by one young enough to elude the intellectual patterns which will make breath rhyme with death. His breathing still belongs so securely to the eternal movements of the earth itself that it suggests no vulnerably individual 'earthly life'.

Only a hundred lines before this passage, Book II of *The Prelude* has admitted the possibility that Wordsworth in his Lake District childhood 'was taught to feel, perhaps too much,/The self-sufficing power of solitude' (77–8). Certainly there are moments in the verse which seem to exaggerate the advantages of feeling that the 'pleasure' and 'joy' available to people is exactly the same as that of all other 'visible things', and at such moments the poet may lean too heavily on simply feeling his own solitude rather than confronting the questions which might be raised by looking at someone else's. Indeed another early manuscript passage, which was also intended for Book II but not finally included, amounts to a radical rejection of the intellectual powers by which we distinguish ourselves from other life-forms as *homo sapiens*:

> I was early taught
> That what we see of forms and images
> Which float along our minds and what we feel
> Of active, or recognizable thought
> Prospectiveness, or intellect, or will,
> Not only is not worthy to be deemed
> Our being, to be prized as what we are,
> But is the very littleness of life.
> Such consciousness I deem but accidents,
> Relapses from the one interior life
> That lives in all things, sacred from the touch
> Of that false secondary power by which
> In weakness we create distinctions, then
> Believe that all our puny boundaries are things
> Which we perceive, and not which we have made.

The human mind's ability to discriminate merely blinds us to the one truth which embraces all truths:

> In which all beings live with god, themselves
> Are god, existing in one mighty whole,
> As undistinguishable as the cloudless east
> At noon is from the cloudless west, when all
> The hemisphere is one cerulean blue.
>
> (*The Prelude*, p. 525, MS. 2)

Here there is nothing which the searching intellect can usefully discover since, as one variant insists, 'all beings' are essentially 'lost / In god and nature'. The 'one mighty whole' cannot be separated into sun-god and worshipper or star and astronomer any more than the sunlit sky can be divided. If we can abandon that 'intellect, or will' which represents individual personality as a 'recognizable thought', then our existence is as demonstrably permanent as the laws of atomic structure which maintain that 'one interior life / That lives in all things'.

The autobiographical verse often uses the imagery of a literally 'interior life' where the poet's heart and lungs make tangible a reciprocation which can hardly be made visible. Vividly visual description almost inevitably records those very distinctions which such poetry seeks to obliterate. So *Tintern Abbey*, for instance, has to speak 'with an eye made quiet' if it is to 'see into the life of things' rather than focus on their surfaces. Its 'blessed mood' is not built into an increasingly clarified vision, but emerges from gradually slackening sensations:

> Until, the breath of this corporeal frame
> And even the motion of our human blood
> Almost suspended, we are laid asleep
> In body.   (*PW*, ii. 260, 43–6)

The plural pronoun is a rhetorical sleight of hand since such moods seem to be enjoyed by a poet who is not at the time vividly aware of other people's existence. Such passages depend upon Wordsworth's being implicitly alone in the landscape. Elsewhere the presence of somebody else tends to intrude a visible physique whose 'forms and images' look specifically human and distinguish a person from that merely 'interior life' which they may share with other creatures. Standing alone, Wordsworth cannot, for instance, see his own tendency to signal emotion by facial expression; but faced by a Leech-gatherer who responds 'with a smile', he admits into the poetry a mirror image of his own peculiarly human tendency to communicate. The meeting between two strangers on the public road gives the poetry a more specific sense of place. However much the Solitaries seem impressively free from the pressures of 'Prospectiveness . . . or will', we must still half-expect to hear of chosen destinations: the Old Man's plan to reach his son in Falmouth, or the Soldier's prospect of returning to his home village, or the workhouse to which at least some think that the Old Cumberland Beggar should be travelling and the circular route of farm houses which he himself means to follow. A man who is discovered in transit cannot look wholly like one who has no other thought than to 'lie in peace on his bed / Happy as they who are dead.' To travel from one place to another is to accept that experience cannot always be a repetition of the same 'Peace, peace, peace'.

The chronology of composition suggests that in his account of the Solitaries Wordsworth increasingly allowed the verse to explore the contradictions of his own response. *Old Man Travelling* had been written by early June 1797 and *The Old Cumberland Beggar* by March 1798. By then many of the 'Discharg'd Soldier' lines had also been composed. But the full *Prelude* account, in which the movements of the poet's mind balance the extraordinary stasis of the Soldier, was not completed until late October 1800.[1] *Resolution and Independence*, composed in 1802, is explicitly curious not only about what the Leech-gatherer is, but about what he can be made to represent in the 'mind's eye' of the poet who meets him.

On 21 April 1802, less than a fortnight before he wrote the poem, Wordsworth had heard Coleridge reciting the bitterly explicit full version of *Dejection: An Ode*. He had listened to his best friend claiming in powerful verse that the strain of an unhappy marriage and a frustrated love affair had destroyed his responsiveness to the landscape's offer of peace. Coleridge even cites his relationship with the Wordsworths as a source of such destructive envy that it contributes to the vicious circle which is blinding him to the beauty of the earth. To continue that relationship, Wordsworth is told in the poem, would be only to infect him too with misery. If Coleridge were right, Wordsworth would risk losing his own sense of 'the one interior life / That lives in all things' were he to go on caring about his increasingly unhappy friend.

The biographical background is important as I myself have argued in a different work.² But it seems only to have intensified Wordsworth's motivation to explore a dichotomy which had long been clear in his own poetry. A knowledge of Coleridge's situation may add a slight extra dimension to a reading of *Resolution and Independence*, but it is equally illuminating to notice how boldly Wordsworth rejects many biographical truths in order to make the poem. We know from Dorothy's Journal that the actual meeting on 3 October 1800 had revealed the Leech-gatherer as having been at one time as much a family man as the 'Old Man Travelling': 'He had had a wife, and "a good woman, and it pleased God to bless us with ten children". All these were dead but one, of whom he had not heard for many years, a sailor.' Wordsworth himself had been being positively sociable on the day of the encounter. Robert Jones, whose presence had had to be eliminated from 'Crossing the Alps', had been to tea and the Wordsworths kept him company on the way home. Returning to Dove Cottage, William and Dorothy together met the Leech-gatherer. Later their brother John came across him.³ Friend, sister and brother are significantly eliminated from a poem whose first seven stanzas are devoted to placing the poet himself in relation to a landscape through which he walks alone.

II

The opening stanzas of *Resolution and Independence* rejoice with the world in welcoming the sun. 'All things' are illuminated and united by the sunlight they celebrate together:

II

All things that love the sun are out of doors;
The sky rejoices in the morning's birth;
The grass is bright with rain-drops; – on the moors
The hare is running races in her mirth;
And with her feet she from the plashy earth
Raises a mist; that, glittering in the sun,
Runs with her all the way, wherever she doth run.

III

I was a Traveller then upon the moor;
I saw the hare that raced about with joy;
I heard the woods and distant waters roar;

> Or heard them not, as happy as a boy:
> The pleasant season did my heart employ:
> My old remembrances went from me wholly;
> And all the ways of men, so vain and melancholy.

The world's boisterously energetic peacefulness is wonderfully caught in the present tense deployed by Stanza II. Each part of the landscape gives life to others. The sun lights the grass through the prism of raindrops which, bounced off the grass by the racing hare, reflect the sun again and pattern out the hare's movements. The present tense, as well as supporting the timeless regeneration of the non-human landscape, does suggest, as Hartman says, that Wordsworth's own 'mind, rejoicing in the beautiful dawn like birds, sky and hare, seems to have imperceptibly entered its own conception'.[4] But that 'seems' is an appropriate caution. The past tense with which Wordsworth explicitly describes his own identification with the scene limits the feeling in time, though leaving its intensity unqualified. Wordsworth records only a momentary glimpse of that eye of nature in which the Old Cumberland Beggar permanently dwells.

It matters no more at this depth of belonging whether the poet 'heard the woods . . . Or heard them not' (17–18) than it would matter to the beggar who should be amongst bird song 'whether heard or not' (*PW*, IV. 240, 184–5). Wordsworth's briefly achieved 'Animal Tranquillity' is perfectly captured in line 16 where we cannot tell whether it is the racing hare or Wordsworth seeing it who has 'the joy'. They cannot be separated out from their shared joy into merely pretty object and blindly detached observer. So Wordsworth regresses from the pointlessly anxious habits of grown-up vision, the 'ways of men' (21), to the immediacies of his childhood when he was 'happy as a boy' (18). F. W. Bateson offers an unsympathetic but accidentally illuminating comment on these lines:

> he seems almost to correlate the adult's happiness with his success in forgetting his social responsibilities:
>
> > My old remembrances went from me wholly;
> > And all the ways of men, so vain and melancholy.[5]

Surely the poet himself admits in so many words that he is enjoying not an 'adult's happiness' but a boy's. Wordsworth momentarily regresses into a state of mind where 'thoughts that are fed by the sun' are not instantly balanced by fears of being 'Dead without any

company'. Clearly at this stage Wordsworth does not concede that
escape from other people's fretfulness may depend on suppressing
his own need to care and be cared for. Later 'the ways of men' are to
be revealed as more of an inseparable package deal than Wordsworth
can acknowledge so long as he is recalling the joy of feelings indistinguishable from those of children and animals.

The past tense warns us that such feelings cannot survive unchallenged in the adult mind. The fourth stanza records the return to a
specially human consciousness, and bleakly emphasizes its tendency
to gloom and worry. Here 'Prospectiveness, or intellect, or will' do
not focus on what is actually present. Such a 'creative' imagination
in fact obliterates the soothing pattern with which the world is
presenting its reality. The poet's anxieties lurk in the dim world of
hypotheses, of futures which may never occur:

> fears and fancies thick upon me came;
> Dim sadness – and blind thoughts, I knew not, nor could name.

v

> I heard the sky-lark warbling in the sky;
> And I bethought me of the playful hare;
> Even such a happy Child of earth am I;
> Even as these blissful creatures do I fare;
> Far from the world I walk, and from all care;
> But there may come another day to me –
> Solitude, pain of heart, distress, and poverty.

Self-consciously making sure that he does hear the skylark and
forcing himself really to notice the hare only define Wordsworth's
separation. Telling himself that he is as much 'a happy Child of earth'
as any other animal only reveals how far he has grown away from it in
growing up to manhood. As he tries to argue himself back into the
felt present of Stanza II, the choice of tense now only evokes the
tension of a mind not at home there. Wordsworth is no longer with
the hare. He is away in gloomy imaginings about 'another day'.

Exiled again into the human time-scheme, Wordsworth feeds his
fear of the future with maudlin thoughts of the past. He harasses
himself with the 'old remembrances' which he had escaped in his
brief rediscovery of integrated life in Stanza III. In Stanza VII he
recalls past examples of promising young poets who have come to
bad ends. He echoes Coleridge's despairing view in *Dejection* that

our elation in the world about us is a subjective product of our own minds. If it is only 'By our own spirits' that we feel 'deified', then there are no realities in the non-human world to prevent any 'despondency and madness' that our minds may inflict (47–9).

But poets who died young like Chatterton and Burns also make a simpler, and no less important, point. The human mind can conceive of and dread its own death and the deaths of those it values. The 'marvellous Boy' who 'perished in his pride' represents a felt loss unknown to the singing birds and racing hare. The human world acknowledges irreplaceably precious individuals in a way that the world of the opening stanzas does not. The raindrops 'glittering in the sun' will disappear painlessly into the force whose glory they reflect. But human beings need to struggle to look after themselves just as their need of love makes them ask to be looked after by others:

VI

My whole life I have lived in pleasant thought,
As if life's business were a summer mood;
As if all needful things would come unsought
To genial faith, still rich in genial good;
But how can He expect that others should
Build for him, sow for him, and at his call
Love him, who for himself will take no heed at all?

This last sentence should surely not be read as a comfortably patronizing rebuke to Coleridge. Wordsworth has been quite explicit that it is he himself who has behaved as if he could be as mindlessly joyful as a hare rather than face up to his peculiar needs as a person. It is Wordsworth who has been living 'As if life's business were a summer mood'. So it is Wordsworth who, immediately before meeting the Leech-gatherer, has recognized that 'needful things' to mankind do not necessarily 'come unsought', and that amongst these is the need to be loved.

This recognition does not however invalidate the yearning towards relaxed identification with the energies of nature. The experience of the opening stanzas, feeling the life of things actually present now, undistracted by imaginings about the needs one may come to feel in some other place and time, is not mocked. It may be revealed as embracing only one side of our nature, but it is not exposed as a delusion. William Heath offers a contrary view. He sees Wordsworth as now reproaching himself for indulging in a 'fantasy':

To be only here, now is in a sense to not exist at all, and to have had one's identity incorporated into general existence. . . . To be a part of what one sees is not to *be* at all. . . . To exist without self-consciousness (stanzas 3, 4 and 5 suggest) is as immoral as it is impossible, for it means participating in the self-defeating selfishness of a Burns, a Chatterton, a Ferguson – and probably Coleridge.[6]

This seems to me to use one side of a generously complex poem to discredit the other. Wordsworth obviously admits that 'To be a part of what one sees' is to cease to be conscious of oneself as a separate identity. But he also points out that self-consciousness involves 'blind thoughts' and prevents awareness of what actually exists here and now. The feelings of the opening stanzas are revealed surely not as 'impossible' but as a convincingly detailed evocation of a world which in one very literal sense is our world. What the later stanzas add is the knowledge that it is only one of two worlds. We cannot choose to exist permanently in one to the exclusion of the other. The human mind's balance has to be dextrous enough to commute between the two inescapable truths. The balance is precarious enough to risk a collapse into 'madness'. Sanity can hardly therefore involve denying the reality of 'All things that love the sun' and recognizing only 'the ways of men'. The reader, after all, must have a response to the simple issue of happiness. The world of 'pleasant noise' which 'rejoices' makes Wordsworth 'as happy as a boy'. Grown 'men' may well have to confront a different world. But since their adult ways of thought are often 'vain and melancholy', they are not simply deluding themselves when they recover some of the child's sense of reality. As Wordsworth's mood shifts from 'gladness' to 'despondency' (48–9), he moves from one way of seeing to another, but each on its own is a partial vision. The poem has its feet firmly on the ground of two realities. It disturbingly shifts its weight at moments from one to the other, but it never quite loses its balance.

III

Balance of course is the essential quality Wordsworth hopes to discover in the Leech-gatherer himself. It is by centring on him that the poet's seesawing mind seeks its equipoise. In the 1815 Preface Wordsworth himself quotes some of the opening description of the

Leech-gatherer to demonstrate how images can be adjusted until their weight is so precisely equal as to 'unite and coalesce in just comparison':

> Take these images separately, and how unaffecting the picture compared with that produced by their being thus connected with, and opposed to, each other!

> As a huge stone is sometimes seen to lie
> Couched on the bald top of an eminence,
> Wonder to all who do the same espy
> By what means it could thither come, and whence,
> So that it seems a thing endued with sense,
> Like a sea-beast crawled forth, which on a shelf
> Of rock or sand reposeth, there to sun himself.

> Such seemed this Man; not all alive or dead
> Nor all asleep, in his extreme old age.
>   . . .

> Motionless as a cloud the old Man stood,
> That heareth not the loud winds when they call,
> And moveth altogether if it move at all.

> In these images . . . The stone is endowed with something of the power of life to approximate it to the sea-beast; and the sea-beast stripped of some of its vital qualities to assimilate it to the stone; which intermediate image is thus treated for the purpose of bringing the original image, that of the stone, to a nearer resemblance to the figure and condition of the aged Man; who is divested of so much of the indications of life and motion as to bring him to the point where the two objects unite and coalesce in just comparison.
>   (PW, II.438)

Wordsworth is clearly able to match modern exponents of practical criticism, but the slightly patronizing admiration this analysis now causes can distract us from the real issue. What do these carefully balanced images end up saying?

To some extent they strive to turn the Leech-gatherer into an anthropomorphic emblem of Wordsworth's fantasy in 'thoughts that are fed by the sun'. Wordsworth dreams there of being 'Happy as they who are dead' and yet sufficiently alive to enjoy it, of combining 'breath with the quiet of death'. On his bed and 'in peace' Wordsworth ceases to be conscious of 'The passion and the sorrow and the strife'. Yet he remains sufficiently awake to relish being 'hush'd and still'. In seeing the Leech-gatherer as 'not all alive nor dead / Nor all asleep', Wordsworth tries to make him image the availability of such a trance not as a fleeting illusion but as a way of life. The terror of absolute oblivion, of the unqualified isolation of death ('I do not wish to lie / Dead, dead, / Dead without any company') looms like the 'huge stone'. But to be serene is not to be petrified, if stone-like placidity can be 'endowed with something of the power of life', if the still mind can yet be 'a thing endued with sense'. The Leech-gatherer may be deprived of just 'so much of the indications of life and motion' as to suggest that borderland of consciousness which Wordsworth and Dorothy tried to achieve in their grave-like trench. The sea-beast, able to commute between the two worlds of land and ocean, is essentially a borderer. Beached on 'rock or sand', it is 'stripped of some of its vital qualities'.

The curiously marginal life which Wordsworth's images seek to discover in the Leech-gatherer is brilliantly caught in the *Prelude* manuscript's description of a horse:

> With one leg from the ground the creature stood
> Insensible and still, – breath, motion gone,
> Hairs, colour, all but shape and substance gone,
> Mane, ears, and tail, as lifeless as the trunk
> That had no stir of breath; we paused awhile
> In pleasure of the sight, and left him there
> With all his functions silently sealed up,
> Like an amphibious work of Nature's hand,
> A Borderer dwelling betwixt life and death,
> A living Statue or a statued Life.   (*The Prelude* p. 624)

Wordsworth tries to sculpt the Leech-gatherer by references to stone and amphibian into a similarly 'statued Life'. But of course the stasis attainable by a horse may be an impossibility for a man. Remembering other young poets who are already dead, Wordsworth is conscious of 'dwelling betwixt life and death' in a sense that a horse by nature cannot be. He does in fact elsewhere use strikingly similar terms to describe a person, but inevitably makes crucial changes:

> A Being breathing thoughtful breath,
> A Traveller between life and death;
>   ('She was a Phantom of delight', *PW*, II. 213, 23–4)

People, for as long as they breathe, are doomed to be 'thoughtful', to structure their existence into terms of purposeful movement. So the Leech-gatherer will eventually speak to his being at least as much 'A Traveller' as 'A Borderer':

> He with a smile did then his words repeat;
> And said that, gathering leeches, far and wide
> He travelled;   (120–2)

Existence in his words is not some silent stasis, 'dwelling betwixt life and death', but a struggle to be expressed in terms of journeying from a remembered past to an anticipated future. In his initial stony silence he may look 'Like an amphibious work of Nature's hand'. But how far is it possible, or indeed desirable, for a man to feel and think as little as an animal?

The boisterously 'playful hare' and the sea-beast which so calmly 'reposeth' are uneasily related in Wordsworth's mind. Full and permanent identification with the joyful energies of the one may be to approach the complacent self-sufficiency of the other, and beyond that to reach the death-like obliviousness of the stone. Wordsworth's 'thoughts that are fed by the sun' had recognized being 'mute as a stone' as close to 'the quiet of death'. To be fully attuned to the non-verbal music with which 'the woods and distant waters roar' may be to be deaf to the peculiarly human needs of oneself and of the people one meets.

So the comparison with an animal is disconcerting to Wordsworth and the reader precisely because we already know that in the Leech-gatherer we are in fact confronted by a human being. Before he offers the images of stone and sea-beast, the poet has stumbled upon a being who is immediately recognized as 'a Man':

> VIII
> Now, whether it were by peculiar grace,
> A leading from above, a something given,
> Yet it befell that, in this lonely place,
> When I with these untoward thoughts had striven,
> Beside a pool bare to the eye of heaven
> I saw a Man before me unawares:
> The oldest man he seemed that ever wore grey hairs.

The mysterious introduction allows the Leech-gatherer to emerge hovering between a 'peculiar grace' and a bluntly palpable sea-creature, and yet he is, with his grey hair, visibly human. For Frederick Garber, it represents 'man as he stands in the cosmos, under the sky in a lonely place beside a bare pool on the moors somewhere between heaven and a beast'. After glimpsing 'the implied source of grace', we are confronted by something almost repellently alien:

> Now suddenly settled to earth, the passage plummets against a huge stone, a hunk of the bottom of things, on which a very different kind of foreignness manages to crawl in order to indulge in a low form of hedonism. . . . The man stands between the source and the beast, related to both though different from each.[7]

This seems to reduce the poem to the extremist dichotomy by which medieval moralists liked to characterize the human condition, but it is, at first sight, a disturbingly tenable reading. Wordsworth's prose comment can easily distract us into thinking that stone and sea-beast are innately contrary images, and that from their meeting some balanced view of the man can emerge. In fact both work to belittle his claims as an individual, sensitive human being.

One does not need to share Gerber's fastidious view of 'a low form of hedonism' to recognize that sea-creatures may offer an unenticing image of 'animal tranquillity'. *Old Man Travelling*'s humanity has to survive comparison with birds. The *Old Cumberland Beggar* juxtaposes birds, dogs and a horse with its human centre. *Resolution and Independence* opens with a man identifying with a hare 'running races in her mirth', but it proceeds to describe the Leech-gatherer by reference to what may be a dozing lobster. Of course the poem refuses to be so specific. We are not challenged to acknowledge that full union with the 'One Life' of 'All things that love the sun' would mean identifying even with a stranded jelly-fish. Wordsworth has not turned from the land creatures – the stock-dove, jay and magpie of Stanza I, the hare of Stanza II, the skylark of Stanza V – so that mankind can be seen as belonging even with superficially less attractive examples of the ecological unity. On the contrary, it is a generality that the more fluid world of the ocean provides in the unspecified 'sea-beast'. As such it can be recognized as essentially outside its most appropriate environment. When Wordsworth wants a sea-beast to suggest the possibility of feeling relaxedly at home in the universe, he predictably lodges it in the sea. In *Song for the Wandering Jew* the Sea-horse

Slumbers without sense of motion,
Couched upon the rocking wave.   (*PW*, ii. 159, 15–16)

As such it supports the poem's pattern in which the deer 'has a home'
on the earth and even apparently restless rivers 'find among the
mountains / Resting-places calm and deep' (10–11, 1–4). In *Resolution and Independence*, by contrast, the sea-beast is not resting upon
the element where it would seem most at home. Like the stone,
whose presence on the hilltop seems so unlikely, the sea-beast,
though able to briefly survive on the land, does not really belong
there.

If Wordsworth were able to liken the Leech-gatherer to a beast
more at home on this ground (the *Prelude*'s horse perhaps), the
implications would be more straightforwardly positive. The man in
his extreme old age might then represent the possibility of a second
childhood, once again able to sustain an animal-like delight in the
universe and to remain 'as happy as a boy'. He might epitomize the
chance of regaining what Wordsworth in *Tintern Abbey* calls 'The
coarser pleasures of my boyish days, / And their glad animal movements all gone by' (*PW*, ii. 261, 73–4). He might seem securely
possessed of that 'consciousness of animal delight', so precariously
achieved by Wordsworth before his meeting with the Discharg'd
Soldier (*The Prelude*, iv. 397). But stone and sea-beast in fact suggest
that, far from being an animal comfortably based in its most natural
habitat, the Leech-gatherer appears as an anomaly in this landscape.
If he could become as mindless as a stone, he by definition would not
feel any discomfort at the oddity of his surroundings. If his moments
of wishing to feel at home on the earth could be as fleeting as those
represented by the occasional visits of an amphibian, then he might
briefly achieve the same sense of repose. But it is only in such limited
ways that Wordsworth can envisage an old man placing himself in
these surroundings. Wordsworth's surprise at the sudden meeting
shows how much his view of the world has been changed by his 'fears
and fancies'. The scenery in which he himself initially felt so at home
now seems the last place in which to find any man living with
apparent ease.

IV

The poet's fears and fantasies may lead him, in the privacy of his own
mind, to imagine the Leech-gatherer as a stone or an animal. But, in

the reality of conversation, the Leech-gatherer has to be approached as a person. When Wordsworth first speaks, he clearly assumes that he is talking to an ordinary post-lapsarian man. After a remark about the changeable weather (84), there is simple curiosity as to what a man whom one might expect to meet elsewhere is up to in such a spot: 'What occupation do you there pursue?/This is a lonesome place for one like you' (88–9). The question sounds normal enough. It is the poet's lack of interest in the answer which seems odd. He does not at first tell us what the Leech-gatherer has to say for himself. We are merely told Wordsworth's view of how he says it.

Stanza XIV's description of the old man's highly civilized speech patterns is almost laboriously emphatic. His words follow each other 'in solemn order'. They are 'Choice' and arranged in 'measured phrase'. This ensures that the composure which might be mistaken for mindlessness acquires a recognizably human dignity. His calm may be important to the poet because it seems attainable not by some silent stone, or the singing birds of the first stanza, but by a man who like others can express himself in words. However, the priority given to the style of his reply, as opposed to its content, allows him to be exalted beyond normal humanity. He is credited with an eloquence 'above the reach/Of ordinary men'. The intractable substance of the Leech-gatherer's answer will later place his life and his livelihood firmly beside the pool where Wordsworth meets him, but for the time being the Leech-gatherer's speech patterns allow the mind to wander to a different place:

> a stately speech;
> Such as grave Livers do in Scotland use,
> Religious men, who give to God and man their dues.   (96–8)

Such people represent a clearly moral way of life which might help Wordsworth in his depression. Their balance between religious and secular values has an inviting explicitness quite different from the Leech-gatherer's own baffling equipoise: 'not all alive nor dead/Nor all asleep – in his extreme old age' (64–5).

Because the first seven stanzas of the poem have been so explicit about Wordsworth's own restlessly imaginative mind, the reader recognizes the Leech-gatherer's ambiguity as a reflection of the poet's own shifting demands. The grey-haired old man Wordsworth sights at the end of Stanza VIII is immediately represented in Stanza IX as something else. There the equivocation between stone and sea-beast suggests that either may be a subjectively chosen point of comparison. It recalls the uncertainty as to whether the meeting is caused 'by peculiar grace, / A leading from above' or 'a something given'. At both moments the posing of alternatives does not just suggest the difficulty of adequately describing the impressions created by the Leech-gatherer. It also voices Wordsworth's hesitation as to what he wishes to find impressive. The Leech-gatherer can be manipulated into a symbol of natural serenity beyond the reach of human communication – 'Motionless as a cloud . . . That heareth not' (75–6). Or, by repeated questioning, he can be made to answer as an image of peculiarly human endurance, exiled like all sons of Adam to 'Employment hazardous and wearisome' (101), yet heroically resolved to 'persevere' (126). So Wordsworth's ability to concentrate on what the old man actually says fluctuates. Curiosity as to what the Leech-gatherer feels himself to be is balanced by a compulsion to discover what he can be made to represent in the minds of those who meet him.

At first the poet chooses to be more interested in the old man's extraordinary speech patterns. But in the next stanza the actual content of the Leech-gatherer's answer compels attention. It returns us from Scotland 'to these waters', from unquestionably religious men to the Leech-gatherer. His piety functions more elusively in an equivocal world of 'choice or chance'. The poetically 'lofty' style 'above the reach of ordinary men' is replaced by a prosaic insistence on the all too common human fate of 'being old and poor':

XV

He told, that to these waters he had come
To gather leeches, being old and poor;
Employment hazardous and wearisome!
And he had many hardships to endure:
From pond to pond he roamed, from moor to moor;
Housing, with God's good help, by choice or chance;
And in this way he gained an honest maintenance.

It is only now, three-quarters of the way through the poem, that the old man is allowed to tell us what he does for a living. He is a collector of medical supplies. His job thus points to a crucial difference between the birds and beasts with whom Wordsworth initially identified and the dying poets he later recalled. The Leech-gatherer works amongst the tranquil world of animals, but he is paid by anxious people who consciously try to escape illness and delay death. Physically he himself has been deformed by 'pain' and 'sickness', and is visibly approaching death 'in his extreme old age'. Unlike the hare, 'running races in her mirth' (11), for whom life seems to be a merely instinctual game, the Leech-gatherer survives by conscious effort. He is proud of maintaining himself by 'honest' work, but he leaves Wordsworth in no doubt that it is 'wearisome' and imposes 'many hardships'.

His words however soon lose their hold on Wordsworth's flickering attention:

XVI

The old man still stood talking by my side;
But now his voice to me was like a stream
Scarce heard; nor word from word could I divide;
And the whole body of the Man did seem
Like one whom I had met with in a dream;
Or like a man from some far region sent,
To give me human strength, by apt admonishment.

In Stanza xv the clear outlines of the Leech-gatherer's own idiosyncratic problems fail to supply an answer to Wordsworth's own. But here, blurred by Wordsworth's imagination into a style of speech or a generalized physical appearance, the man can be made to image 'human strength'. The simile which tries to move the actual confrontation to a meeting in 'a dream' suggests not only intensity but illusion. Wordsworth's mind is audibly struggling to replace anxiety with resolution. The verse tries to push the Leech-gatherer with his familiar needs into 'some far region' from which cheering messages can come.

But the attempt fails. Anxiety returns and with it the willingness to once again listen to what the old man actually has to say:

XVII

My former thoughts returned: the fear that kills;
And hope that is unwilling to be fed;
Cold, pain and labour, and all fleshly ills;
And mighty Poets in their misery dead.
– Perplexed, and longing to be comforted,
My question eagerly did I renew,
'How is it that you live, and what is it you do?'

The sources of anxiety are partly objective 'fleshly ills', but they are partly subjective phantoms, created by an imaginative intellect which manufactures more problems than it solves. 'Cold, pain and labour' are less explicitly fatal than 'the fear that kills'. The poet who is in fact still young and healthy repeats the destructive process of anticipating 'another day', exiling himself from his present surroundings to a mental landscape of 'mighty Poets in their misery dead'. The mind, simultaneously conceiving an ambition and discovering the improbability of its fulfilment ('hope that is unwilling to be fed'), recognizes its self-torturing restlessness. It longs for a way out of its own vicious circle.

The Leech-gatherer's response to the appeal is therefore appropriately rather mindless:

XVIII
He with a smile did then his words repeat;
And said that, gathering leeches, far and wide
He travelled; stirring thus about his feet
The waters of the pools where they abide.
'Once I could meet with them on every side;
But they have dwindled long by slow decay;
Yet still I persevere, and find them where I may.'

For the first time, the Leech-gatherer is allowed to intrude his own direct speech into the poem. Where before the distracted poet had been unable to distinguish 'word from word', he now hears distinctly enough to record the speech verbatim. It does not sound like the 'lofty utterance . . . above the reach / Of ordinary men' with which Wordsworth sought to credit the Leech-gatherer in Stanza XIV. It could only seem to have the fluent energy of the non-human world and sound 'like a stream' when it was 'scarce heard' (107–8). But any speech, as in *Old Man Travelling*, identifies poet and old man as belonging to the same unique species. Moreover the Leech-gatherer expresses his contentment 'with a smile'. No hare can convey 'her mirth' in that way. No sea-beast can use such a signal to communicate the comfort with which it reposes on a rock. The two men are now clearly capable of a far more particularized and personal dialogue than that available to the birds in the general harmony of the first stanza where 'The Jay makes answer as the Magpie chatters' (6).

So Wordsworth's 'longing to be comforted' at last receives some sort of audible answer. To the extent that he fears 'fleshly ills', he can

find in the Leech-gatherer's words apt encouragement. In spite of
past 'pain' and 'sickness' the old man sounds placid. The 'Cold, pain,
and labour' that Wordsworth can only fearfully imagine for himself
in the future has already been survived by the old man in his struggle
to make a living on the moors. His work has not only become more
difficult as old age saps his strength. He now reveals that the sources
of his livelihood have dwindled too. Yet still he perseveres. The harsh
physical pressures of his own nature and the landscape on which he
depends make him living proof of how much can be endured.

V

Wordsworth's fear of the future is not, however, confined to its
physical difficulties, and the next stanza reveals him as still distracted
and dissatisfied:

XIX

> While he was talking thus, the lonely place,
> The old Man's shape, and speech – all troubled me:
> In my mind's eye I seemed to see him pace
> About the weary moors continually,
> Wandering about alone and silently.
> While I these thoughts within myself pursued,
> He, having made a pause, the same discourse renewed.

The problem with which Wordsworth still wrestles is isolation. It is
imaged by his again being unable to listen to the Leech-gatherer. The
'stranger's privilege' he claimed in initiating the conversation (82) has
failed to release him from his own anxious mind, and the 'thoughts
within' keep him a stranger even as they chat. The 'speech' ceases to
be heard as a statement of how the Leech-gatherer endures his own
particular problems. It fades into an evocation of his separateness in
that 'lonely place'. The phrase echoes Wordsworth's opening enquiry as to what the Leech-gatherer could be doing in such 'a
lonesome place' and defines the extent to which Wordsworth is still
baffled. Once again Wordsworth's vision blurs man into image. He
no longer focuses on the encouraging human face which in the
previous stanza offered him 'a smile'. Instead 'The old Man's shape'
evokes a body compelled to 'pace . . . about alone'.

Wordsworth, blind to the present meeting, is carried by his
'mind's eye' to a bleak world of loneliness. The restless imagination,

which had earlier exiled him from the joy of animals, now distances him from the old man's friendliness. The mind had then deprived him of the present morning's sunshine and hypothesized 'another day' of 'Solitude, pain of heart, distress, and poverty' (35). Now it turns the actual relaxation of the chatting Leech-gatherer into the imagined restlessness of an endless and silent 'Wandering'. The physical problems of 'distress and poverty' may have been proved manageable, but the emotional fear of 'Solitude, pain of heart' seems to have been intensified by the meeting. The opening stanzas had deployed the present tense to give the natural world's delight a glorious permanence. Now the present tense is used to suggest the awesome immutability with which lonely men must 'pace / About the weary moors continually'. Present participles, which had once maintained a continuing dream of the sun 'rising', the birds 'singing' and the hare 'running races in her mirth', now become an unending nightmare in which man is 'Wandering about alone'.

The Leech-gatherer himself has not described his life in terms of either of these permanences. William Heath notes that Stanza XVIII implies the ordinary adult consciousness of past and future as well as present:

> Past ('Once I could meet'), present ('But they are dwindled') and future ('Yet still I persevere') are ordered by lines, grammar and tone. The assertion of confidence in the midst of adversity is a matter of style as well as belief for the Leech-gatherer.

Heath suggests that this provides a relatively smooth transition to Wordsworth's vision of isolation:

> because this is – in the rather simplified terms of the old man – an imaginative act, it is relevant to the poet, who begins himself to move from anxiety to perplexity, then to imaginative composition of his own in the lines that Coleridge praised in Chapter 22 of *Biographia Literaria*;

> In my mind's eye I seemed to see him pace
> About the weary moors continually,
> Wandering about, alone and silently.[8]

But Coleridge in fact quotes the two stanzas as an example of Wordsworth's 'incongruity' in moving so unpredictably from the 'unimpassioned' and 'undistinguished' to the 'striking and original'.

What Heath calls the 'rather simple terms' used in the Leech-gatherer's own speech do seem to me almost defiantly prosaic, grounded in the mundane palpabilties of his trade. As such they are surely not 'an imaginative act'. It may even be true to say that his resolution derives from his being less imaginative than the poet who in the next stanza is 'troubled' by a vision of his own devising.

We must notice the gulf between Stanzas XVIII and XIX, and accept it as part of the poem's meaning. It is not sufficient merely to observe, as Bradley does, that the 'pedestrian' gives way to 'lines of extraordinary grandeur'.⁹ The 'grandeur' imposed by Wordsworth is clearly absent from the old man's words. The Leech-gatherer's own speech is pedestrian in the precise way it keeps his feet on the ground of practical purpose. He says that it is his trade of 'gathering leeches' which necessitates his travelling around, 'stirring thus about his feet / The waters of the pools where they abide'. This pragmatic sense of direction is then obscured by Wordsworth's implying that the travelling is an almost aimless 'Wandering'. What the Leech-gatherer thinks he has adequately explained is made mysterious. The Leech-gatherer sees things in terms of the literal world 'about his feet'. To him 'slow decay' is a mundane problem of a decline in the supply of leeches. But Wordsworth, as if demonstrating the creative processes that composed *Old Man Travelling: Animal Tranquillity and Decay*, sees in his 'mind's eye' something very different: an awesome 'shape', imaging partly an alarming decay into total isolation from other people and partly the grandeur of release into a non-human tranquillity.

Yet it is a chillier grandeur than that evoked by earlier Solitaries. The energetically interdependent plurals in which Lucy is 'Roll'd round in earth's diurnal course / With rocks, and stones, and trees' are quite different in tone from the strikingly singular 'huge stone' so inexplicably 'couched on the bald top of an eminence'. The richly varied landscape where the Old Cumberland Beggar lives in the eye of nature is far from the moorland pool 'bare to the eye of heaven'. Both men seem more at home in their natural settings through being so distant from other people, but intimacy with such different settings makes one share his meal with 'the little woodland birds', while the other merges with the rock-like resilience of a sea-beast. To the extent that both are lonely travellers whose efforts we pity, they echo each other but with a significant modulation: the Beggar 'plies his weary journey' (54), but the Leech-gatherer has to 'pace / About the weary moors' (130). It is only the Leech-gatherer's landscape which can in its own right seem so bleakly monotonous as to be called weary. It is a measure of how far Wordsworth has now come to see another man's solitariness as a stimulus to questions about his own.

   Wordsworth's earlier confusion as to where he should place himself in relation to an apparently joyous natural landscape is reproduced in this later doubt as to where to place the Leech-gatherer. Does he belong in a human conversation, answering a young man's over-imaginative anxieties with an old man's practical wisom? Or is his true station an irredeemably 'lonely place' whose silence makes any attempt at verbal communication an anomaly, a world too large to be narrowed to human relationship? Poetry, being chronological, has difficulty in maintaining a balance between such alternatives since one must be placed first and concede to the other the strength of the last word. So Wordsworth insists that Stanzas XVIII and XIX are simultaneous. He pursues his own thoughts in Stanza XIX at the same time as the Leech-gatherer makes his speech in Stanza XVIII: 'While he was talking thus' (127).

VI

The poem has thus far been dynamic in its shifting emphases. Now this tense energy is dissipated in a last stanza whose relaxed piety foreshadows the overall decline of Wordsworth's verse:

XX

And soon with this he other matter blended,
Cheerfully uttered, with demeanour kind,
But stately in the main; and when he ended,
I could have laughed myself to scorn to find
In that decrepit Man so firm a mind.
'God,' said I, 'be my help and stay secure;
I'll think of the Leech-gatherer on the lonely moor!'

The uncomfortable phrasing of the penultimate line should not confuse us. Wordsworth is praying. 'God,' is not some casual exclamation but a sober vocative. Wordsworth asks Him to be a reliable prop to his own frailty. This is something quite new in Wordsworth's verse. Of course the Leech-gatherer himself has earlier offered conventional pieties, claiming that it is 'with God's good help', as well as 'by choice or chance', that he finds his lodgings (104). His speech patterns recalled 'Religious men who give to God and man their dues' (98). But both moments had seemed fairly insignificant. The 'Discharg'd Soldier' had similarly claimed to put his trust 'in the God of heaven' as well as 'in the eye of him that passes' (494–5), and one rightly in that case foresees no religious conclusion being drawn by the poet himself. In *Resolution and Independence* it seems even safer to assume that it is not as a Christian that the Leech-gatherer will finally matter to Wordsworth. So much of the poetry centres on the poet's own reactions, and none of these foreshadow this centring on religious inspiration. Whatever the poem's conflicts have been they are not of a kind that seem likely to be resolved by giving both 'God and man their dues'. Yet this is what the last two lines attempt, the priority being given to religious faith, backed up by the need to meditate upon the human exemplum of the Leech-gatherer.

The last word does however go to a phrase, 'the lonely moor', which recalls the tension of the poem. It is in this alienating locale and not the joyously shared landscape of the opening stanzas that Wordsworth seeks his happy ending. The self-critical mood in which he now thinks he should 'have laughed himself to scorn' is far from his unselfconscious delight in the hare's 'mirth'. The poem closes with a conscientious intention to concentrate the mind upon a proper object: 'I'll think of the Leech-gatherer'. Yet it had begun with a spontaneity in which consciousness was a relaxedly marginal consideration: 'I heard the woods and distant waters roar;/ Or heard them not, as happy as a boy: (17–18). The mind had been an untrustworthy source of distracting 'blind thoughts' which blurred one's vision; now to 'think' about the old man having 'so firm a mind' is to see clearly. But what? The Leech-gatherer, seen in the 'mind's eye' of the previous stanza, 'troubled' Wordsworth as an enigmatic 'shape'. In the stanza before that he had been visibly an ordinary person, talking 'with a smile' about the difficulties of his trade. Each had been, in its own way, a fitting climax to one of the poem's conflicting tendencies. In one the Leech-gatherer had finally been distanced into an awesome image of silent isolation, pacing into a grandeur beyond the reach of human relationship. In the other his reality as a person with bluntly realistic problems had finally impinged on the wandering mind of the poet. In one the soundlessness of the old man's solitude or his loneliness had seemed clinched into a permanence which could not now be interrupted. In the other his humanity had at last been voiced in the palpability of direct speech. Before these rival conclusions he had been imaginatively manipulated in various ways to make him answer to Wordsworth's fretful doubts. He had been a sea-beast, a rock, a body whose deformity witnesses to past suffering, a cloud, an echo of Scottish courtesies and a figure in a dream.

The last stanza gives us no guidance as to which of all these images we are to see as helping Wordsworth to religious faith. Nor does it give us any clue as to how this religion relates either to the joys or to the anxieties of earlier stanzas. We can, of course make guesses, and they bode ill for Wordsworth's future power as a poet. The existence of a separate Heaven may reduce the importance of an animal-like joy in the earth. The unspeakable significance of God may make the selective concerns about which individualistic men speak to each other relatively insignificant. The serene beauty of the integrated landscape and the poignant frailty of people who seem so separate from it create ambivalent feelings which within these new religious dimensions may be treated with 'scorn'. If security is to be sought only in God, then perhaps poems should not maintain the uneasy equipoise of their polarized insights but relax into single-minded moralism. The 'meddling intellect' should not be balanced by more elusive intuitions, but admired as the 'firm . . . mind' of an exemplum about which one should 'think'. Neither the grandeur of the living universe nor the pathos of human tenderness can jostle for the central role in a world whose new monarchs are to be God and the intellect which imitates Him.

In important senses, each of the last three stanzas of the poem asserts its own claim to be a fitting conclusion. Neither the old man's finally audible speech nor the culminating silence of his pacing about the moors can on its own do justice to what has gone before. Together they at least avoid the injustice of over-simplification. The stanza which follows and is technically allowed to end the poem could only be an apt conclusion to a quite different work. Though Wordsworth was all too soon to write just such works, he had not yet done so. Grateful for this, we should not allow the last stanza of *Resolution and Independence* to make us forget the poem's power. To do so would be to read backwards.

VII

In some ways *The Prelude*'s description of the London Beggar re-establishes a pattern broken by *Resolution and Independence*.

Unlike the Leech-gatherer, the Beggar has no job. In this he resembles not only the Cumberland Beggar but also the presumably retired old man of *Animal Tranquillity and Decay* and *The Prelude*'s old soldier who has been explicitly 'discharg'd'. Since they do not work for their living, it is possible to see them as having retired into a 'settled quiet' where 'All effort seems forgotten' (*Old Man Travelling: Animal Tranquillity and Decay*, 8–9). The Leech-gatherer alone has the audibly resolute independence of a man who supports himself, and his stance reflects this: 'Himself he propp'd, limbs, body and pale face / Upon a long grey staff of shaven wood' (91–2). The ex-soldier, on the other hand, had been discovered in an essentially more dependent pose: 'from behind / A mile-stone propp'd him' (*The Prelude*, IV.411–12). It is this passive reliance on external support which is echoed by the London Beggar: Wordsworth sees him 'propp'd against a wall' (*The Prelude*, VII.612). Such postures may suggest a pathetic need to trust to other people rather than their own poignantly diminished strength. Or perhaps their leaning so heavily on inanimate objects evokes an awesome inertia, an impressively achieved peace which bypasses all understanding of life as necessarily demanding an effort. But whatever its implications, their posture is quite different from that of the Leech-gatherer, who is determined to move on, providing for himself by 'Employment hazardous and wearisome' (101).

He is also remarkable for his 'yet-vivid eyes' (91). The London Beggar has by contrast 'sightless eyes'. These have been fore-shadowed by the Cumberland Beggar's 'languid orbs' and 'Old Man Travelling'''s 'face' and 'look' in which there is no more 'expression' than in his 'bending figure'. But even more relevant is the situation created by the old soldier's 'look' of 'ghastly mildness': 'I could mark him well, / Myself unseen' (*The Prelude*, IV.493, 404–5). The reduced vision of such figures allows Wordsworth to focus on them with a bewildered but unwavering concentration. Where the Leech-gatherer is able to look back at Wordsworth with 'a flash of mild surprise' (90), the other Solitaries hardly notice the poet.

In the extreme case of the blind Beggar, Wordsworth even before the confrontation is explicitly troubled by the apparent impossibility of awareness becoming mutual. Though himself willing to look and go on looking, he feels surrounded by people who remain totally opaque.

How often in the overflowing Streets,
Have I gone forward with the Crowd, and said
Unto myself, the face of every one
That passes by me is a mystery.
Thus have I look'd, nor ceas'd to look, oppress'd
By thoughts of what, and whither, when and how,
Until the shapes before my eyes became
A second-sight procession, such as glides
Over still mountains, or appears in dreams;
And all the ballast of familiar life,
The present and the past; hope, fear; all stays,
All laws of acting, thinking, speaking man
Went from me, neither knowing me, nor known.
                              (*The Prelude*, VII. 594–606)

The shift of mood here is portrayed with such subtle economy that a hasty reading can miss it. Yet the shift is crucial. At first the paradox of isolation when surrounded by people is painful. Wordsworth is 'oppress'd' by a frustrated need to communicate. He records what he 'said / Unto' himself not just to allow the feeling the immediacy of the present tense ('*is* a mystery'), but more importantly to evoke the loneliness of those compelled to talk to themselves. At first there is no resignation to the difficulty of getting to know anything about other people. He goes on searching the blank faces ('nor ceas'd to look'). He continues to ask the unanswered questions 'of what, and whither, when and how'. The unguessable errands of 'late and soon, / Getting and spending' are not here comfortably patronized as moving at a tangent to the poet's proper concerns as they are in 'The World is too much with us' (*PW*, III. 18). Wordsworth is initially curious about the 'when' of the London crowd's 'late and soon', the 'what' and 'whither' and 'how' of their 'getting and spending'. As so often in Wordsworth, the brain has to exhaust itself with unsatisfied thoughts before it can relax and make room for a calmer state of mind. The restlessly searching eye has to be blinded before a very different way of seeing can be gained.

Eventually Wordsworth gives up the struggle to distinguish. Instead of looking at the singular 'face' of each person, he allows them to blur into plural 'shapes'. This satisfyingly unified 'procession' is literally 'A second-sight', a different way of seeing a crowd which at first Wordsworth longed to separate into individuals, each with his own separate sense of importance. His ignorance of the particular destination which had seemed tantalizingly hidden behind each face no longer frustrates him. The poet relaxes as the spectator of a unified movement of merely ritual display. Instead of feeling 'oppress'd' by the limits of 'overflowing Streets', Wordsworth's mind is released into a world as spaciously expansive and as soothingly fluid as mists gliding over mountains or dreams ignoring 'All laws of acting, thinking, speaking man'.

Incisively Wordsworth reminds us of the main features of this mental landscape where he enjoys a solitude which is almost the exact opposite of his initial loneliness. Not only is the second landscape one of natural mountains rather than man-made streets, of the relaxed unconscious mind rather than strenuously conscious curiosities. It also escapes from a linear sense of time ('whither, when'). 'The present' does not belong in a sequence with 'the past' and the imaginatively anticipated future of 'hope, fear'. The 'thinking' man who had tried to make some chronological sense of his experience retires. Wordsworth is no longer lured by 'hope' into effort or distracted away from available peace into imaginatively anticipated 'fear'. Resigned to being thus cut off from the experience of other people ('neither knowing me, nor known'), Wordsworth has no use for verbal communication. It is 'speaking man' who must vanish before the serene silence of a world which 'glides / Over still mountains' can be felt. To speak the human language, asking the ultimately unanswerable questions about what it feels like to be somebody else, is to focus on separation. It creates a self-consciousness in which one hears one's own baffled thoughts ('said / Unto myself'). Only deafness to such sounds allows one to hear what *The Prelude* elsewhere calls 'The ghostly language of the ancient earth', and there Wordsworth says of such moods:

> Oft in those moments such a holy calm
> Did overspread my soul, that I forgot
> That I had bodily eyes, and what I saw
> Appear'd like something in myself, a dream,
> > (*The Prelude*, II. 328, 367–70)

In Book VII too Wordsworth closes his 'bodily eyes', merging the physical differences around him into a 'dream'. He thus deploys an essentially ambiguous frame of reference in which 'Abruptly to be smitten with the view / Of a blind Beggar'. On the one hand, he is shockingly unprepared for a confrontation with an essentially singular man for whom blindness is a brutally simple disaster. On the other hand, Wordsworth is aptly open to the possibility that the Beggar's disability protects him from the delusions of all those other 'acting, thinking, speaking' people who hurry past him, each fantasizing that the universe is centred on his own localized destination. The Beggar, undistracted by all that they can see in this particular street, may more clearly sense the sustaining forces of that overall ecosystem on which everyone in the street depends.

The others imagine that they can see where they now are and can successfully find their way to some other place where they would rather be. By contrast, the poet, in the sentence which first confronts the Beggar, confesses himself to be 'lost'. The word here has some curiously positive connotations. In the London streets, Wordsworth could be as comfortably 'lost ... without a struggle to break through' as he had been in the Alps. There, losing his own sense of direction, he had found a truer image of his place amongst 'the types and symbols of Eternity' (*The Prelude*, VI. 529–30). Here too he may feel that his identity is as securely 'lost in god and nature' as the *Prelude* manuscript claims 'all beings' are if, instead of looking out at the 'puny boundaries' which seem to divide them, they sense within the 'undistinguishable' parts they play in that 'one interior life / That lives in all things' (*The Prelude*, p. 525). Those who blindly trust to the merely external indications of so-called 'common' sense, imagining that a street sign is sufficient statement of their present place in the world, might think that to be 'lost' is to get nowhere. The poet feels that he is travelling further, through being 'lost', into that unity which exists everywhere:

> And once, far-travell'd in such mood, beyond
> The reach of common indications, lost
> Amid the moving pageant, 'twas my chance
> Abruptly to be smitten with the view
> Of a blind Beggar who, with upright face,
> Stood propp'd against a Wall, upon his Chest
> Wearing a written paper, to explain
> The story of the Man, and who he was.
> My mind did at this spectacle turn round
> As with the might of waters, and it seem'd
> To me that in this Label was a type,

Or emblem, of the utmost that we know,
Both of ourselves and of the universe;
And on the shape of the unmoving man,
His fixèd face and sightless eyes, I look'd
As if admonish'd from another world.
                              (*The Prelude*, VII.607–22)

Unburdened by 'the ballast of familiar life', Wordsworth has been
light-headed almost to the point of feeling disembodied. Now the
sudden appearance of the Beggar smacks his eyes open with a brutally physical forcefulness. Where in the consciously curious earlier
lines he was able to 'look' actively, his seemingly 'wise passiveness'
now lays him open to a quite unlooked-for ambush and he is 'smitten
with the view'. Without warning, he is plunged into an experience
which compels his mind to 'turn round/As with the might of
waters'. The 'overflowing streets' had at first seemed frustratingly
remote and then as welcoming as the elegantly indistinct invitation
offered by the gliding mists. Now this fluidity is instantly chan-
nelled: whether into the creative energy of a waterwheel or a destructive whirlpool of despair is carefully left as an open issue. Hartman
suggests a third equally apt implication: 'Turned round' could suggest 'being turned back to a prior, neglected significance'.[10] The one
initial certainty is not what the Beggar signifies but the sheer power
of the turbulent impact he has upon the poet's mind. Amongst the
'procession' or 'moving pageant' passing by in dignified predictabil-
ity, this deviantly 'unmoving man' is a 'spectacle' which paradoxically leaps out at its witness.

One side of the Beggar's ambiguous immobility is in fact its power
to move us. The physically mobile crowd had eventually merged into
the undisturbing stasis of 'still mountains', with no more power to
arouse compassion than 'shapes' in 'dreams'. But the physically
'unmoving' Beggar, as palpably real as the wall on which he leans,
spells out his demand for pity in the notice he wears 'upon his
Chest'. The notice is intended 'to explain the story of the Man', to
answer the kind of curiosity which Wordsworth had earlier felt
about other people's 'when and how'. As a 'story' it trusts to the
chronological sense that the 'present' needs the explanation of 'the
past', the linear sense of time which Wordsworth had gradually lost
in his daydream. Hidden behind 'His fixed face and sightless eyes',
the Beggar has to try to express himself in the pathetically limited

format of the few words that can fit on the paper and which others are likely to pause long enough to read. So 'the utmost that we know' is negatively defined as no more than this. The sad sense that 'the face of every one / That passes . . . is a mystery' returns in this cruelly clear exemplum. We express as little of ourselves as can be contained in such a notice. It is a 'Label' which reveals no more about inner feelings than the label on a suitcase exposes its contents. The Beggar, 'propp'd against a wall' incapable of sight or movement, unable to claim relationship with any of the passers-by, does resemble a piece of left luggage. But the inadequacy of his being so labelled, of 'The story' which Wordsworth does not think worth passing on to the reader, paradoxically turns the mind to the fact that this is not an inanimate object but a 'Man' with a man's peculiar right to be recognized as an individual, to explain not only his 'story' but 'who he was'. This feeling of distinct identity and the will to express it may be peculiar to the 'thinking, speaking' species of *homo sapiens*. Certainly we identify with it, and Wordsworth precisely describes the label as something we know not only of the Beggar but 'of ourselves'.

His frailty is recognized as a version – however magnified – of our own. But his self-assertion – however feeble – is ours too. His need to be 'propp'd' is preceded by the assertion that he 'Stood'. He literally stands up in order to be counted as a fellow human being who deserves concern. With his label he explicitly appeals for sympathy. The appeal of course is made by such an alienatingly strange and opaque figure that it amounts to a challenge. The utmost that we can know of the feelings lurking behind 'His fixèd face and sightless eyes' is very little. But the anonymity of the earlier street scene has alerted us to the fact that all faces are to some extent a mystery, that the Beggar's blindness is only a more physical version of our own. To deny him may thus be to deny our own human nature. To try to escape our human language 'of what, and whither, when and how', helplessly limited though the Beggar's label proves it to be, may deprive us of the compassion which he, and all of us, need. To try to suppress the imagination which colours 'The present' with the 'past' and forces us on to the restless seesaw of 'hope, fear' about the future may make us inhumanly unimaginative about each other's needs. To this extent Wordsworth is snapped out of his daydream and 'admonish'd from another world' which is paradoxically the ordinary world. It is the world 'of familiar life' from which he had separated himself. It is the human version of what *The Prelude* later calls:

> The very world which is the world
> Of all of us, the place in which, in the end,
> We find our happiness, or not at all.   (x. 726–8)

The Beggar's forlorn isolation, cut off by poverty and blindness
from other people and yet striving to reach them with his label,
makes Wordsworth's comfortable solitude 'beyond/The reach of
common indications' curiously limited. The mental landscape of
mountains and dreams may now seem narrowed by its lack of human
figures. Indeed Wordsworth, 'lost/Amid the moving pageant',
seems in one sense to have had a narrower vision than the Beggar. The
dream of solitude is challenged here in a way that foreshadows its
final rejection in *Elegiac Stanzas*:

> Farewell, farewell the heart that lives alone,
> Housed in a dream, at distance from the Kind!
> Such happiness, wherever it be known,
> Is to be pitied; for 'tis surely blind.
>
> (*Elegiac Stanzas suggested by a Picture of Peele Castle*,
>   57–60, PW, IV. 260)

The Beggar's label witnesses to his awareness of his own suffering,
and to his faith in the fellow members of a species defined by its
capacity for kindness.

However, the Beggar epitomizes our knowledge 'both of
ourselves *and of the universe*'. Since the poetry has already defined
that universe as infinitely more than the confined human world of
London's 'overflowing Streets', Wordsworth is 'admonish'd from
another world' in two quite different senses. It is partly the human
world's reimpingement on a mind that had been alienated beyond its
reach, but it is also the essentially non-human world in which that
mind had been, and perhaps still should be, wandering. The Beggar
himself may long ago have learnt how to see his own mind as securely
lodged within that 'second-sight procession' which 'appears in
dreams'. The Leech-gatherer had been able to convey 'apt admonishment' only when his human voice faded and his 'whole body' could
be seen as 'one whom I had met with in a dream'. Then he seems to be
'from some far region', remote from his own verbalizable difficulties.
The Beggar too is 'from another world' partly because of the distance
between the noisy self-pity we might expect and the silent placidity he seems actually to image. The 'written paper' – unlike its

unrecorded words – is opaque enough to reflect a far more inclusive account of man's place in a larger universe than the Beggar's innately personal and selective autobiography with which Wordsworth does not distract us. If the label is looked at as an inclusive archetype of all statements rather than read as his own personal plea, it can reflect the fluidity of the world on which men feebly try to make their finite distinctions legible. When Wordsworth ceased to distinguish 'word from word' in the Leech-gatherer's voice it became 'like a stream' in its forcefully fluent wisdom. The Beggar's label has 'the might of waters' partly because it too is not confined by the distinctions of language to expressing the limited human point of view. Wordsworth's final vision perhaps moves over the Beggar as impassively as the lofty skyscape of his dreams 'glides / Over still mountains'. The ultimate knowledge represented by this 'type / Or emblem' may be close to the insight that discovered in the Alpine landscape 'the types and symbols of Eternity'. Later in Book VII Wordsworth asserts that the characters inscribed upon that larger universe, outlined for instance in the mountains of his home country, had shaped his mind to recognize the encoded patterns of unity even in London:

> By influence habitual to the mind
> The mountain's outline and its steady form
> Gives a pure grandeur, and its presence shapes
> The measure and the prospect of the soul
> To majesty.   (721–5)

'The forms / Perennial of the ancient hills' allow the mind to find even in

>   the press
> Of self-destroying, transitory things
> Composure and ennobling Harmony.
>   (*The Prelude*, VII. 738–40)

The presence in Wordsworth's imagination of the 'mountain's outline' does perhaps allow him to shape the Beggar's clumsy label into 'a pure grandeur', to recognize in the Beggar's stasis a composure which impressively reflects an indestructible harmony.

To the extent that the Beggar is an emblem of such knowledge, we would be quite wrong to approach him as a helpless individual who typifies all peculiarly human vulnerability. Composure cannot be met by compassion, and the voice of human tenderness would seem only an impertinent irrelevance when addressed to a being of mountainous grandeur. Yet we dare not use him only as an exemplum of how we ourselves can achieve peace of mind since, in his mind, the label is clearly designed to disturb us into active concern. Staring at the Beggar's 'sightless eyes', we glimpse quite contrary visions and are left quivering between incompatible responses. Wordsworth will not release the tension here as he does in *Resolution and Independence* by closing his own eyes to pray. He holds his gaze, stressing its unswerving focus by reiterating in three consecutive phrases what he sees: 'on the shape of the unmoving man, / His fixed face and sightless eyes, I look'd.' What the Beggar reveals 'of ourselves' remains opaque. We may belong only with each other in a community of undiscoverable suffering and inexpressible sympathy. Or we may be at home in a universe which answers to our dreams. But Wordsworth has the courage and the candour to face this mystery to the end. I cannot share John Jones's view that the Beggar is simply 'inauspicious' and Wordsworth's encounter with him is 'instinct with defeat'.[11] It seems truer to say that, in poetry which eschews all easy triumphs, Wordsworth continues to hold his ground. His strenuous debate is in fact grounded in the equal rights of composure and compassion. Each is raised in its extremest form by the Beggar and has its claims to be 'the utmost that we know'. Their coexistence can hardly be peaceful. But Wordsworth confronts their conflict in poetry of undefeated power.

✦ 7 ✦

THE REACH OF WORDS

'SPOTS OF TIME' IN 'THE PRELUDE'

I

The frankly tentative style of *The Prelude*'s greatest moments is
matched by the unpretentious structure in which they are so loosely
assembled. It is a disorderly poem. So I make no apology for trying to
understand Book XI's famous reference to 'spots of time' (258) by
first looking at a crucial passage in Book III. There Wordsworth
stresses that this autobiography is not a simple record of ambitions
fulfilled:

> Not of outward things
> Done visibly for other minds, words, signs,
> Symbols or actions.   (III. 174–6)

Dismissing external, causally linked events, *The Prelude* confronts
private, and apparently disconnected, moments of feeling. As 'spots
of time', they claim to epitomize our confused response to both the
spatial and the temporal. On the one hand, their arresting intuitions
do grasp the stasis which lies within the earth's self-sustaining unity.
The 'spots' do ground experience on essentially unchanging locali-
ties. On the other hand, such moods seem incongruously short-lived.
So they evoke the transitoriness of human experience as well as the
stability of the earth it explores. Moreover Wordsworth's frame of
mind at a 'spot of time' is curiously alert to the possible, and often the
actual, presence in the landscape of other people. So the mood clearly
belongs to a consciousness which, though pausing to glimpse the
eternal, is easily distracted by that sense of linear time, which seems
to be a peculiarly human experience.

Language might seem better suited to some implications of such
ambiguous moments than to others. A mood which is evocatively 'of
time' may find apt 'words, signs, / Symbols or actions' in which to

snare intimations of mortality with 'other minds', and to demonstrate 'visibly' an interest in other people. But the often remote 'spots' which in one memory function as the 'symbols' of eternity may sometimes constitute a less sharable vision:

> It lies far hidden from the reach of words.
> Points have we all within our souls,
> Where all stand single; this I feel, and make
> Breathings for incommunicable powers. (III. 184–7)

Our concern for each other tends to be more vocal than our awed recognition of the world's indivisibility. So a verbal statement like *The Prelude*, which has to address itself not to mountains who cannot read but to people who can, may be under constant risk of sounding unbalanced.

However, *The Prelude*'s sense of audience is more affectionately specific than this might suggest. In places it is clearly 'the Poem addressed to Coleridge', which is how Dorothy described it in making the first fair copy in 1805.[1] We are probably indebted to Coleridge for the fact that *The Prelude* exists at all. Without his encouragement, Wordsworth might never have had the confidence that his own fascination with such superficially trivial incidents of his past could be shared. He still found the project 'alarming' when it was nearly completed since it was 'a thing unprecedented in Literary history that a man should talk so much about himself'.[2] Yet Coleridge's arguably mistaken view as to precisely what made Wordsworth such a great poet may have lured the poem into some of its more disastrous attempts to assert a clarity and coherence of thought which is quite at odds with the poet's own conflicting intuitions. Wordsworth's genius, according to Coleridge, could best be demonstrated in a work which would reveal him as a 'philosophical Poet', characterized by 'Unity of Interest' and 'Homogeneity', and offering 'a compleat and constant synthesis'.[3] This tells us far more about Coleridge himself, who confessed that he indeed 'ached to behold & know . . . something *one & indivisible*',[4] than about Wordsworth, whose best verse dares to face the impossibility of resolving the incongruities of human response into any comfortably consistent synthesis. Yet Coleridge, on his own admission, nagged Wordsworth with 'urgent & repeated – almost unremitting – requests & remonstrances' to get on with 'A Great work, in which he will sail; on an open Ocean, & a steady wind; unfretted by short

tacks, reefing & hawling & disentangling the ropes.'⁵ In fact many
readers now value the complex 'disentangling' which Wordsworth's
most thoughtfully zigzagging verse pursues, and regret those
relentlessly straightforward passages where he tries to sound as
'unfretted' as Coleridge demands and to assert that all mankind's
disparate emotions really blow us along the same undeviating
course.

   The Prelude is sometimes a 'conversational' poem in the precise
sense that it evokes a dialogue between the natural tendency of its
author and the acknowledged requirements of its addressee. There is,
for instance, the interchange which closes Book VI's account of the
walking tour through the Alps. Here Wordsworth is at first so
willing to follow his own instinct for discrimination that he even tries
to see the human mind's ability to identify with the grandeur of the
Alps as deserving a 'different worship' from that appropriate to the
Alps themselves:

> Not prostrate, overborn, as if the mind
> Itself were nothing, a mean pensioner
> On outward forms, did we in presence stand
> Of that magnificent region. On the front
> Of this whole Song is written that my heart
> Must in such temple needs have offer'd up
> A different worship.   (VI. 666–72)

The Prelude did not, of course, gain its title until after the poet's
death. Wordsworth may already be thinking of the 'Growth of a
Poet's Mind' which was eventually to stand on 'the front' of his poem
as a subtitle. Yet in manuscript B of 1805, the title page offered only
'Poem, Title not yet fixed upon, by William Wordsworth, Addressed
to S. T. Coleridge'. However unconsciously, the poet seems to have
felt that a significantly 'different worship' from that inspired by
mountains might be not so much the generalized maturing of the
human mind as its particular ability to grow into affection for other
people. Certainly the poem here immediately turns away from the
relationship between grandiose landscape and the grandeur of the
intellect which identifies with it. Instead, Wordsworth tries to relate
both of these to the potentially quite different moods in which we
feel 'tender thoughts'. Since Coleridge is not only a tenderly loved
friend but also the examiner of the poem's ideological efforts, this
new juxtaposition leads Wordsworth dutifully to attempt the re-

quired synthesis. He begins confidently enough, but ends up sounding hopelessly bewildered:

> Finally whate'er
> I saw, or heard, or felt, was but a stream
> That flow'd into a kindred stream, a gale
> That help'd me forwards, did administer
> To grandeur and to tenderness, to the one
> Directly, but to tender thoughts by means
> Less often instantaneous in effect;
> Conducted me to these along a path
> Which in the main was more circuitous.
> Oh! most beloved Friend . . .   (672–81)

The Alps' ability to evoke 'Directly' a sense of grandeur seems to
Wordsworth so self-evident as to need no further comment. He
cannot convince himself so easily that his capacity for 'tenderness'
derives from the same source. Two streams of feeling, however
bravely they may claim to flow into each other, are not so 'kindred' as
to have set out from the same point. Coleridge's image of the consistently 'steady wind' pushing in one direction is imperfectly echoed
by the 'gale'. Its turbulent associations may surreptitiously claim the
need of more 'short tacks, reefing & hawling & disentangling the
ropes' than Coleridge would approve. Indeed the causal link between
grandeur and tenderness is so laboriously far from being 'instan-
taneous', so explicitly 'circuitous' that one is bound to be suspicious.
Perhaps, in spite of Coleridge's desire to be shown it, Wordsworth in
all honesty cannot make his poem trace such an unlikely 'path'.

Certainly the very next lines change the subject with a suddenness
which sounds like relief. Wordsworth turns to politics and the re-
volutionary zeal which had been visible in the local population at the
time of his walking tour. However, his stubborn pursuit of candour
soon brings the poem back to the same problematical point. It is as if
he is incapable of leaving even the 'most beloved Friend' under any
comforting illusion that these crucial experiences in the Alps always
encouraged feelings of human love. Wordsworth confesses how
slightly he had been moved when he and Jones saw, on their home-
ward journey, people marching off to risk their lives in defence of
what they presumably took to be the liberty of their families. The
poet himself, being still 'Scarcely of the household then / Of social
life', had been busy enjoying, 'as a bird' or 'as a fish' does, 'the

ever-living Universe' and so took relatively little interest in such
essentially human commitments:

> I look'd upon these things
> As from a distance, heard, and saw, and felt,
> Was touch'd, but with no intimate concern;
> I seem'd to move among them as a bird
> Moves through the air, or as a fish pursues
> Its business, in its proper element;
> I needed not that joy, I did not need
> Such help; the ever-living Universe,
> And independent spirit of pure youth
> Were with me at that season, and delight
> Was in all places spread around my steps
> As constant as the grass upon the fields.   (694–705)

Wordsworth's earlier claim that all he 'saw, or heard, or felt' in the
Alps equally led to 'tender thoughts' is recalled by the verbal echo
only to be discredited. In fact, the closer he had felt to the grandeur of
'the ever-living Universe', the more distantly he 'heard and saw, and
felt' the community spirit of those who actually lived in 'that magnificent region' and the passions which made them willing to face death
in defence of their belief in 'social life'.

His ability to feel at least 'touch'd' had not been helped by moments in which 'delight' seemed as reliably 'constant as the grass
upon the fields'. On the contrary, if any experience on that tour had
led him to care about the fear of death which all men can share and the
need of personal relationship which all men can feel, it is likely to
have been one in which the natural scenery of the Alpine wilderness
had struck him as inhospitable, uncomfortable and perhaps so downright dangerous that he and Jones had felt a nervously conscious need
of each other. One such moment has in fact been described just
before the sequence I have been discussing. Jones and Wordsworth
found themselves misled by the public clocks into leaving the safety
of a town under the illusion that dawn was about to break. In fact it
was still the middle of the night and they were soon 'lost, bewilder'd
among woods immense' and depressed by the sight of Lake Como far
beneath them. Its 'sullen water' seemed to be sinisterly coloured by
the 'dull red image of the moon' moving 'Like an uneasy snake'
(621–38). They dared go no further and resigned themselves to
spending the rest of the night where they were:

                    On the rock we lay
And wish'd to sleep but could not, for the stings
Of insects, which with noise like that of noon
Fill'd all the woods; the cry of unknown birds,
The mountains, more by darkness visible
And their own size, than any outward light,
The breathless wilderness of clouds, the clock
That told with unintelligible voice
The widely-parted hours, the noise of streams
And sometimes rustling motions nigh at hand
Which did not leave us free from personal fear,
And lastly the withdrawing Moon, that set
Before us, while she still was high in heaven,
These were our food, and such a summer's night
Did to that pair of golden days succeed,
With now and then a doze and snatch of sleep,
On Como's Banks, the same delicious Lake.   (641–57)

The lake for two sunlit days, had seemed a delightful image of the 'ever-living Universe', reassuring the 'independent spirit of pure youth' that he is always and everywhere securely linked to 'symbols of Eternity' even when he is in the most depopulated scenery. Yet the same lake can also look so like 'an uneasy snake' that 'rustling motions nigh at hand' impose an essentially 'personal fear'. The same young men who sometimes feel that they are living 'as a bird / Moves through the air' at other moments see each other as the only reassuringly familiar figures in an alien landscape of 'unknown birds' and stinging insects. The same poem whose sense of endlessly recycled energy can pace itself to 'steps / As constant as the grass upon the fields' can elsewhere yearn to tell 'The widely-parted hours' of linear time which must eventually bring all bad experiences, as well as good ones, to an end. The same world from which we seem to breathe all life and joy in moments which make the earth seem heavenly is also a 'breathless wilderness' where Milton's phrase for hell – 'darkness visible' – seems all too appropriate. It is this sense of wonderment at the baffling incongruity of human experience which seems to me the essential Wordsworth. So Coleridge's occasional successes in making *The Prelude* claim that, after all, grandeur and tenderness work in a comprehensibly 'kindred' way, can make some passages of the poem mumble as meretriciously as a ventriloquist's dummy.

II

Wordsworth's own preference often seems to be for a frank admission that some of what he feels cannot be clearly articulated. Book II, for instance, recalls a friendship which predates those with Jones and Coleridge, and confesses that it may make no sense at all to the ordinary reader. Wordsworth remembers that walks taken before morning school were often

> more dear
> For this, that one was by my side, a Friend
> Then passionately lov'd; with heart how full
> Will he peruse these lines, this page, perhaps
> A blank to other men!   (II. 351-5)

The Prelude's frequent references to past or present friends, to Wordsworth's wife and sister, speak to the innately selective tenderness which at once unites and divides us. At such moments, the reader is touched as much by specific intimacies which distance him into an eavesdropper as by the general tendency to personal affection with which he naturally feels at home.

Only Wordsworth and one other person can really know about the early morning walks of that particular friendship. Yet, when Book II, with characteristic inconsistency, moves straight from moments shared with the 'Friend / Then passionately lov'd' to other early morning walks which were enjoyed alone, it becomes only partly more accessible. Most of Wordsworth's readers can presumably remember going for a walk alone, but words which could make the experience of isolation sharable seem in practice almost as hard to find as those which could admit the reading public to the secrets of a private relationship. So Wordsworth still complains about the problems of communication when he recalls leaving the house 'Far earlier' than the time of rendezvous with his friend:

> when the Vale
> Lay quiet in utter solitude.
> How shall I trace the history, where seek
> The origin of what I then have felt?
> Oft in those moments such a holy calm
> Did overspread my soul, that I forgot
> That I had bodily eyes, and what I saw

> Appear'd like something in myself, a dream,
> A prospect in my mind.   (ii. 360–71)

In spite of this passage's enigmatic charm, readers do not seem to count it amongst *The Prelude*'s great 'spots of time'. Their judgement seems to be based on a test which is presumably unconscious since I have never seen it identified in published commentary. Each kind of early morning walk described in the sequence is alive with Wordsworth's struggle against the limits of language, but the two kinds remain firmly separated. There is a clear, chronological division between the excitement of walking with someone 'passionately lov'd' and the 'holy calm' of being abroad early enough to enjoy 'utter solitude'. The most impressive 'spots of time' seem to make their feelings for relationship and for isolation almost simultaneous.

Unquestioning acceptance of a depopulated landscape is only one of the feelings we can bring to such a place. Scenery so approached may allow a rediscovery of silent values. But it inevitably will suppress those feelings which only mankind can express. Book ii's child, unambivalently relishing 'utter solitude', is at that moment still only half-awake. He moves, like a sleepwalker, through a world which resembles his own 'dream'. Like sleep, a wild landscape offers an experience which both opens and closes the mind. The woods, for instance, of Book xi threaten (or promise) to come between a man and much that he would otherwise be feeling; they 'interpose' their 'shades':

> Even as a sleep, betwixt the heart of man,
> And the uneasy world, 'twixt man himself,
> Not seldom, and his own unquiet heart.   (xi. 17–19)

The selective patterns of such a dream certainly derive from only a partial consciousness, but Wordsworth finds it far harder to decide whether their unfamiliar emphases constitute a revelation or a delusion. Do such dream-like moments illuminate the usually hidden truth that 'the heart of man' belongs with that essential quiet which pulses at the heart of nature? Or do they disguise the inevitability of our waking again to those concerns which make the human world 'uneasy' and human emotion 'unquiet'?

The answer of the *Elegiac Stanzas* seems clear enough. Here only the young are ignorant enough to imagine that 'the Poet's dream' should be to pursue 'the soul of truth' in 'silent Nature's breathing life' (*PW*, IV. 258, 13–31). Experience teaches us to confess our often painful need of other people and to reject daydreams:

> Farewell, farewell the heart that lives alone,
> Housed in a dream, at distance from the kind!
> Such happiness, wherever it be known,
> Is to be pitied, for 'tis surely blind.   (*PW*, IV. 260, 53–6).

These lines, however, are almost unique in their decisiveness. Elsewhere, whenever Wordsworth tries to say goodbye to either the natural or the human world, his voice tends to modulate into the ambivalence of an *au revoir*. The Pedlar of *The Ruined Cottage* may once have 'turned away' from the merely human as no more than 'an idle dream that could not live / Where meditation was' (524–5). Yet he still compulsively returns to the 'momentary trance' in which 'human life', and Margaret's devotion to the man 'For whom she suffer'd', do seem to have enduring significance (368–75). Similarly, the child of the *Immortality Ode* may at first seem to be rejecting his true 'glory' as part of the world's 'freshness of a dream', by rehearsing instead his fragmented 'dream of human life' (*PW*, IV. 279, 5, 93); but the *Ode* still ends by accepting the reality of 'the human heart by which we live' and the realism of a vision which 'hath kept watch o'er man's mortality' (197–204).

Dreams, which are emotionally convincing and yet observably incongruous in their reordering of reality, become almost inevitable points of reference for Wordsworth in *The Prelude*. The 'spots of time' juxtapose such conflicting visions that each is defined as partial, and the dreamer is poised between rival insights. For the nine-year-old Wordsworth, spending his first week in Esthwaite, 'its paths, its shores / And brooks, were like a dream' (v. 452–3). The most memorable occasion involves a concentrated focus over long distance in poor visibility:

> Twilight was coming on; yet through the gloom,
> I saw distinctly on the opposite Shore
> A heap of garments, left, as I suppos'd,
> By one who there was bathing; long I watch'd,
> But no one own'd them; meanwhile the calm Lake
> Grew dark, with all the shadows on its breast,
> And now and then, a fish up-leaping, snapp'd
> The breathless stillness.   (v. 459–66)

In the dreaminess of his 'half-infant thoughts' (454), the boy can focus on the singular evidence of an absent human being, or he can concentrate on the natural sound of the fish which seems to confirm 'The breathless stillness' it is interrupting. Either can be seen, even in the thickening dusk, 'distinctly'.

This dichotomy is given a life-or-death significance next morning. The owner of the clothes has been drowned, and the search party is at work with 'grappling irons, and long poles' (469). They bring to light, from the very depths of an unalterably beautiful scene, the anomalously ugly fact of human transience:

> the dead Man, 'mid that beauteous scene
> Of trees, and hills and water, bolt upright
> Rose with his ghastly face;   (470–2)

The landscape's loveliness, which had been dimly sensed through the shadows of the previous evening, is now exposed in daylight vividness. But the preciousness of clumsily vulnerable human bodies has also become more awesomely clear. The abandoned clothes had only been vaguely suggestive. They had seemed hardly worth claiming – 'no one owned them' – and the discrete pun had denied their role as personal belongings. But now 'his ghastly face' defines them as all too visibly personal.

The businesslike adults presumably concentrate on this discovery of a specific human tragedy. But the imaginative boy has seen 'Such sights before' in 'the Forests of Romance'. To him, the corpse is not only a 'shape / Of terror'. It also recalls 'The breathless stillness' which he had noticed in the peaceful twilight. So Wordsworth's 'inner eye' paradoxically 'saw' in the dead man 'A dignity, a smoothness, like the works / Of Grecian Art, and purest Poesy' (480–1). The poet's duty is apparently to both the eternal life asserted by the 'up-leaping fish' and the undeniable mortality pointed by the 'bolt upright' human corpse. His task is to crystallize both into a single 'spot of time'.

But as *The Prelude* complains elsewhere, it is indeed a 'Hard task to analyse a soul, in which'

> each most obvious and particular thought,
> Not in a mystical and idle sense,
> But in the words of reason deeply weigh'd,
> Hath no beginning.   (II. 232–7)

The paradoxical origin of intense emotion is not to be caught in the single-minded vocabulary of those who

> class the cabinet
> Of their sensations, and, in voluble phrase,
> Run through the history and birth of each,
> As of a single independent thing.   (II. 228–31)

'The mind of man', according to Book I, is as elaborately and elusively structured as 'the breath / And harmony of music'. Its 'dark / Invisible workmanship', like the twilight which joins the leaping fish and the bundled clothes, 'reconciles / Discordant elements, and makes them move / In one society' (I. 351–5). Admiration for the landscape's beauty and fear for mankind's vulnerability can both seem moving on the same occasion. So Wordsworth's famous claim that he 'grew up / Foster'd alike by beauty and by fear' (I. 306) is not some Pavlovian response to the delight which his Augustan predecessors took in antithesis. It signals a profoundly thoughtful attempt to expose the dream-like incongruities of those moments which Wordsworth most vividly remembers.

III

The Prelude is often about a child who really does feel scared. The incident which inspires the remarks about 'dark / Invisible workmanship' is literally a cliff-hanger. Trying to reach the eggs in a raven's nest, Wordsworth finds himself clinging precariously to a windswept rock face:

> by knots of grass
> And half-inch fissures of the slippery rock
> But ill sustain'd, and almost, as it seem'd
> Suspended by the blast which blew amain,
> Shouldering the naked crag; Oh! at that time,
> While on the perilous ridge I hung alone,
> With what strange utterance did the loud dry wind
> Blow through my ears! the sky seem'd not a sky
> Of earth, and with what motion mov'd the clouds!
>   (I. 342–50)

To express in words the mental acrobatics which render such a moment exciting, and yet alarming, requires a poetry which is deftly aware of its own limitations. Language can articulate no more, though perhaps no less, than the boy can decipher of the wind's 'strange utterance'. The wind is partly a helping hand by which the boy is 'almost, as it seemed, / Suspended'. Yet it is also 'the blast' which threatens to hurl him to destruction.

The cliff itself is as confusing. It seems to welcome the daring embrace of the boy who is 'Shouldering it'. Yet it also images the natural world as treacherous ground where a human being is 'But ill sustain'd' by 'slippery rock'. The 'naked crag' stands for both intimacy and exposure. The boy hangs essentially and yet ambiguously alone. He is exhilarated by an independence where survival depends only on his own grasp of the landscape's palpabilities. Yet he is alarmed by his isolation from any other human being who might care to rescue him.

Re-enacting the dizziness of this dream or nightmare, Wordsworth can at first say of the sky only that it did not resemble itself. Then the reader's eye is lurched to the beginning of the next line in a kind of vertigo, where even normal skies hurtle to earth, and the motion of the clouds moves only to the inexpressible. Yet Wordsworth wrenches victorious meaning from the very defeat of language. Where words tend to come down on one side or the other, his verse compels them to remain suspended, loyal to an experience of precarious poise, clinging to the complexities of a world which is at once a gloriously infectious energy and a ruthlessly hostile environment.

The passage provides no evidence to support that off-putting account of nature in *The Prelude* which is still offered to so many puzzled schoolchildren. They are invited to imagine a Lake District transformed into some bizarre village policeman who takes the law into his own hands, twisting the young Wordsworth's arm until he accepts authority, and giving him an instructive psychic clout whenever the lad shows disrespect.

The poem in fact builds its effects out of far more credible experiences. Wordsworth seldom seems afraid of some pantheist deity's obscure hunting laws like those imagined by Coleridge's Ancient Mariner.[6] But the boy is sometimes scared, and with good reason, that his pranks may have infuriated some all too real human being. When he has stolen the birds that some other boy has snared (1. 324–32) or the boat that belongs to the Patterdale shepherd (1. 372–427), he is understandably nervous. If the night-time landscape conceals

some human witness, there will be trouble. After his raid on the
snares, he unsurprisingly imagines the sounds of pursuit:

> when the deed was done
> I heard among the solitary hills
> Low breathings coming after me, and sounds
> Of undistinguishable motion, steps
> Almost as silent as the turf they trod. (1. 328–32)

The actual response of the hills themselves seems less predictable.
Natural laws are not usually thought to embrace mankind's (arguably odd) laws of property.

A chicken farmer harassed by a fox, or indeed a shepherd, like
Michael, hastening to save his sheep from a snowstorm, wisely relies
upon his own skills. The rules of the ecological game have not been
rigged so as to protect their property. The countryside probably
accepts a juvenile delinquent with much the same inhuman equanim-
ity that it allows either boy to snare birds in the first place. It permits
the Patterdale shepherd to house his boat fastened 'to a Willow tree
. . . Within a rocky Cave' (1. 374–5), but not presumably because he
seems respectable. The wilderness may be at least as open to a wild
boy as to a law-abiding adult. Its streams, for instance, allow nude
bathing, and Wordsworth remembers the freedom with which afterwards he

> stood alone
> Beneath the sky, as if I had been born
> On Indian Plains, and from my Mother's hut
> Had run abroad in wantonness, to sport,
> A naked Savage, in the thunder shower. (1. 300–4)

Such a neutral landscape is unlikely itself to punish thieves. Yet it
equally has no reason to protect a guilty little boy. At best its 'solitary
hills' may turn out, after all, to be free of enemies. But at worst,
mountains in the middle of the night suggest an alien, unwelcoming
environment. They can image the dark ostracization that may eventually penalize anti-social acts.

When Wordsworth steals the boat, it is his own frenzied rowing
that creates the nightmare of mountains on the move. Like any
oarsman, he takes up a position in the boat which blinds him to where
he is going, and compels him to face his starting-point. As he rows
out from the shoreline, his angle of vision changes, revealing more

and more of the huge cliff which had at first been concealed behind
the lower crags in the foreground:

> from behind that craggy Steep, till then
> The bound of the horizon, a huge Cliff,
> As if with voluntary power instinct,
> Uprear'd its head. I struck, and struck again,
> And growing still in stature, the huge Cliff
> Rose up between me and the stars, and still,
> With measur'd motion, like a living thing,
> Strode after me. (1.405–12)

The mountain's ominous gesture does not announce anything so
simple or so out of character as 'stealing is wrong'. That idea had been
in the boy's mind from the outset, and he had hoped that it would
turn mere fun into delicious drama: 'It was an act of stealth / And
troubled pleasure' (1.388–9). But the massive scale of the scenery
proves intractable. It will not be contained as a fitting background to
a mere escapade.

The boy has also underestimated the range of his own emotions.
The feeling that other people may, after all, matter cannot be suppressed. It comes to life in the mountain's insistently anthropomorphic stride. As a literal fact, the more he tries to flee the scene of the
crime, the larger he makes it loom. This self-inflicted pursuit never
looks like the retaliation of the whole natural world. The cliff actually
obliterates the stars, and the after-effect is blindness to trees and sea
and sky and fields:

> after I had seen
> That spectacle, for many days, my brain
> Work'd with a dim and undetermin'd sense
> Of unknown modes of being; in my thoughts
> There was a darkness, call it solitude,
> Or blank desertion, no familiar shapes
> Of hourly objects, images of trees,
> Of sea or sky, no colours of green fields;
> But huge and mighty Forms that do not live
> Like living men mov'd slowly through my mind
> By day and were the trouble of my dreams. (1.417–27)

What was planned as a titillatingly stealthy act of 'troubled pleasure'
gets the boy into trouble which feels all too real. The nightmare

images to which he is awake by day stalk as relentlessly through his dreaming sleep.

Wordsworth evokes this disturbingly indistinct frame of mind with remarkable precision. The line endings, for instance, are meticulously deployed. William Empson comments on the positioning of 'sense': 'There is a suggestion here from the pause at the end of the line that he had not merely "a feeling of" these unknown modes but something like a new sense which was partly able to apprehend them – a new kind of sensing had appeared in his mind.'[7] Christopher Ricks observes an even greater fertility of implication in the placing of 'live':

> As we move forward through the lines, it seems that they are asserting, and not just intimating, that the huge and mighty forms do not live; then as we reach the next line, we realize that what may be being said is rather that they live but do not live as men live – or is it that they do not live whereas men do . . . the question of whether such mighty forms do not live or whether they do indeed live but not as men live (rather as 'unknown modes of being') is one which his poetry never ceased to revolve.[8]

Yet even such a shrewd and sensitive account as this may omit one of the meanings by which we are trapped into feeling the boy's own restless confusion since the mighty forms may be all too recognizably human – at least sometimes it is 'Like living men' that they 'mov'd'.

The paradox is as much in Wordsworth himself as in the ambiguous world he explores. It is the child's own 'brain' which 'Work'd' to create nightmare, just as it had been his own efforts with the oars which made the cliff appear to rise. The cliff had looked nothing like the outraged Patterdale shepherd, and yet its strides do suggest the 'measur'd motion' of a human being who deliberately keeps pace with every oar stroke which seeks escape. The trees no longer have their 'familiar shapes' nor the fields their green colour. Yet they survive in the child's keen sense of loss. Their 'desertion' echoes in the tramp of the forms that have replaced them. Wordsworth's 'dim and undetermin'd sense' is baffled by a world which increasingly seems to have human values at its centre, and yet in the process seems rapidly to disappear. A mind haunted by 'living men' is banished to a 'solitude' where the stars vanish, and one's grip on even the most familiar 'hourly objects' is loosened.

Hurling out alternative verbalizations, since none seems adequate on its own, Wordsworth invites us to 'call it solitude'. Here solitude is neither the serene isolation of feeling at home among the hills nor the loneliness of missing the people one loves. It is the self-inflicted alienation of a greedy child. In trying to grab the best that both the landscape and people possess, he has deprived himself both 'of grandeur and of tenderness'. His dreams are troubled by conflicting needs which have been equally frustrated.

The casual thief who cares so little about what is personal to somebody else, and the acquisitive tourist who tries to pick the most dramatic feature out of an interlocked landscape, are curiously similar. The selective stance of both is a costly insensitivity. For Wordsworth, the enrichingly creative artist should not be so predatory on either front. But in off-moments he may become so, and dwindle into a mere connoisseur. Elsewhere in *The Prelude*, Wordsworth confesses that his response to a world which does in fact 'overflow/With passion and with life' has often been mean-mindedly 'feeble' (XI. 145–9). He quickly explains that he does not here mean that partial blindness in which he has sometimes been too absorbed in compassion for people to notice the beauty of the landscape. The 'stroke/Of human suffering' is a proper distraction which 'justifies/Remissness and inaptitude of mind' (XI. 149–51). The regrettable moments are those where pride in his own ability to spot an aesthetic bargain diminished the scenery and his own response:

> presumption, even in pleasure pleas'd
> Unworthily, disliking here, and there,
> Liking, by rules of mimic art transferr'd
> To things above all art.   (XI. 152–5)

The modish taste of the times has too often made Wordsworth evaluate 'the life of things' with the deadening intellect of an art critic appraising two-dimensional fragments of landscape:

> giving way
> To a comparison of scene with scene
> Bent overmuch on superficial things,
> Pampering myself with meagre novelties
> Of colour or proportion.   (XI. 157–61)

Such childish egotism reduces the earth to a theatrical game.

We tend, of course, according to a Wordsworthian paradox, not to grow out of, but further into, such childishness. It is the adult tourist's approach to the Alps which, in its self-pampering search for a magical moment, may seem patronizably infantile. It is the adult of *Anecdote for Fathers* who makes the damaging comparison of the present scenery with the past, and tries to teach a destructive curiosity as to which is to be preferred. His son, like the innocent children of the *Ode* and *The Idiot Boy*, is still young enough to demand less and thus find out more. So in *The Prelude* the growing boy who tries to make life more colourful by grabbing the boat just hurries himself into a world of 'no colours'. The attempt to manipulate experience into some neatly proportioned 'act of stealth / And troubled pleasure' merely produces a nightmare where all sense of proportion is lost. Similarly the presumption of trying to extract a sense of achievement from a rival's snare cheats not only others but oneself. It is a delinquent suppression of the boy's own responsiveness to both society and the natural world.

IV

Wordsworth's behaviour seems to have been no more often antisocial than that of any normal child. He admits that his abnormal environment provided such extreme opportunities for 'independent musings . . . That spells seem'd on' him when he was alone (III. 229–32), but he goes on to describe himself as by nature gregarious:

> Yet could I only cleave to solitude
> In lonesome places; if a throng was near
> That way I lean'd by nature; for my heart
> Was social, and lov'd idleness and joy.   (III. 233–6)

In Book II Wordsworth remembers the fun of belonging to a gang of boys who had boat races against each other on Windermere. The children were too content in their friendship to be seriously competitive, and, whatever the result, they ended up resting together in happy exhaustion, 'all pleas'd alike' (II. 65–9). Yet Wordsworth, even here, sometimes felt a restless wish to be apart. After a description which has sounded like an unreserved celebration of communal games, the unexpected comment is: 'And I was taught to feel, perhaps too much, / The self-sufficing power of solitude' (II. 77–8). Later in Book II this conflicting pattern is repeated. The boy, playing with his friends on an island in Windermere, seems absorbed in their shared amusements. These seem relaxedly banal – eating strawberries

and cream, for instance – and the games sound too deafeningly
boisterous to allow for quiet meditations on the beauties of landscape: 'the shouts we sent / Made all the mountains ring' (II. 169–70).
Such wildly active sociability thus produces a grammar which seems
quite opposed to 'wise passiveness'. Yet the day ends with a curious
ritual which allows the group to focus on an image of human isolation.

It is an image to which each child responds alone. So Wordsworth's language loyally moves from first person plural to first
person singular:

> But ere the fall
> Of night, when in our pinnace we return'd
> Over the dusky Lake, and to the beach
> Of some small Island steer'd our course with one,
> The Minstrel of our troop, and left him there,
> And row'd off gently, while he blew his flute
> Alone upon the rock; Oh! then the calm
> And dead still water lay upon my mind
> Even with a weight of pleasure, and the sky
> Never before so beautiful, sank down
> Into my heart, and held me like a dream.   (II. 170–80)

The boy is suspended in a dream which is as ambiguous as that which
hangs him on the cliff face in Book I, or places the drowned man
within the scenery's 'breathless stillness' so as to create a single
'dream of novelty' (v. 466, 453). Now Wordsworth himself seems
almost immersed in the weighty depths of the lake.

Jonathan Bishop perhaps goes too far in saying that the Book II
lines 'place the boy first under the water, then identify him with it;
imaginatively he dissolves into the element that drowns him'.[9] This
does capture one of the implications. But the moment concentrates as
much on an individual human being in all his frailty as on any
tendency to merge with the scenery's strength. The artificial 'music
of humanity' supplied by the flautist, as well as the natural harmony
of the landscape, coincide to trigger the intensity.

The boys have deliberately put themselves at a distance from their
musical friend so as to be moved by the sounds of peculiarly human
isolation. The musician sounds impressively self-reliant, and yet
enacts a poignantly vulnerable role in this stage-managed fantasy of a
castaway. Stressing that the child 'blew his flute / Alone', Wordsworth

extracts from the adjective a potent duality which can sound at once securely independent and touchingly lonely. The dream in which the young Wordsworth need have no more fearful sense of death than that enjoyed by 'the calm / And dead still water' is partly asserted as a revelation and partly admitted to be a consciously contrived manipulation of experience.

In the skating episode, it is Wordsworth's own choreography which enacts not only his social instinct but also intimates the power of solitude. Initially he skates as part of a team, dancing out their shared fantasies:

> We hiss'd along the polish'd ice, in games
> Confederate, imitative of the chace
> And woodland pleasures, the resounding horn,
> The Pack loud bellowing, and the hunted hare.
> So through the darkness and the cold we flew,
> And not a voice was idle; with the din,
> Meanwhile, the precipices rang aloud,
> The leafless trees, and every icy crag
> Tinkled like iron, while the distant hills
> Into the tumult sent an alien sound
> Of melancholy, not unnoticed, while the stars,
> Eastward, were sparkling clear, and in the west
> The orange sky of evening died away.   (1. 461–73)

The landscape's echoes grow into a summons. But Wordsworth is still close enough to his frolicking friends to hear the landscape's invitation as 'alien' and 'melancholy' in its divisiveness. The clumsy double negative of 'not unnoticed' jars us into recognizing that Wordsworth cannot guess how much his friends register the 'distant hills' or the colour of the evening sky. He can speak for all in recalling 'the din' of human voices, but to the extent that any other boy was moving towards 'an alien sound', he too was disappearing into an essentially private experience.

Wordsworth himself sometimes literally withdrew, 'leaving the tumultuous throng' of other skaters so that he could play private games with the landscape. He 'retired / Into a silent bay' (1. 474–5) or joined the patterns of the scenery by trying 'To cut across the image of a star / That gleam'd upon the ice' (1. 476–7). Sometimes the need to cast off from the fellow human beings on whom he had been relying was felt without warning while they were still skating together in formation. Then he would instantly fall back upon nothing but his own physique and the energies of the natural world:

> When we had given our bodies to the wind,
> And all the shadowy banks, on either side,
> Came sweeping through the darkness, spinning still
> The rapid line of motion; then at once
> Have I, reclining back upon my heels,
> Stopp'd short, yet still the solitary Cliffs
> Wheeled by me, even as if the earth had roll'd
> With visible motion her diurnal round;
> Behind me did they stretch in solemn train
> Feebler and feebler, and I stood and watch'd
> Till all was tranquil as a dreamless sleep.   (1. 479–89)

Like Lucy, 'rolled round in earth's diurnal course/With rocks, and stones, and trees', the child discovers his real involvement with a life force that genuinely exists. The optical illusion of a revolving earth evokes a normally invisible truth.

Yet it also deludes the boy into feeling that his personality has already suffered a kind of death. For only in death can a human being really find a 'dreamless sleep' that will last. While he still lives, his dizzying dreams must turn on conflicting centres, 'spinning still' with a need to keep in line with his fellows, and yet 'reclining back' to reach some primal role amongst the forces by which the cliffs are 'Wheeled' and the whole earth 'roll'd'. His destiny is more complex than that of 'The orange sky of evening' which, having 'died away', will after yet another 'diurnal round' be as vividly alive again. Inviting as it seems, the setting sun points a 'melancholy' contrast between those 'symbols of Eternity' with which we can briefly identify, and their 'alien' ignorance both of our mortality, and of the ritual affections with which we strive to make it tolerable.

V

These various kinds of death, both literal and metaphorical, permeate the two incidents which *The Prelude* explicitly labels as 'spots of time'. In one, Wordsworth remembers waiting to be collected at the end of a school term. Leaving his brothers, he took up a position on a high crag so that he could watch both roads on which the horses to take him home might appear. The boy was thirteen. His mother had

died when he was seven. Now, though he could not guess it at the time, he was about to embark upon the holidays during which his father would die. Ignorant of the disaster which would overtake the family only ten days later, the boy waits, poised between the present companionship offered by the wilderness and the human friends whose arrival he awaits:

> 'twas a day
> Stormy, and rough, and wild, and on the grass
> I sate, half-shelter'd by a naked wall;
> Upon my right hand was a single sheep,
> A whistling hawthorn on my left, and there,
> With those Companions at my side, I watch'd,
> Straining my eyes intensely, as the mist
> Gave intermitting prospect of the wood
> And plain beneath.   (XI. 356–64)

When his father dies, the child looks back to the scenery from which he had been partially distracted by 'anxiety of hope' for his family, and by 'desires' which have now been brutally frustrated (XI. 370–5):

> And afterwards, the wind and sleety rain
> And all the business of the elements,
> The single sheep, and the one blasted tree,
> And the bleak music of that old stone wall,
> The noise of wind and water, and the mist
> Which on the line of those two Roads
> Advanced in such indisputable shapes,
> All these were spectacles and sounds to which
> I often would repair and thence would drink,
> As at a fountain;   (XI. 376–85)

The verse pulls in two quite different directions. On the one hand, adopting an isolated stance besides 'The single sheep' and 'the one blasted tree' may be the only escape route from awareness of mortality. Hope and fear can be ridiculously wasteful. So it may be wise to drown the timorous human language, which anticipates the death it fears by clinging so vocally to life. To deafen oneself amongst 'the noise of wood and water' may be to join the grandeur of an indivisible orchestration.

On the other hand, the boy can only feel 'half-shelter'd by a naked wall'. One part of his vision may see his existence as securely centred between the sheep on his right hand and the 'whistling hawthorn' on his left; but another part is looking away, 'Straining . . . eyes intensely' to catch the earliest possible glimpse of people whom he longs to see. To look to their unique preciousness may be to face the pain of separation and even the inevitability of death. Certainly such a point'of view must blind one to most of that surrounding life which is never absent. Yet to be absorbed by all the fascinating 'business of the elements' is to risk missing a rendezvous with those one loves. We cannot feel absolutely attuned to the natural harmony since its undeviating rhythms will never be quickened by an individual's impatience or suddenly halted by his discovery of personal loss. Such movements can seem remorselessly callous as they advance in their 'indisputable' progress. The weather which at first sounds so exhilaratingly 'stormy, and rough, and wild' can seem a chillingly 'bleak music' in its carefree ignorance of all our vulnerable loves.

However, as *Tintern Abbey* insists, that rival 'music of humanity' can itself sound innately 'sad' (*PW*, ii. 261, 91). Secure joy may only be found by those minds which can recognize even in 'sleety rain' the stimulus and sustenance of a world which they would choose to 'drink'. The boy's own mind discovers 'indisputable shapes' in the mist. He feels that they are unquestionably present. What the poetry with fertile indecision does maintain as an open question is whether those shapes are the massive patterns of the living universe or the diminutive outlines of the human figures which the boy's eager anticipation keeps imagining are already in sight. Together both these very different 'spectacles' form that insight into his own conflicting needs 'to which' the boy so 'often would repair' and to which the work of the maturing poet would so compulsively return.

VI

The only other incident which *The Prelude* specifically identifies as a 'spot of time' is also about a child scanning a wild landscape in the hopes of spotting a friend. But the incident is at once more emotionally intense and more intellectually complex. The boy is lost on the moors above Penrith. Searching for the companion from whom he has become separated, he stumbles instead upon the site of an old gallows where a murderer's corpse had been left to rot. In flight, he clambers up to a summit marked by an ancient beacon and sees at a distance a complete stranger. She is perhaps a teenager, for the verse equivocates, calling her at first a 'girl' and then a 'woman'. She is carrying a pitcher of water from some unseen well to some unknown dwelling and passes on, apparently unaware that the panicked child even exists.

The Prelude chooses to explore this moment in the context of Wordsworth's love for Mary Hutchinson who became his wife. After describing his loneliness at Penrith Beacon, he goes on to remember 'the blessed time of early love' when he often revisited the place with both Mary and his sister, 'those two dear Ones, to my heart so dear' (XI. 317). But, even more importantly, he has already paid affectionate homage to Mary before he invites us to understand his feelings as a lost child. Mary's own childhood in the countryside had supposedly taught her not just to cope with but actively enjoy an unpeopled landscape. The sequence begins by praising her for having been 'Nature's inmate' long before she met Wordsworth (XI. 214). But how are we to relate her childhood intimacy with the landscape to her adolescent ability to have a love affair with Wordsworth?

Wordsworth was Mary's almost exact contemporary, having been born only four months before. So *The Prelude* is able to claim that their similar childhoods ensure that they were made for each other. But Mary's approach to the landscape is admired as having been even more consistently undemanding than the poet's own. He pleads guilty to more destructively acquisitive moments: he was 'often greedy in the chace', restlessly moving 'from hill to hill, from rock to rock'. So, 'craving combinations of new forms,/New pleasure', he suppressed his 'inner faculties' (XI. 190–5). Mary, by contrast, 'Was wholly free' from 'critic rules'. She did not let 'barren intermeddling subtleties/Perplex her mind' (XI. 203–5). To borrow the phrasing of *The Tables Turned*, she allowed no 'meddling intellect' to misshape 'the beauteous forms of things' (*PW*, III. 57, 27–8). In fact *The Prelude* asserts that she actually 'conversed with things' (XI. 200). But as Wordsworth spells out the implications of this, he indirectly praises not only the child who is so conversant with the natural world, but the adult lovers who can provide each other with a literal dialogue and make affection audibly reciprocal:

> she was Nature's inmate. Her the birds
> And every flower she met with, could they but
> Have known her, would have lov'd. Methought such charm
> Of sweetness did her presence breathe around

That all the trees, and all the silent hills
And everything she look'd on, should have had
An intimation how she bore herself
Towards them and to all creatures.   (XI. 214–21)

Birds and flowers, unlike people, cannot recognize this special child
and so cannot return her love. Even the poet's own imagination
admits that it can offer only a doting fantasy whose fulfilment would
be conditional upon an impossibility. If they had human powers,
'could they but / Have known her', then they 'would have lov'd'. The
'silent hills' have no vocabulary in which to acknowledge Mary's
unique charm and cannot show the kind of appreciation which the
poet is here verbalizing. Yet Mary herself of course did not open her
mouth to talk to the trees but to 'breathe around' them. So Wordsworth's assertion that the hills should have had some sense of 'how
she bore herself / Towards them' is not a serious rebuke. What they
are offered would only be misunderstood by any attempt to treat it as
the kind of specific affection which people can consciously feel for
each other. Mary herself is not said to have loved but to have 'met
with' the natural world, and it is only her human lover who can
imagine that world responding with love.

What the poetry is about to explore is how far this promiscuous
response 'to all creatures' which both Mary and Wordsworth felt in
childhood can have been a useful preparation for their later commitment to finding happiness with each other in a monogamous
marriage. This question which seems so complex to Wordsworth in
The Prelude is given a startlingly simple answer by Coleridge in *The
Ancient Mariner*. Convinced that even adults must learn to care
equally for 'Both man and bird and beast', the Wedding-Guest
finally turns away from the marriage feast. *The Ancient Mariner*, in
turning its back on the celebration of human love so as to smile upon
'All things both great and small', makes a decisive choice at the very
point where *The Prelude* so endlessly hesitates.

At first *The Prelude*'s praise for Mary's sensitivity to the natural
world may seem to celebrate an undiscriminating stance which can
have little connection with the way in which two people, in
preference to everyone else, fall in love with each other:

She welcom'd what was given, and craved no more.
Whatever scene was present to her eyes,
That was the best, to that she was attuned.   (XI. 207–9)

Puberty, of course, would have led Mary to distinguish the excitement she felt at the place where her lover had agreed to meet her, and
the presumably less impatient, if equally impassioned, welcome she
could give to scenery in which she expected to walk alone. But a man
who loved her would hope that she could still often feel the ubiqui-
tously available joy of the world even though, at such times, he must
resign himself to being of less central importance in her mind, and
even indeed to being, for the moment, wholly forgotten. The Lucy
poems are still arguably love poems even when they rejoice at Lucy's
self-sufficient delight in a natural unity which excludes all thought of
her human lover being uniquely precious. Similarly Lucy herself is
expected to be pleased that *Strange Fits of Passion* sometimes allow
the poet to sleep in the 'sweet dreams' of 'Kind Nature', even though
they make him temporarily forget her existence while he is actually
riding to meet her (*PW*, ii. 29, 17–18). Human love, of course, is more
than such selflessness. It involves two people accepting each other's
selfish need to feel needed. So the Lucy poems also encompass
complaints at being abandoned and anticipate Lucy's own wish to be
reassured that her lover does not always indulge in the kind of
'slumber' which lets his 'spirit seal' itself far from all 'human fears'
(*PW*, ii. 216, 1–8). She is told too that he is often awake to how empty
life would seem 'if Lucy should be dead' (*PW*, ii. 29,28). Yet the
hypothesis of Lucy literally having died is used partly to emphasize
the extent to which lovers do wish each other to have a carefree life.
The last stanza of *Three Years She Grew*, for instance, is not
devoted solely to the grieving 'memory of what has been, / And never
more will be' (*PW*, ii. 216, 41–2). It also celebrates the serenity which
survives even where someone is mourning the loss of the most
beloved person: 'She died, and left to me / This heath, this calm, and
quiet scene' (*PW*, ii. 216, 39–40). When Lucy disappears into her
total identification with 'the calm / Of mute insensate things', she
deprives the poet only of her own presence as an individual (17–18).
She does not take away the 'calm, and quiet' world which he still
audibly lives to enjoy. She may even have left it to him as if it could be
hers to give as some affectionate bequest. Lucy's last wish may
admittedly have been an egotistical hope that her memory would be
cherished by a suffering lover as proof of how much she had been
loved; but it may have been a self-effacing prayer that after her death
he would often forget her in his continuing enjoyment of all that can
never go away.

It is hardly surprising, then, that when Book XI of *The Prelude*
turns from Mary's childhood of all-embracing joy to the poet's own,
it offers a complementary ambivalence. Since the poet's early enthusiasm for 'things' was like his wife-to-be's in its very lack of any
power to choose, it does – and yet does not – explain why his choice
of a marriage partner was so successful:

> I worshipp'd among the depths of things
> As my soul bade me; could I then take part
> In aught but admiration, or be pleased
> With anything but humbleness and love;
> I felt, and nothing else; I did not judge,
> I never thought of judging, with the gift
> Of all this glory fill'd and satisfied.
> And afterwards, when through the gorgeous Alps
> Roaming, I carried with me the same heart: (XI. 234–42)

Was this the same heart that years later was to fall in love with Mary?
Perhaps from the Alps 'admiration' can seem almost synonymous
with a remarkably inclusive usage of the word 'love'. But marriage requires a more selectively defined tenderness which presup-
poses an adult sense of priorities.

So Mary may well have relished the poet's reassuring use of the
past tense when he credits himself with once having had a wholly
undiscriminating capacity for love:

> I lov'd whate'er I saw; nor lightly lov'd,
> But fervently, did never dream of aught
> More grand, more fair, more exquisitely fram'd
> Than those few nooks to which my happy feet
> Were limited. I had not at that time
> Liv'd long enough, nor in the least survived
> The first diviner influence of this world,
> As it appears to unaccustom'd eyes;   (XI. 226–33)

To some extent this has the normal Wordsworthian connotations of
nostalgia. The freshness of his boyish delight is evoked with the
familiar elegiac tone of one mourning a loss. But there is the hint of
something positive in having at last 'survived/The first diviner influence'. The phrasing of 'I had not at that time/Liv'd long enough'
does momentarily suggest a sense of deficency in the childhood idyll,
an awareness of having been incomplete. Wordsworth, who once

never dreamt of anything 'More grand, more fair, more exquisitely fram'd/Than those few nooks to which my happy feet/Were limited', does suggest that his dreams were then indeed limited, that one day he would look for something more.

The uneasiness clearly derives from the context. Whatever he and his wife found sufficient in their separate childhoods would not have remained adequate indefinitely. Their marriage as adults is a tacit claim that they have grown to desire a relationship which more precisely reflects their own individualities. The sense that one particular person is 'more exquisitely fram'd' to one's needs than anyone else can be is obviously the premise on which romantic notions of marriage are based. Equally obviously the girl who consistently felt 'attuned' to everything, and the boy who with even fervour 'loved' whatever he met, had to grow out of their childhood vision before they could accept such a premise. There are in fact two kinds of marriage. The poet, by at first confining this enquiry to the happier moments of childhood, is able to concentrate on only one. He can celebrate the magnificent compatibility between one solitary human being and the landscape which that person inhabits and witnesses. He can attempt another version of the 'spousal verse of this great consummation' proclaiming 'How exquisitely the individual Mind . . . to the external World / Is fitted' (*PW*, v. 4, 56–71). But the disturbing, and yet affectionate, implication creeps in that each child was bound to end up requiring something more, something 'More grand, more fair, more exquisitely fram'd', something like the ordinary human marriage they have found with each other.

For the time being, Book XI offers no view as to how the two marriages interrelate. Instead Wordsworth merely congratulates himself on the survival of his first union with the external world and attributes it wholly to the innate strength of that relationship. There is no hint that its survival has been helped or hindered by his later commitment to Mary. It is not this love affair but the general distractions of 'custom, that prepares such wantonness / As makes the greatest things give way to least' that once threatened to divorce him from nature, and the risk anyway passed because:

> I had felt
> Too forcibly, too early in my life,
> Visitings of imaginative power
> For this to last: I shook the habit off

Entirely and for ever, and again
In Nature's presence stood, as I stand now
A sensitive, and a creative Soul.
There are in our existence spots of time. . . .   (XI. 251–8)

It is an extraordinary sequence, leading as it does to what must be one of the most famous lines of English poetry.

The reference to 'our existence' is the only use of the plural first person pronoun, and there is no hint, even here, that the 'we' is Wordsworth and his wife, rather than the general audience whom Wordsworth means to inform. One is braced for some grotesque egotism on Wordsworth's part. It sounds as if eagerness to relish moments spent alone in the poet's own childhood has cleared his mind of any interest in Mary or the peculiarly human kinds of love which his marriage to her might typify. But this is not to be. After a few generalizations, he offers one specified example of these early 'Visitings of imaginative power', and then baffles himself by trying to relate it explicitly to his later courtship of Mary Hutchinson.

The example constitutes a bold admission that Wordsworth's account of childhood has so far been misleadingly one-sided. He had not always 'fervently' loved whatever he saw, nor felt 'attuned' to 'Whatever scene was present'. The chosen 'spot of time' demonstrates that he had sometimes felt abandoned in a bleakly alien world where all he wanted to find was a particular friend.

When he was five years old, Wordsworth was taken horse-riding by one of his father's servants. On the wild moors above Penrith, the boy accidentally gets separated from 'honest James' whom he likes and trusts (XI. 279–86). Already scared, the child wanders alone until he finds himself in a grisly place:

> where in former times
> A Murderer had been hung in iron chains.
> The Gibbet-mast was moulder'd down, the bones
> And iron case were gone; but on the turf,
> Hard by, soon after that fell deed was wrought
> Some unknown hand had carved the Murderer's name.
> The monumental writing was engraven
> In times long past, and still, from year to year,
> By superstition of the neighbourhood,
> The grass is cleared away; and to this hour
> The letters are all fresh and visible.   (XI. 289–99)

The 'Faltering, and ignorant' child panics on seeing the letters (XI. 300–2). We are not told what name they spell, any more than we are told what was actually inscribed on the Blind London Beggar's 'written paper'. Both impinge with an unspeakable force which could only be betrayed by verbatim repetition of mere words.

The unnamed murderer stands for all outrages against human relationship. As a victim himself, he evokes the horror we feel at the death of any person, however deserved or 'natural' it may seem. The fact that he does have a name stresses the individualism of human beings and the peculiar costliness of their mortality. We care less about the transience of, for instance, the tree which, though once given a new life as a gibbet mast, has now 'moulder'd down'. We are more disturbed by the disappearance of the bones: they once belonged to someone who, like 'honest James' or Wordsworth himself, had a name. But a name, especially the name of a dead stranger, reminds us that the individualistic feelings which we have in common can also separate us. Names distinguish. They are labels by which we identify the one person a lost child needs to find or – at the scene of a hanging – the one person whose ghost he might fear. Our curiosity in a graveyard may prove 'That we have all of us one human heart' (PW, IV. 239, 153). But the questions which we bring to the head stones remain unanswered; the inscriptions often evoke only the exclusiveness of human passion, the privacy of each love or hate, and the inaccessible silence to which all personal life tends.

In flight from the bleak implications of the murderer's epitaph, the child clambers away, up the hillside, to an experience of bewildering intensity:

> forthwith I left the spot
> And, reascending the bare Common, saw
> A naked Pool that lay beneath the hills,
> The Beacon on the summit, and more near,
> A Girl who bore a Pitcher on her head
> And seem'd with difficult steps to force her way
> Against the blowing wind. It was, in truth,
> An ordinary sight; but I should need
> Colours and words that are unknown to man
> To paint the visionary dreariness
> Which, while I look'd all round for my lost Guide,
> Did at that time invest the naked Pool;

The Beacon on the lonely Eminence,
The Woman, and her garments vex'd and toss'd
By the strong wind.   (XI. 302–16)

The beacon's function as a signalling device stresses distance as much as communication. Like the gibbet, it speaks of a vanished past. As an anomalous man-made object on this otherwise intractably 'rough and stony moor', the beacon evokes the absence of people who at some earlier time must have been working on this summit. Then they must have made it seem a less 'lonely Eminence' than it now feels. The present, alarmingly depopulated landscape seems emptier too because of three other figures who flicker tantalizingly at the edge of the child's vision. There is the desired image of the absent James; there is the felt presence of the murderer whose bones may have vanished but whose name is still legible; finally there is the evidence of the 'unknown hand' which, acting on the superstitions of some local community, regularly visits this desolate spot to keep those letters 'fresh and visible'.

So the girl is a stark exception, a person in 'ordinary sight' intruding on a landscape which is otherwise populated only by the phantoms of the child's own miserably creative imagination. She alone exists independent of his fear. Her sheer physicality is stressed by her straining to walk against the wind. She moves into the boy's vision by her own forceful stride, and remains undeniably invested with significance even when the child is consciously looking only for James: 'while I look'd all round for my lost Guide . . . at that time.' The pool's nakedness may have been created largely by the child's own feeling of exposure. But the girl, purposefully making her way against the wind which tosses her clothes, is strikingly tangential to his mood. The child, 'Faltering' and lonely, is confronted by an image of resolution and independence.

But there is no claim that his mood is relieved as the adult poet's is by the Leech-gatherer. Presumably ignored, perhaps not even seen, by the girl, he still searches for his friend. He senses the impressiveness of the girl's appearance in such a place. But he finds it 'visionary' in a way which crystallizes, as much as it qualifies, the 'dreariness' of his own situation. She seems to have – almost enviably – merged with the landscape, appears no more anxious than the mute beacon, no less responsive to the windy world than her own flapping clothes. She evokes the stasis of the view glimpsed in the Simplon Pass, an image of 'tumult and peace'. But here it is a view that fascinates, but cannot wholly dominate, Wordsworth. The child is alone and afraid, unhappy in a way that can only be fully answered by the sight of a known and affectionate face. Even at the age of five, Wordsworth is older than his own Idiot Boy. Where Johnny, alone in the landscape, has no fear and needs no friend, Wordsworth is already aware of his own fragility – an awareness doubtless reinforced by the gibbet's evocation of violence and mortality – and desperately aware of the importance of companionship. To this extent he is more estranged from the landscape than Johnny, and indeed than the girl who seems to feel so much at home here. But if his relationship with the world about him is less satisfying, his ability to enjoy a relationship with another person is far greater. When James and Wordsworth find each other, the rejoicing and relief will be mutual. When Betty Foy finds her son, there can only be a welcome whose one-sidedness defines the gulf between them.

Yet Wordsworth offers no decisive resolution of his paradox. Being terrified of dead murderers evoked by one's own alienated imagination is no fun. Fearing death while surrounded by the One Life is obviously wasteful. Needing the love and concern of another human being does clearly give hostages to fortune.

The girl's seeming acceptance of her situation suggests that she enjoys the contentment with which the poet has earlier credited Mary as a child:

> She welcomed what was given, and craved no more.
> Whatever scene was present to her eyes,
> That was the best, to that she was attuned.   (XI. 207–9)

But of course the girl beneath her distantly glimpsed exterior could have been feeling as lonely as the young Wordsworth, and, as the whole sequence uncomfortably suggests, this would hardly have made her less potentially suitable as the future wife of that unhappily alone little boy. Even the way in which the poetry nudges her to grow from 'A girl' into 'The Woman' hints the complexity of a marriage which seeks to keep both partners in contact with the innocence of their childhood and yet fulfil the more selective and more sexual love of their maturity. The 'naked Pool' whose exposure in line 304 merely typifies the 'bare Common' where the girl is first sighted reappears ten lines later to supply a context which can hint at the separability of 'The Woman, and her garments'. Her clothes are now so 'vex'd and toss'd / By the strong wind' that sometimes they must be forced to mould themselves to the outline of her visibly feminine figure. Even the change from indefinite to definite article may discretely suggest the growth from a child's inclusive acceptance of the sight as just 'A girl' to the man's eventual ability to make a decisive choice as to which person will be for him 'The Woman'.

So it is hardly surprising that the poet's attempt to relate this moment to 'the blessed time of early love' with Mary leaves him baffled by the 'mystery of Man' (XI. 318–30). The 'naked pool and dreary crags' and 'the melancholy Beacon' remain when he returns in his late teens with his beloved sister and his future wife (XI. 321–2). Only that distantly independent girl is missing. Her place is taken by two people whose precious company invests the bleak landscape with 'The spirit of pleasure and youth's golden gleam' (XI. 323). But Wordsworth, with an honesty that leaves him and the alert reader somewhat bewildered, insists that the original sombre scene to which the girl contributed still has a relevant emotional power.

The childhood admiration for the stranger in the landscape and the adult love by which he now means to live are hopefully expressed as mutually reinforcing:

> So feeling comes in aid
> Of feeling, and diversity of strength
> Attends us, if but once we have been strong.   (XI. 326–8)

The hope is tenuous enough. Within a couple of lines Wordsworth admits with magnificent candour 'I am lost'. 'Faltering and ignorant' he may have been searching the horizon for his 'lost Guide' in the very act of being fascinated by someone who seems to need no friends. But now decades later he can make no more sense of what seem to be the conflicting 'hiding-places' of his 'power':

> The days gone by
> Come back upon me from the dawn almost
> Of life: the hiding-places of my power
> Seem open; I approach, and then they close;
> I see by glimpses now; when age comes on,
> May scarcely see at all, and I would give,
> While yet we may, as far as words can give,
> A substance and a life to what I feel: (XI. 334–41)

Wordsworth has difficulty in making sense of his powerful emotions largely because they seem to originate in more than one 'hiding-place'. His imperfect vision already fluctuates between rival insights. Experience is cyclical: the past does 'Come back'. Yet it is also inexorably linear: the daunting future of 'age' inescapably 'comes on'. There is a limit to how far words can reach into such paradoxes, and Wordsworth audibly appeals for our active participation. His shifting pronoun insists that only teamwork can give substance to suggestion: 'I would give / While yet we may'.

By announcing that he is himself 'lost', Wordsworth appeals to the reader's own most searching intellect for the recovery of emotions which are pregnant with contradiction. Some of the emotional groundwork of our life is laid in the 'wise passiveness' of an infant's undiscriminating joy. But we learn also to stand by the selfishly selective generosities of a more actively human love:

> Oh! mystery of Man, from what a depth
> Proceed thy honours! I am lost, but see
> In simple childhood something of the base
> On which thy greatness stands, but this I feel,
> That from thyself it is that thou must give,
> Else never canst receive.   (XI. 329–34)

There is an essential duality at the base of Wordsworth's feelings for Mary. He respects her childlike ability to feel 'attuned' to 'whatever scene was present to her eyes', but he can never wholly forget what he learnt as a lost little boy. So he also needs to give her his love, and to receive the reassurance that she has grown up to feel uniquely attuned to him.

However, the exchange of gifts is not only suggestive of Wordsworth's marriage to Mary. He is also concerned with that other marriage through which landscape must be approached in a sufficiently generous frame of mind if it is not to seem as lifeless as one's mood. A manuscript version of *Dejection: An Ode*, which is perhaps Coleridge's most movingly honest work, reads: 'O Wordsworth! we receive but what we give, / And in our life alone does Nature live.'[10] Coleridge proceeds to argue that if we are alert to the life about us, our joy is like a 'Wedding-garment' which makes the landscape visibly lovable. But a mean-minded approach is like a 'Shroud' which transforms the living universe into 'that inanimate cold world allow'd / To the poor loveless ever-anxious Crowd'. Wordsworth's experiences at Penrith Beacon enact just such a contrast. The morbid imagination of the lost child at first centres the scenery on the gibbet mast even though it has disappeared. Revisited with his future bride, the same landscape is dressed in 'youth's golden gleam' and its glory revealed 'in the blessed time of early love'.

But Wordsworth makes the two experiences pivot on the elusive implications of the unknown 'Woman, and her garments vex'd and toss'd / By the strong wind'. The poet of the Solitaries is able to glimpse images of self-sufficient power not only in the natural world but in some of the more impressive strangers who are seen making their way through it. Such innate strength dwells in a silence beyond the reach of Coleridge's vocal plea that experience is created within the observer's mind. The girl is not to be manipulated by the young Wordsworth's mood any more than she herself can determine the way in which the elementally 'strong wind' hurls itself upon her.

In the spots of time, Wordsworth has little to offer those who seek the decisive lucidity of a singular vision. The relationship between the world and the mind which struggles to comprehend it seems to him essentially ambiguous. Perception is partly composed of subjective visions of dead bogeymen. Yet it can suddenly be confronted by strikingly independent strangers. We may long to feel as unselfconscious and as invulnerable as the blowing wind. But we also yearn for that vivid awareness of mortal individuality which human beings can give each other in 'the blessed time of early love'.

Clearly it is debatable whether 'words can give / A substance and a life' which embraces all the implications of such complex moments. The poet would perhaps 'need / Colours and words that are unknown to man' to recapture a 'visionary dreariness' which he still finds at once inspiring and depressing. Greater clarity might only evade or oversimplify the 'mystery of Man'.

Language can make our experience seem less mysterious than it feels. Words often separate emotions whose contrasting shades together give one moment its colour. Grammar may allocate experience into distinct periods of time, and tenses misrepresent the tension with which memory and anticipation make us strain to understand our present feelings. But Wordsworth's understanding at Penrith Beacon relates his feeling of now being 'lost' not only to his lonely childhood but also to the happiness he later found in courting Mary, and to his fear that in old age he may become too blind to find anything. *The Prelude* enables us to see, if only 'by glimpses', the elaborate interconnectedness of our apparently most distinct emotions. To do so, Wordsworth stretches language beyond its usual limits. In lazy usage, 'I am lost' announces nothing but ignorance. But *The Prelude* expands such simple phrases to bring within our grasp knowledge which normally 'lies far hidden from the reach of words' (III. 185).

THE BURTHEN OF THE MYSTERY

'TINTERN ABBEY', 'SURPRISED BY JOY' AND 'AFTER-THOUGHT'

I

The *Lines Written a Few Miles above Tintern Abbey* are justly famous for offering some of Wordsworth's most powerfully positive rhetoric about the natural world's power to soothe and nourish the human mind. However, the reputation leans heavily on two enormously impressive and yet relatively short passages – the evocation of 'that blessed mood' which enables us to 'see into the life of things' (*PW*, II.260, 37–49) and the description 'Of something far more deeply interfused / Whose dwelling' seems to be equally 'the light of setting suns' and 'in the mind of man' (93–111). Both these climactic sequences have been discussed in earlier chapters, and since together they constitute less than a fifth of *Tintern Abbey*'s 159 lines, I want to emphasize now how *un*confident the poem as a whole seems to me to be. Its own description of its hesitant progress is disarmingly accurate:

> with gleams of half-extinguished thought,
> With many recognitions dim and faint,
> And somewhat of a sad perplexity, (58–60)

The poem admits that its most optimistic assertion may 'Be but a vain belief' (50), and deploys 'perhaps', 'perchance' and 'I would believe' amongst its language of hope (31, 111, 87).

The opening verse-paragraph might, at first glance, be mistaken for a relaxedly affectionate description of the immediate scenery. Yet its tendency is to obscure all visual detail and distinction or even to look away to what is, at the moment, not visible at all:

> Five years have past; five summers, with the length
> Of five long winters! and again I hear
> These waters, rolling from their mountain-springs
> With a soft inland murmur. – Once again

Do I behold these steep and lofty cliffs,
That on a wild secluded scene impress
Thoughts of more deep seclusion; and connect
The landscape with the quiet of the sky.
The day is come when I again repose
Here, under this dark sycamore, and view
These plots of cottage-ground, these orchard-tufts,
Which at this season, with their unripe fruits,
Are clad in one green hue, and lose themselves
'Mid groves and copses. Once again I see
These hedge-rows, hardly hedge-rows, little lines
Of sportive wood run wild: these pastoral farms,
Green to the very door; and wreaths of smoke
Sent up, in silence, from among the trees!
With some uncertain notice, as might seem
Of vagrant dwellers in the houseless woods,
Or of some Hermit's cave, where by his fire
The Hermit sits alone.   (1–22)

'These waters' of the foreground are no sooner acknowledged than they are traced back to 'their mountain-springs'; and then, through the comparison implied by their 'murmur' being an 'inland' one, they are further distanced into that absent ocean whose sounds they so distantly echo. This 'wild secluded scene' seems impressive not because of the degree of seclusion which it actually offers but because its massive rock faces stop the eye travelling too far and leave the mind free to wander beyond them to 'Thoughts of more deep seclusion'. Eventually the paragraph will indeed ramble to its apparently desired conclusion and arrive at that favourite word 'alone', a term given almost tautological emphasis since it comes immediately after the repeated use of the word 'Hermit', which in itself epitomizes an extremist commitment to 'seclusion'.

Throughout, Wordsworth himself is clearly present in the stress he lays on his own senses – 'I hear', 'I behold', 'I . . . view', 'I see'. The point of view is specific in place – 'Here, under this dark sycamore' – and in time – 'Five years have past', 'The day is come when', 'at this season'. The angle of vision might seem so admittedly personal, so static in its claimed 'repose' that one should not be surprised to find Wordsworth overcoming his normal distaste for the terminology of the pictorial arts. He uses 'landscape' here, repeats it at line 24, and is prepared to mention 'The picture of the mind' in line 61. Words-worth's subjectivity of vision in the first paragraph involves so much busily creative redefinition that the associations seem appropriate enough. As the verse nervously wriggles to discipline its image of the world into a profounder 'quiet' which can match the poet's desire for 'repose' and 'seclusion', we can sense the painter's hand manipulating untidy reality into patterned calm. The apparently focused epithets of 'steep and lofty' might suggest that we are to visualize these particular 'cliffs', but the concreteness of that noun is instantly dissolved as the cliffs obliterate the distinction between two unqual-ified abstracts 'and connect / The landscape with the quiet of the sky'. 'These plots of cottage-ground', if left to their own latent suggestive-ness, might evoke the families who live in the houses and work in the gardens to grow their vegetables and flowers. The gardens are, how-ever, immediately transformed into 'these orchard-tufts' so that, before tilled earth can admit what *The Ruined Cottage* calls 'the touch of human hand', it is grassed over. Of course even fruit trees have to be deliberately planted and carefully tended in the British climate, so orchards, though less obviously man-made, could still be distinguish-able from wilder woodland. Wordsworth, however, seems to relish the fact that at this time of year the eye can choose to ignore that distinc-tion. Since the trees 'with their unripe fruits, / Are clad in one green hue', they can seem to 'lose themselves / 'Mid groves and copses'.

The vanishing gardens and orchards are followed by runaway hedges. These are not maintained as the artificially woven boundaries which they must seem to the farmers who regularly cut and lay their growth. Instead they are allowed to unravel into frolicking exten-sions of the untamed woodland: 'These hedge-rows, hardly hedge-rows, little lines / Of sportive wood run wild'. Even the farm houses themselves are merged with the wilderness since they are 'Green to the very door'. The nostalgic tourist of *Tintern Abbey* will not cross that threshold to consider the people who live within. To the story-teller of *Michael* those 'wreaths of smoke' would presumably have suggested the warming hearth where the integration of work and home allows father and son to sit 'by the fire-side' equally prepared:

> to card
> Wood for the Housewife's spindle, or repair
> Some injury done to sickle, flail, or scythe,
>
> (*PW*, II.83, 106–9)

Michael is subtitled 'A Pastoral Poem' and one might expect 'these pastoral farms' to similarly evoke the ways in which 'fields and hills' are the 'occupation and abode' of working families (*PW*, II. 81, 22–6). However, in *Tintern Abbey*'s first paragraph fire, is not used to suggest the communal habits of human society but the deviant isolationism of those who opt out of it. The 'vagrant dwellers' are presumably gipsies, and when writing elsewhere about that secretive tribe Wordsworth cannot decide whether to condemn them for opting into 'Their bed of straw and blanket-walls' because they prefer 'this torpid life' to civilized productivity or to pity them as victims of their 'birth / And breeding'. For whatever cause, they are essentially 'Wild outcasts of society' (*PW*, II. 26–7, 8, 20–8). *Tintern Abbey*'s gipsies suggest that people themselves can 'run wild' as happily as the 'sportive wood' which sounds eager to overrun the line so laboriously drawn between each fruitful field and the barren wilderness. The Hermit prefers his natural 'cave' amongst 'the houseless woods' to any artificial home, even one 'Green to the very door'.

Wordsworth stresses that he is choosing to turn from what he can with certainty observe to imagine tentatively what the distant woods may or may not contain. Yet in spite of the 'uncertain notice', the reader is left in no doubt of the poet's chosen movement away from the ordinary sociability of mankind. The audible effort to rearrange the scene of the first paragraph is sufficiently successful to enact a celebration of the human mind's power to think itself into identification with the natural world. Yet the dexterity required admits that such vision needs to suppress our tendency to be distracted by the things which people have made and cared for. Unlike the Hermit who manages to go on sitting 'alone' and unseen, most of us feel too strong a need of company and of communication to be more than visitors to that 'secluded scene', however intensely we sometimes long for an even 'more deep seclusion'.

The poet himself seems able to escape such ambivalence only in memories of childhood. In describing that time when 'nature . . . was all in all' to him, he can strip even the most intractable words of their tendency to reverberate against the need of human relationship (72–5). The 'lonely streams' to which 'nature led' him as a boy have no connotations of frustrated longings for companionship since he did not then approach them as a person but 'bounded' beside them 'like a roe' (66–70). To his joyfully mindless eyes, to feel 'haunted' is not to be frightened of death but enamoured of life, and to see a wood as 'gloomy' is not to be depressed but invigorated by its profound ability to nourish the appetite which it stimulates:

> I cannot paint
> What then I was. The sounding cataract
> Haunted me like a passion: the tall rock,
> The mountain, and the deep and gloomy wood,
> Their colours and their forms, were then to me
> An appetite; a feeling and a love,
> That had no need of a remoter charm,
> By thought supplied, nor any interest
> Unborrowed from the eye. – That time is past,   (75–83)

The grammar of the sensual past is a 'wise passiveness' – 'The sounding cataract / Haunted me' – and so is quite different from the consciously active senses which dominate the present – 'I hear' (2). The adult poet of the first paragraph cannot afford to resign himself to the impossibility of acting like a painter. He apparently chooses what he will 'behold' and 'view' and 'see' (5, 10, 14). He colours the scenery with 'Thoughts' of that 'more deep seclusion' (7) which may be hidden in the remote centre of the woods, whereas the boy's vision explicitly 'had no need of a remoter charm, / By thought supplied'. He has no interest in what the human mind can conceive beyond its ability to register what the eye sees. He has no more curiosity about the lives of men and women than is felt by the galloping deer with whom he identifies, so he does not need to manipulate the landscape into some demonstrated compatibility with suitably selected examples of human life.

The mature poet, by contrast, forces himself out of the cautious rearrangements of *Tintern Abbey*'s first paragraph and confronts far less tractable aspects of humanity – 'the din / Of towns and cities', for instance (25–6). Yet the poem's stance towards people and their need to care for one another remains unsettled. No sooner has *Tintern Abbey* praised 'acts / Of kindness and of love' as the 'best portion good man's life' than it hastens on to offer a much fuller celebration of what sounds like a withdrawal from the anxieties of the social world:

> that blessed mood
> In which the burthen of the mystery,

> In which the heavy and the weary weight
> Of all this unintelligible world,
> Is lightened: (35–9)

In this 'serene and blessed mood', released from the effort of trying to understand each other, we are alerted to the larger reality that lies about us:

> we are laid asleep
> In body, and become a living soul:
> While with an eye made quiet by the power
> Of harmony, and the deep power of joy,
> We see into the life of things.   (45–9)

The soothingly unified life of things intrudes a comparison which can make recognition of individual human lives seem of debatable value.

At best, people too can merge their voices into one. But the needs they have in common attune them to sadness rather than joy. So their harmony is not soporific, but sobering:

> The still sad music of humanity,
> Nor harsh nor grating, though of ample power
> To chasten and subdue.   (91–3)

Here too, although Wordsworth confesses to 'hearing oftentimes' the touching sounds of peculiarly human experience, they cannot keep his undivided attention. In such a context, he may at first feel that the 'joy' of the larger world is almost an intruder – 'A presence that disturbs' – but he is soon concentrating wholly on all that in truth can never go away, however often we may be distracted into not noticing it:

> a spirit, that impels
> All thinking things, all objects of all thought,
> And rolls through all things.   (100–2)

The 'music of humanity' cannot always sound in tune with such harmony. So *Tintern Abbey* hears also the fragmented sound of people who have separated into discordant egotisms: 'the sneers of selfish men' (129). Speech can degenerate into a meaningless noise which defines only our isolation: 'greetings where no kindness is' (130). Sometimes 'The dreary intercourse of daily life' merely confirms the alienation of human communities where all live in their own 'lonely rooms' (131, 25).

Such generalizations are bound to undervalue the singular intensity with which one person can care about another, and *Tintern Abbey* goes on to close as a love poem to Wordsworth's sister, Dorothy. So tentatively fluctuating a poem can offer only the most inconclusive conclusion, and it finally gestures towards a future which remains frustratingly opaque. Its last paragraph is an ambivalent 'prayer' about Dorothy's 'after years'. On the one hand, Wordsworth hopes that she will remember the extreme claims he now makes:

> that Nature never did betray
> The heart that loved her; 'tis her privilege,
> Through all the years of this our life, to lead
> From joy to joy: (122–5)

He offers his sister a sweeping faith 'that all which we behold / Is full of blessings' (133–4). The fact that sometimes people desperately need each other's 'acts of kindness and of love' could obviously be a distraction from such a vision. So Wordsworth prescribes an invigorating isolation:

> Therefore let the moon
> Shine on thee in thy solitary walk;
> And let the misty mountain-winds be free
> To blow against thee: (134–7)

The grammar seems to recommend an undemanding passivity. Perhaps Dorothy is meant to seek the comfort which Michael found:

> alone
> Amid the heart of many thousand mists,
> That came to him, and left him, on the heights.
> (*PW*, ii. 82, 58–60)

She could even try to imitate the Idiot Boy's mindlessly open-minded journey into the moonlight.

But *Tintern Abbey* is not addressed to a child, let alone a retarded one whose mental growth has ceased. Dorothy has already grown up and is doomed to grow old. Her brother knows that the 'wild ecstacies' which he wishes on her must eventually be, at best, 'matured / Into a sober pleasure' (137–9).

So the poem also anticipates a far less promising old age. The energetic independence of a 'solitary walk' through a beautifully interdependent world may dwindle into an enfeebling loneliness. Being alone can initiate a series of peculiarly human vulnerabilities: 'Solitude, or fear . . . or grief' (143). Wordsworth could die before Dorothy. Then she might not find enough consolation in her own love for the natural world. She might also need to remember that she had herself been loved by a fellow human being. She might have to depend on memories of happier times when Wordsworth demonstrably needed to hear her 'voice', and to see her 'wild eyes' (147–8). If so, he insists that she must recall not only his exhortations about landscape but also the man who made them (145–6). She must remember that he cherished 'these steep woods and lofty cliffs', not just 'for themselves', but also for the sake of the sister he loved (157–9).

The poem so candidly confuses itself that one is not surprised by its ability to confuse others. The Duke of Argyll records being embarrassed by hearing Wordsworth read *Tintern Abbey* aloud.[1] This was in 1848, fifty years after the work had been composed. At first all went well. For most of the recital, Wordsworth's 'fervour and almost passion of delivery' sounded 'beautiful'. But he pronounced the vocatives of the last paragraph with a climactic intensity which was too much for the Duke: 'The strong emphasis . . . struck me as almost unnatural at the time – "My dear *dear* friend" ran the words, – "in thy wild eyes".' The Duke seems to have initially misunderstood, and thought that the 'words addressed personally' invoked no more than some imaginary companion. When he was later told that the addressee was Dorothy, all seemed clear. He had just met Wordsworth's aged sister and had been shocked. The years had reduced her to a helplessly decrepit body and an inaccessibly senile mind: 'Her condition accounted for the fervour with which the old poet read the lines which reminded him of better days . . . the vacant silly stare which we had seen in the morning was from the "wild eyes" of 1798.' The Duke thus assumed that Wordsworth's passionate reading was directed, not to this 'old paralytic and *doited* woman', but to a wholly different Dorothy remembered from 'better days'. Wordsworth was supposedly trying to escape the bitter fact of the present by an incantatory chant which might carry him safely away into a regressive fantasy. But was the Duke right? To Wordsworth, his sister's state of mind in old age may have seemed too opaque to justify such a single-minded retreat. The poem to which he was returning had, after all, offered more than one guess as to how Dorothy might feel in her 'after years'.

On the one hand, it had anticipated the Duke's assumption. Perhaps Dorothy really was trapped, somewhere behind those vacant eyes, into a 'Solitude' which imposed 'fear, or pain, or grief', and which prevented any serene identification with moon and wind. On the other hand, the poem offered Wordsworth the, hope that Dorothy inhabited a quite different kind of isolation. What from the outside looks like a gradual fading of life may be experienced by the person inside the trance as the dawning of emotional rebirth:

> Until the breath of this corporeal frame
> And even the motion of our human blood
> Almost suspended, we are laid asleep
> In body and become a living soul: (43–6)

Apparent paralysis may in fact be a movement towards inner energies. The mask of senile decay can seem like brain death, but behind it the mind may be recovering its primal liveliness in a secret second childhood.

We pity those who can no longer speak to clear distinctions between their minds and the world they experience. We mourn their lost ability to define each object as a firmly separated noun. But they may be privately enjoying

>   a sense sublime
> Of something far more deeply interfused,
> Whose dwelling is the light of setting suns,
> And the round ocean and the living air,
> And the blue sky, and in the mind of man: (95–9)

They may have journeyed beyond the reach of our language. But they may have arrived where they can feel a secure part of the 'motion . . . that impels / All thinking things, all objects of all thoughts' (100–1). So Dorothy might sometimes be enjoying her world as happily, if as undemonstratively, as the Idiot Boy.

Such hopes, as well as the fears surmised by the Duke, may have led Wordsworth back to the aptly ambiguous prayer of *Tintern Abbey*. Ideally, Dorothy should be able to feel as untroubled as moonlight and mountain winds. But if instead she still felt pain, then he could only hope that she would remember how much he loved her. Either plea could be equally appropriate because she was now stranded on the far side of silence. The one certainly fulfilled hypothesis of *Tintern Abbey* was the loss of communication:

> If I should be where I no more can hear
> Thy voice, nor catch from thy wild eyes these gleams
> Of past existence (147–9)

Dorothy was, in *The Prelude*'s terms, at one of those 'Points . . . within our souls,/Where all stand single', and might remain 'far hidden from the reach of words' (III. 185–7). Fifty years after he had written *Tintern Abbey*, Wordsworth felt bound to recite his love, and his respect, for someone who could give no sign that they were understood.

Even if she noticed its existence, would Wordsworth's love matter to Dorothy? Confusingly, the hypothesis that it would seem relatively unimportant to her could have struck Wordsworth as the more cheering answer. If Dorothy was unaware of other people's concern, she might feel also numb to pain. Her mind might be absorbed in an unselfconscious intimacy with its own experience. It could be enjoying that totality of relationship in which the winds define themselves against the mountains and the moon expresses itself as light. Only an uncomfortably conscious sense of isolation could force Dorothy to feel in real need of her brother's love.

The eventual appropriateness of these lines which Wordsworth had written so long ago is not some freakishly isolated coincidence. His greatest early verse is often as much about the helplessness of adult loneliness as the self-sufficiency of childlike joy. He had, for instance, in the same year that he wrote *Tintern Abbey*, completed both *The Ruined Cottage* and *The Idiot Boy*. In one a proud husband will not, and in the other a happy child cannot, recognize how much they are loved. Yet the people whom they unwittingly abandon to grief do not want the wanderers to suffer any of that anxious sense of isolation which they have imposed. The Duke of Argyll might have been asked to endure a far lengthier recital which could still have sounded touchingly relevant to the old poet's own puzzled affection.

II

In a self-defeating attack on Wordsworth, A. P. Rossiter rashly quotes the Duke's anecdote and then complains:

> I do not see how anyone who *thinks* about Nature can have any faith in the famous lines:

Knowing that Nature never did betray
The heart that loved her; 'tis her privilege
Through all the years of this our life, to lead
From joy to joy.

. . . Dorothy became a paralytic imbecile: Nature only led from
joy to joy if we accept Meredith's bitter lines in *Modern Love*:

If any state is enviable on earth,
'Tis yon born idiot's, who, as the days go by
Still rubs his hands before him, like a fly
In a queer sort of meditative mirth.

And although Wordsworth sedulously revised *The Prelude*, no
line of his to Nature ever touched the notes of

No, no, no life!
Why should a dog, a horse, a rat have life,
And thou no breath at all? Thou'lt come no more,
Never, never, never, never, never.

That is a statement about Nature, if we *think*;[2]

Rossiter hopes to make Wordsworth sound silly. But in fact both the
range and depth of Wordsworth's achievement is pointed by each of
the four works cited.

Tintern Abbey is itself shrewdly sceptical of what may turn out to
be only 'a vain belief'. It fears that in her 'after years' Dorothy may
not be able to keep to the 'solitary walk' laid out by the inviting
patterns of the landscape. She may instead be pushed into 'fear, or
pain, or grief'. Elsewhere Wordsworth explicitly says that it could be
only by a 'special privilege' which is not in fact granted to human
beings that someone could grow older without becoming a

partner in the years
That bear us forward to distress and guilt,
Pain and abasement,   (*The Prelude*, VII. 403–5)

Tintern Abbey as a whole manages more faith in the natural world's
privileged power to lead from joy to joy than in our ability to follow.
Wordsworth's verse also attempts a full exploration of the
challenge which in Meredith's lines remains merely a glib gesture.
Rossiter ignores the very existence of *The Idiot Boy*. Yet that poem is
arguably centred on the idea that uninterrupted joy may be available

only to those whose brains have been damaged into 'a queer sort of meditative mirth'. Elsewhere, Wordsworth probes the issue from thoughtfully varied points of view. Most of his characters, unlike Johnny, who is indeed simply a 'born Idiot', have grown up. They have discovered peculiarly human needs and vulnerabilities, both in themselves and in others. However, each seems able at some stage to again be freed from, or deprived of, such awareness. Margaret in *The Ruined Cottage* can retreat, but only sometimes, into 'The careless stillness which a thinking mind / Gives to an idle matter' (382–3). Approached one way, Michael's misfortunes do seem likely 'to overset the brain' (450). The Old Man Travelling looks, but does not sound, 'insensibly subdued to settled quiet' (7–8). Complex questions of response are raised by *The Prelude* Beggar's 'fixed face and sightless eyes' (VII. 621). We can be sure of only a 'half-absence' in the Discharg'd Soldier's 'tone / Of weakness and indifference' (IV. 475–6). We wonder how far the Leech-gatherer's good humour depends on a consciousness which is now 'not all alive, nor dead / Nor all asleep in his extreme old age' (64–5).

Rossiter seems to discover an admirably bitter realism in Meredith's image of the fly. But the idea that peace is only bought at the cost of all that makes us human is not evaded by Wordsworth. It is confronted in detail and in depth. The narrator of *The Ruined Cottage*, for instance, at first seems endearingly human in his clumsy battle with the flies buzzing around his head. Yet his friend, who finds ways of positively enjoying 'this multitude of flies' and of feeling comfortably at home with their 'happy melody', is no fool. The flies, after all, are an inescapable part of the place where both men stand. Similarly, in *The Prelude* Book VI, it is only human of Wordsworth and Jones to regard 'the noise' and 'stings of insects' as disturbingly alien so long as the two friends feel 'personal fear' at being 'lost, bewilder'd' in an apparently dangerous wilderness. Yet, less than a hundred lines earlier, Wordsworth has convincingly shown that the same kind of terrain has such a 'lovely countenance' when seen in the different light of day that man can so far forget his nervous humanity as to feel ecstatically 'lost . . . without a struggle to break through', content to accept even 'winds, bewilder'd' as reassuring 'symbols of Eternity' (617–57, 525–72).

Much of Wordsworth's verse searches for answers to the question which Rossiter praises both Meredith and Shakespeare's Lear for merely raising. Wordsworth often asks how far people are naturally led to identify with the other forms of life which constitute our world – 'a fly', 'a dog', 'a horse', 'a rat' – and how far we are instead bound to feel distinctly, even aggressively, different. We approach Margaret's past in the context of animals who at present enjoy the ruins of her home (108–16). We watch Michael's obsession with his son in the light of a more rewarding, if less accessibly familiar, love for sheep, and for all that they require and represent. Both the serious challenge and the comic charm of *The Idiot Boy* derive partly from the hazy distinction between Johnny and his pony. The Old Man Travelling and the Cumberland Beggar are confusingly like the small birds about their feet. The Leech-gatherer is disturbingly compared to a sea-creature. In 'The Discharg'd Soldier' Wordsworth's own comfortably dehumanized mood, with its 'consciousness of animal delight', is at once destroyed, and yet perhaps retrospectively validated, by the meeting. *Tintern Abbey* itself explicitly tries to relate the 'glad animal movements' of an unthinking childhood to conscious fears of old age (74). *The Prelude* insists not only on our suppressed affinities with other creatures, but also on our ultimately irrepressible feeling that people matter more. The drowned man's clothes visibly belong to the same twilight world as the leaping fish. But the lake where a fish swims in its element can be either a stimulating delight or a fatal disaster to a human being, and perhaps rather more readers have felt it appropriate to refer to this 'spot of time' as 'the drowned man' rather than 'the leaping fish' (*The Prelude*, v.450–81). Yet, as one *Prelude* manuscript points out, 'the fish that moves / And lives as in an element of death' is an intriguing example of 'Nature's unfathomable works.' It is only the 'refin'd astonishment' of the human mind which can appreciate, in a 'spirit of thoughtful wonder', the baffling variety of ways in which so many species play their parts within the drama of one living world (*The Prelude*, p. 572, 40–7).

The flute player whom the boys leave alone on the island demonstrates that people themselves are ultimately confined to needing solid ground beneath their feet. Yet the music submerges Wordsworth's thoughts, 'Even with a weight of pleasure', into the lake's 'dead still water' (II. 170–80). The boy who perches precariously on the cliff is excitingly close to the raven whose nest he means to reach. But, unlike the bird, he can never feel completely above either his own fear of death or his feeling that he is 'alone' and far from the help of other people (I.333–50). The attempt to seize not just eggs but actual birds by raiding another boy's snare produces a similarly partial escape from humanity. He sees the birds partly as a fox might: they are simply his 'prey' (I. 328). But the 'sounds/Of indistinguishable motion' by which he is then pursued are too vague to suggest only an instinctual fear of rival predators. They also image a guilty anticipation of disapproval and the loss of friends (I. 322–32).

Wordsworth may have enjoyed a sense of animal cunning in the 'stealth' with which he steals the boat, and does indeed enjoy identifying with a vessel which goes 'heaving through the water like a Swan'. But the boy can take only a consciously 'troubled pleasure' on such waters, and soon feels out of his depth. His imaginative mind works to create 'living men' who move far too alarmingly to be mistaken for swans sailing on in elegant mindlessness (*The Prelude*, I. 372–427). Skating invigorates the boy until he feels like an 'untired horse', and the friends who skate together deliberately fantasize that they have become a pack of hounds. But then they relax and instinctually glide like birds who have 'given' their 'bodies to the wind'. Only in such a moment can the boy feel fully convinced that his life is as 'tranquil' as the 'dreamless sleep' which animals can enjoy (I. 452–89). Wordsworth's hopes at the end of the school term are dependent on 'the expected steeds', and he feels 'impatient for the sight/Of those two Horses which should bear us home'. Yet both the hopes and the subsequent shock of a parent's death are peculiarly human. Neither the sheep at Wordsworth's side nor the horse he awaits can look forward so excitedly over a long distance, nor experience such disappointment (XI. 346–89).

At the start of the Penrith Beacon episode, Wordsworth and James are essentially 'a pair of Horsemen'. A centaur-like identification with the horse's movements, rather than any detached sense of skill, must have been felt by a child who 'scarcely . . . could hold a bridle'. But once separated from his friend, the boy finds that sitting on a horse only adds to his sense of alienated insecurity:

> Disjoined . . . from my Comrade, and, through fear
> Dismounting, down the rough and stony Moor
> I led my Horse, and stumbling on, at length
> Came to a bottom, where in former times
> A Murderer had been hung in iron chains.   (XI. 286–90)

The sentence staggers, clause by clause, down to its disturbing conclusion, just as the boy descends, thought by thought, from fear to morbid panic. The mistrust of his horse is not balanced by confidence in himself. When the horse which cannot be trusted to carry him back to James has to be 'led' by the 'stumbling boy', we sense the helplessness of the blind leading the blind.

Yet the boy is already sufficiently knowledgeable to see uncomfortably more than his horse can. He recognizes the implications of an ugly past in the site of the gallows, and discovers in himself peculiarly human longings. It is not to an animal, or even to an unnamed stranger who happens to be passing through the same landscape, that people look in their darkest moments. At such times the human need is for a known friend like 'honest James'. To a newborn baby, emotional life may seem to be nourished equally and inseparably by both his mother and by all other forms of life as 'One beloved Presence' (II. 250–60). But even a young child is under pressure to see himself as separate from his world, to value other people for reasons which make *homo sapiens* an anomaly in the universe, and to care for them in ways which can make even a populated scene echo hollowly to one particular absence.

However, the innocence of the newborn is never wholly abandoned by the maturing consciousness. Intelligence, which is so tangled with the powers of memory, can make the primal intensities 'come back . . . from the dawn almost / Of life' (XI. 335–6). So an endlessly unresolved 'diversity of strength' constitutes the 'mystery of Man' (XI. 327–9): a need to explore quite different, if equally elusive, kinds of experience.

III

In his final quotation, Rossiter cites *King Lear*, and its tragic juxtaposition of animals and human beings. Vividly aware of the difference in their preciousness, the verse rages at the similarity of their ultimate fates. But the quoted lines voice what is Lear's, rather than Shakespeare's, touchingly blind alley of a merely rhetorical question. It is a suddenly shattered old man who wails at his daughter's corpse:

> Why should a dog, a horse, a rat have life,
> And thou no breath at all? Thou'lt come no more,
> Never, never, never, never, never.   (v. iii. 306–8)

Wordsworth too can evoke the intolerable transitoriness of individual life, and the reiterated negation in which it ends for those who feel as bereaved as Lear. To Margaret of *The Ruined Cottage* 'never' can sound like an almost unendurably apt term:

> My tears
> Have flowed as if my body were not such
> As others are, and I could never die.   (355–7)

Perhaps closer to Lear's pained certainties are those moments when Michael 'never lifted up a single stone', and so acknowledged that his son would come no more. Even *The Idiot Boy* finds room amongst its jokes for the tragi-comic bluntness with which a distraught parent is unhelpfully reminded that her son 'may perhaps be drowned/Or lost perhaps and never found' (II.173, 179–80).

Wordsworth does pause to concentrate on the intensity of pain to which Lear speaks. But the shifting enquiry of Wordsworth's best verse advances on far more fronts. He himself had to endure the loss of a favourite daughter. But the year before she died, his poetry had positively celebrated her ability to live the unthinking life which is enjoyed by animals: 'Light are her sallies as the tripping fawn's/Forth-startled from the fern where she lay couched' (*Characteristics of a Child Three Years Old*, PW, I.229, 15–16). Catherine is still young enough to escape the self-consciousness which distinguishes human beings from the other forms of life which comprise our world. Her games are 'Unthought-of, unexpected, as the stir/Of the soft breeze ruffling the meadow-flowers' (17–18). Her flirtation with language has not advanced beyond the innocence of 'involuntary songs' (14). So she reacts not only as spontaneously but also as independently as a wild animal. Love cannot mean to her all that it means to an adult: 'Loving she is, and tractable, though wild' (1). Conscious needs of relationship have not yet tamed her into feeling dependent. In her self-reliant liberty she cannot conceive of isolation as loneliness:

> this happy Creature of herself
> Is all-sufficient; solitude to her
> Is blithe society,   (11–13)

So, 'when both young and old sit gathered round/And take delight' in watching her, she plays just as she would when 'unattended and alone' (8–10). Wordsworth loves this animal-like freedom from self-consciousness, although it effectively allows his daughter to ignore him. He himself is not permanently imprisoned in the intellectual detachment of maturity. He can often identify with her. He can recover enough of the joy he had learnt in his own childhood to share something of her experience.

Within a year of the poem's completion, Catherine died. Wordsworth was left to fluctuate between the mercies of forgetfulness and those moments when memory made a surprise attack under the cover of unexpected happiness:

> Surprised by joy – impatient as the Wind
> I turned to share the transport – Oh! with whom
> But Thee, deep buried in the silent tomb,
> That spot which no vicissitude can find?
> Love, faithful love, recalled thee to my mind –
> But how could I forget thee? Through what power
> Even for the least division of an hour,
> Have I been so beguiled as to be blind
> To my most grievous loss! That thought's return
> Was the worst pang that sorrow ever bore,
> Save one, one only, when I stood forlorn,
> Knowing my heart's best treasure was no more;
> That neither present time, nor years unborn
> Could to my sight that heavenly face restore.   (PW, III. 16)

This does touch the note of Lear's anguish. The insight which only human intelligence can gain is bitterly exposed as a knowledge of 'grievous loss' which only human love can suffer.

But 'Surprised by Joy' is more than this. It is not only about the ugly truth that we shall be separated from each other. Its starting point is that beautiful common sense through which, often as children and too rarely as adults, we notice that we are not separate from our world.

Wordsworth can still be moved to feel the elemental excitement of the earth. He can still occasionally be surprised into responding 'as the Wind'. At such moments he experiences the seemingly irrepressible spontaneity of the child: 'Unthought-of, unexpected, as the stir / Of the soft breeze' (PW, I. 229, 17–18). So his bewilderment that he has ever been able to forget her death is partly answered by the earlier poem. He delighted in Catherine's life because she was able to disregard all that can make an adult feel 'grievous loss'. She had been his 'Heart's best treasure' largely because of an endearing and inspiring independence. She herself had no vulnerable sense of the preciousness and precariousness of those on whom her happiness depended. The joy by which Wordsworth can even now feel surprised is partly of this kind.

But Wordsworth, as an adult, sometimes needs to share experience. As poet and as lover he longs to hear in someone else's response the proof that his feelings are understood. So 'Love, faithful love', even before the tragedy of Catherine's death, had been for him essentially different from any 'Loving' known by a three-year-old who had been still sufficiently 'wild' to feel 'of herself . . . all-sufficient' (PW, I. 229, 11–12). Affection, for an adult, is bound to infringe liberty. Joy which is partly dependent on being shared implies an acceptance of vulnerability. At moments it must nervously anticipate the inevitable separation to which all mortal relationships move. It cannot always 'be blind' to the possibility of 'grievous loss'.

In the graveyard of To a Sexton Wordsworth sees a bleak image of the only lasting unity which families, in spite of all their efforts, can achieve. 'Father, sister, friend, and brother' ultimately share only the common ground of being buried as 'Neighbours in mortality' (PW, II. 134, 8, 28). The poet himself, though he is writing in 1799 before he is even married, can anticipate the pain he may have to endure as a widower before fate will 'Let one grave hold the Loved and Lover' (32). Here a father must acknowledge that, even if his tender-hearted stamina has been such that he has for 'twenty years tended' his 'sickly daughter', the only absolute way for her to be 'defended' from 'weakness' and 'pain' is for her to lie in the graveyard where he will eventually join her (14–17). The deaths which gradually dismantle a man's 'whole fire-side' of loved dependants are ironically reuniting them in a more permanently shared place – 'eight feet square' of cold ground (9–12). Yet even this chilling intimacy is not always safe from disturbance since the poem's protest is against a sexton whose insensitive digging is even now muddling up the bones of different families.

The poet, unlike the rebuked sexton, may piously wish to know more about the particular feelings which made each group of long dead people choose to be buried here side by side. But in fact he can make only a general surmise based on what seem to be primal affections in 'the heart of man', the perennial causes of 'his tears', 'his hopes', 'his fears' (21–2). When Wordsworth himself is faced by the death of his own son and daughter within a single year, he writes a poem addressed by name to the only person who could fully understand his own desperate need of 'solace' as he could understand hers, the 'Beloved Wife' whose own 'tender heart' is having to endure precisely the same 'lamentable change' (*PW*, III. 281–3, 2, 22, 63–4). It is only for William and Mary that the loss of Catherine and Thomas proves so conclusively:

> How nearly joy and sorrow are allied!
> For us the stream of fiction ceased to flow,
> For us the voice of melody was mute.   (22–4)

If the mind which focuses on such private and precarious relationships is carried inexorably towards bereavement, we are bound sometimes to look beyond one chosen 'partner in the years / That bear us forward to distress' (*The Prelude*, VII. 403–4). If happiness in human love can at the cruellest moments seem no more than 'a stream of fiction', we inevitably try to identify instead with a world whose real rivers can never be stilled into silence but will always run round a painless cycle 'Of first and last, and midst, and without end' (*The Prelude*, VI. 572).

In *After-Thought* Wordsworth explores his ambivalent response to the River Duddon in the light of the fact that people, unlike rivers, move irreversibly 'towards the silent tomb' which in 'Surprised by Joy' had engulfed Catherine. Walking out of the Duddon valley, Wordsworth has the momentary illusion that the river has come to an end merely because he has turned his back on it. But he turns to see that the natural world offers us a more permanent partnership than people can provide. So he addresses the river in a tone whose tender vocatives significantly echo his cry to Catherine:

> I thought of Thee, my partner and my guide,
> As being past away. – Vain sympathies!
> For, backward, Duddon! as I cast my eyes,
> I see what was, and is, and will abide;
> Still glides the Stream, and shall for ever glide;
> The Form remains, the Function never dies;
> While we, the brave, the mighty, and the wise,
> We Men, who in our morn of youth defied
> The elements, must vanish; – be it so!
> Enough, if something from our hands have power
> To live, and act, and serve the future hour;
> And if, as toward the silent tomb we go,
> Through love, through hope, and faith's transcendent dower,
> We feel that we are greater than we know.   (*PW*, III. 261)

Like so many of Wordsworth's more thoughtful poems, this is far more than either an elegy for human transience or a celebration of the world's immortal energies. Because *After-Thought* is about both, it transcends the simplicity of either stance.

The 'Vain sympathies' in which Wordsworth at first thinks of a river passing away do indeed constitute a pathetic fallacy. But it is not vanity in the poet to recognize then in the actual permanence of the river something which is in his own nature. The terms in which the river can be accurately praised are equally apt in describing peculiarly human emotions and the poetry which records them: 'The Form remains, the Function never dies.' Individual men and women, whether in real life or fictional narrative verse, may move relentlessly 'toward the silent tomb'. But however fleetingly each personal life runs 'Through love, through hope', those feelings survive in the common experience of a species. It is a species which could be defined by reference to the conscious 'love' and 'hope' which distinguish its drive to reproduce itself.

Moreover the insight of a single mind can, however briefly, grasp this permanence. Wordsworth's own brain eventually 'must vanish', but while consciousness lives there, it can recognize 'first and last, and midst, and without end'. The individual mind can learn to sometimes 'be blind' to the threat of its own 'grievous loss', and instead 'see what was, and is, and will abide'. Such vision glimpses two eternal and yet quite different realities. One is the visible world exemplified by a literal stream which 'shall for ever glide'. There are patterns in our mind which identify with its serenely stable rhythm, and recognize it as a 'partner' and a 'guide'. But succeeding generations of humanity have validated as equally permanent truths those emotions which have always resisted the limits ordained by nature and 'defied/The elements'. The natural laws which sentence all personal feeling to death are our enemies as well as our friends. Our 'love' and 'hope' compel us to treat as hostile an environment which will not discriminate the preciousness of personalities as we do in cherishing 'the brave, the mighty, and the wise'.

So two opposed intensities make us 'feel that we are greater than we know'. At times we are 'Surprised by joy'. We can be jerked out of our obsession with personal life and into the impersonal glories of the world which we must, whether we notice it or not, inhabit. But sometimes we cannot value ourselves and each other so lightly. Then our language seems bound to denounce an unsympathetic landscape and 'the silent tomb' which is all it will ultimately allow us. Wordsworth hoped his verse would 'serve the future hour', and the lasting value of his most potent language is that it still has the 'power/To live, and act' on both fronts. It is grounded on bold curiosity about an earthly paradox which is more intriguing than any dream of paradise:

> Not in Utopia, subterraneous Fields,
> Or some secreted Island, Heaven knows where,
> But in the very world which is the world
> Of all of us, the place in which, in the end,
> We find our happiness, or not at all. (*The Prelude*, x. 724–8)

In the steady vision of such stoicism 'Heaven' means very little. It is no more than a casual colloquialism by which all realms of fantasy can be dismissed.

But *After-Thought*, which was written some time after 1806, can no longer maintain quite such a consistent realism. In one unexpected phrase, it hints at a Christian heaven. The unqualified and plaintive monosyllables of 'love' and 'hope' are followed by the deviant grandiloquence of 'faith's transcendent dower'. The implications of such jargon are innately vague, but Wordsworth is audibly gesturing towards faith in an afterlife. The clumsy shift of style admits that the poem is attempting to change its subject. Wordsworth increasingly needed to alter the stance of his poetry so as to make bereavement seem tolerable. The evidence does not suggest that he *thought* his way into a new religious position. On the contrary, he apparently came to find some thoughts so painful that he was driven to escape them in dogma.

When his brother John was killed, Wordsworth admitted to a friend that life with unanswered questions no longer seemed bearable:

A thousand times have I asked myself, as your tender sympathy led me to do, 'why was he taken away?' and I have answered the question as you have done. In fact there is no other answer that can satisfy and lay the mind at rest. . . . Why have we sympathies that make the best of us so afraid of inflicting pain and sorrow, which yet we see dealt about so lavishly by the supreme governor? Why should our notions of right towards each other, and to all sentient beings within our influence, differ so widely from what appears to be his notion and rule, if everything were to end here? Would it not

be blasphemy to say that . . . we have *more of love* in our Nature
than he has? The thought is monstrous; and yet how to get rid of it,
except on the supposition of *another* and a *better world*, I do not
see.[3]

Wordsworth can see only this one exit from intolerable grief, so he
wills himself to believe in the resurrection of those whom he has
loved. But to embrace that 'supposition' is 'to get rid of' uninhibited
thought and to 'lay the mind at rest'. It is to close down the intellectual energy which had given the earlier verse its strength.

Wordsworth had once been able to respond differently to such
questions largely because they had been phrased differently. They
had once excluded any reference to an anthropomorphic God. Then
the verse had admitted that people do offer *'more of love'* to each
other than could ever be felt by the earth whose 'motion' so indis-
criminately 'rolls through all things' in *Tintern Abbey*, and whose
imperishable form is exemplified by the River Duddon in *After-
Thought*. This world of impersonal creativity reassimilates the dead
until they are lost to us amongst its 'rocks, and stones, and trees'. Yet
while we breathe, we are alive to the majestic impartiality of its
reciprocal relationships. Its natural laws give us life as surely as they
will one day require our death. Their even-handed justice ignores all
personal considerations. It preserves without affection and destroys
without malice. To credit it with kindness or accuse it of cruelty
would be an equally inappropriate sentimentality. *Tintern Abbey*'s
'life of things' is too vast and too various to resemble a person.

So the letter's substitution of 'He' for 'It' radically alters the terms
of debate and epitomizes the process which gradually transforms
Wordsworth's verse. The ambivalent feelings for an earth which is
endlessly re-creating its ever-changing self are abandoned. Wordsworth turns instead to faith in an anthropomorphic and yet unchanging creator. It would be unthinkable to approach such a humanoid
'supreme governor' as inhumanly callous. But if He resembles us in
wanting the people whom He cherishes to have eternal life, He must
be distinct from most of His creation. The poetry which honours
Him is bound to have its mind on higher things than the concrete
glories of 'that very world which', at least for the time being, 'is the
world of all of us'. Moreover it is not just the earth's grandeur which
is belittled by comparison with *'another* and a *better world'*. Our
own tenderness, so idiosyncratic in its passions, so specific in its

preferences, is also diminished by a God of infinite love. Wordsworth's 'supreme governor' either wants us all equally to live for ever
or, if He does choose some and not others, His selection is rational
and moralistic. As such, it is quite different from the instinctual and
uncritical affection which is felt by the protagonists of the narrative
poems, and voiced in the more intimate moments of the autobiographical verse.

Moreover the divine enigma, unlike the human paradox, does not
stimulate Wordsworth's creative approach to language. Instead of
forcing language to define new questions, Wordsworth eventually
finds more than enough old answers in the ready-made vocabulary of
a traditional religion. By 1842 he is capable of quoting within a single
sonnet not only 'I know / That my Redeemer liveth' but also 'O
Death / Where is thy Sting? – O Grave, where is thy Victory?' (*PW*,
III. 399, XXXI. 5–6, 13–14). A search for more precise or more original
definitions than 'faith's transcendent dower' might have suggested
an almost irreverent scepticism or even stumbled into heresies. So
Wordsworth's verse became more nebulous in vocabulary as it
became more conventional in thought. Behind such well-established
lines, Wordsworth may have felt less danger of feeling ambushed by
'grievous loss'. But his verse had less chance to sound convincingly
'Surprised by Joy'. Wordsworth's growing certainty about a God in
whose image we are made, and about '*another* and a *better world*'
which we can know He has prepared for us, dilutes and finally
destroys the earlier vision. Dogma has little respect for those elusive
and conflicting instincts by which we can only 'feel that we are
greater than we know'.

IV

Wordsworth's most thoughtful poems do reward a reader 'who
thinks about Nature'. But since nature's invitation is also a challenge,
Wordsworth requires us to think too about the complex equivocations in which our own human nature responds. The requirement has
seldom been met by published criticism. Even those who admire him
have often praised his work in terms which evade the verse's intelligent untidiness, and have thus imitated the older Wordsworth's own
damaging commentaries. Yet it is now a century and a half since John
Keats observed in Wordsworth's poetry a challengingly 'complex
mind'.[4]

Keats was then young enough to approach Wordsworth unin-
hibitedly as a contemporary poet. But he was already old enough to base
his assessment on wide reading in earlier literature. He judged poets
on the one quality 'which Shakespeare possessed so enormously':

> *Negative Capability*, that is when man is capable of being in
> uncertainties, Mysteries, doubts, without any irritable reaching
> after fact and reason – Coleridge, for instance, would let go by a
> fine isolated verisimilitude caught from the Penetralium of mys-
> tery, from being incapable of remaining Content with half
> knowledge.[5]

On this approach, Wordsworth surpasses not just Keats' other con-
temporaries like Coleridge but all earlier poets except Shakespeare
himself. Even Milton, according to Keats, suffers from a more limited intellectual curiosity, and his verse is too 'content' with the
'Dogmas and superstitions' of its times. It relies too heavily on
'resting places and seeming sure points of Reasoning'. So Milton 'did
not think into the human heart, as Wordsworth has done'.[6]

Wordsworth, for Keats, has the restlessly 'explorative' genius
which can reveal the mysteriousness of our paradoxical insights. In
the emotional nursery of childhood, we at first learn only how to get
drunk on the joyous beauty of the world:

> we become intoxicated with the light and the atmosphere, we see
> nothing but pleasant wonders, and think of delaying there for ever
> in delight: However among the effects this breathing is father of is
> that tremendous one of sharpening one's vision into the heart and
> nature of Man – of convincing one's nerves that the world is full of
> Misery and Heartbreak, Pain, Sickness and Oppression – whereby
> this Chamber of Maiden Thought becomes gradually darken'd and
> at the same time on all sides of it many doors are set open – but all
> dark – all leading to dark passages . . . We feel the "burden of the
> Mystery", to this Point was Wordsworth come, as far as I can
> conceive when he wrote 'Tintern Abbey' and it seems to me that
> his Genius is explorative of those dark Passages. Now if we live,
> and go on thinking, we too shall explore them – he is a Genius and
> superior to us, in so far as he can, more than we, make discoveries,
> and shed a light in them.[7]

Tintern Abbey seems to Keats a clear example of a poem where
Wordsworth challengingly admits to offering only half knowledge.

But Keats, congratulating himself on not having given away his medical books, argues that any knowledge is useful: 'Every Department of knowledge . . . is needful to thinking people . . . it takes away the heat and fever; and helps, by widening speculation, to ease the Burden of the Mystery.'[8] For Keats, knowledge is far from certainty and very close to 'widening speculation'. So he sees where *Tintern Abbey*'s self-confessed limitations point: 'When we come to human life and the affections it is impossible . . . to know how far Knowledge will console us for the death of a friend and the ill "that flesh is heir to",'[9] Keats wonders whether Wordsworth's audible 'anxiety for Humanity'[10] is disproportionate or all too apt. The remembered knowledge of childhood joy in 'the light and the atmosphere' which was once a literal part of our 'breathing' may or may not console.

Wordsworth explores not only our memory of the earth's 'pleasant wonders' but also our discovery 'that the world is full of Misery and Heartbreak'. In *Tintern Abbey* a brother, moving through a landscape which should 'lead' Dorothy 'from joy to joy', arrives instead at 'Solitude, or fear, or pain, or grief'. 'Surprised by Joy', a father is almost simultaneously ambushed into reliving the moment when he first knew that Catherine was dead. A poet, recording 'what was, and is, and will abide', may be concentrating on a river whose endlessly fluent movement contrasts so absolutely with 'the silent tomb' in which our own transient voices must end. But he could equally be turning away, and addressing himself to those irrepressible aspirations and affections by which human beings have always 'defied/The elements' and lived as if they, and those they loved, need not be subject to natural laws. Such incongruities remain for Wordsworth 'the burthen of the mystery'.

Keats does not hope for verse which could reach further than the enigmatic points uncovered by Wordsworth. No poem can hope to convince one wholly of generalized truths. Those can only be evaluated against our own experience: the test which Wordsworth, in his most demandingly tentative lines, is always, however indirectly, requiring us to apply. The Wordsworth who wrote the great poems would have welcomed Keats's approach:

In regard to his genius alone – we find what he says true as far as we have experienced and we can judge no further but by larger experience – for axioms in philosophy are not axioms until they are proved upon our pulses: We read fine things but never feel them to the full until we have gone the same steps as the Author.[11]

Wordsworth often does presuppose an experienced reader: one old enough to have learnt how contradictory our feelings can be, and how inadequate any one settled understanding of our world must seem. His poetry, in spite of its profoundly moving respect for the simplest human emotions and the most ordinary features of the landscape, is seldom itself simple. To approach it with renewed curiosity is to discover how intricately it manipulates small detail for large effect, and how original, or even downright odd, are some of its implications. Each time we return to one of Wordsworth's most intelligent poems, it can surprise us by how much it actually has to say. It can also, of course, disconcertingly expose how little we had previously noticed. But this should not dismay us. Instead, the verse's resilient power to surprise should be enjoyed as proof of its greatness. Keats himself, after looking again at some of Wordsworth's poems, made a bewildered, and yet delighted confession: 'I may have read these things before, but I never had even a thus dim perception of them.[12]

NOTES

CHAPTER 1: THE TYPES AND SYMBOLS OF ETERNITY

1 Quoted by Hazlitt, *Works*, ed. P. P. Howe, London 1930–4, vol. 17, p. 117.
2 *The Poems of Tennyson*, ed. Christopher Ricks, Longman 1969, p. 1114, l. 1.
3 'Essay supplementary to the Preface', *PW*, II. 423.
4 William Blake, *The Marriage of Heaven and Hell*, II, ll. 7–9.
5 Roger Sharrock, *Essays in Criticism*, III. 396–412.
6 John Jones, *The Egotistical Sublime*, Chatto & Windus 1964, p. 65.
7 Editions 1802–1832; see *PW*, II. 394.
8 *PW*, I. 62.
9 Jones, op. cit., p. 103.
10 Christopher Ricks, 'Wordsworth: "A pure organic pleasure from the lines"', *Essays in Criticism*, vol. 21, 1971.
11 Geoffrey Hartman, *Wordsworth's Poetry 1787–1814*, Yale University Press 1964, p. 17.
12 Mary Moorman, *William Wordsworth: A Biography*, vol. 1: *The Early Years, 1770–1803*, Oxford University Press 1957, p. 140n.
13 William Empson, *The Structure of Complex Words*, Chatto & Windus 1969, pp. 294–5.
14 Preface to editions 1815–1836, omitted 1845, *PW*, II. 440.
15 See Moorman, op. cit., p. 130.
16 *The Letters of William and Dorothy Wordsworth: The Early Years 1787–1805*, ed. Ernest de Selincourt, rev. Chester Shaver, Clarendon Press 1967, p. 169.

CHAPTER 2: THE WEAKNESS OF HUMANITY

1 Jonathan Wordsworth, *The Music of Humanity*, Nelson 1969, p. 152.
2 ibid., p. 118.
3 Mary Jacobus, *Tradition and Experiment in Wordsworth's Lyrical Ballads (1798)*, Clarendon Press 1976, p. 176.
4 Mary Moorman, *William Wordsworth: A Biography*, vol. 1: *The Early Years, 1770–1803*, Oxford University Press 1957, pp. 51–2.

5 David Ferry, *The Limits of Mortality*, Wesleyan University Press 1959, p. 63.
6 ibid., p. 64.
7 ibid., p. 65.
8 ibid., p. 106.
9 ibid., p. 173.
10 David Perkins, *Wordsworth and the Poetry of Sincerity*, Harvard University Press 1964, p. 116.
11 Wordsworth, op. cit., p. 153.
12 Paul D. Sheats, *The Making of Wordsworth's Poetry, 1785–1798*, Harvard University Press 1973, p. 178.
13 ibid.
14 Wordsworth, op. cit., p. 93.
15 In Jonathan Wordsworth's edition, ibid., pp. 172–83.
16 *Religious Musings*, ll. 126–30, in *The Complete Poetical Works of Samuel Taylor Coleridge*, ed. E. H. Coleridge, 2 vols, Oxford University Press 1912, I, pp. 113–14.

CHAPTER 3: THE STRENGTH OF LOVE

1 *The Letters of William and Dorothy Wordsworth: The Early Years 1787–1805*, ed. Ernest de Selincourt, rev. Chester Shaver, Clarendon Press 1967, p. 315.
2 ibid., pp. 314–15.
3 ibid., p. 322.
4 *Journals of Dorothy Wordsworth*, ed. Helen Darbishire, Oxford University Press 1958, p. 60.
5 David Perkins, *Wordsworth and the Poetry of Sincerity*, Harvard University Press 1964, pp. 16, 170.
6 Donald Wesling, *Wordsworth and the Adequacy of Landscape*, Routledge & Kegan Paul 1970, p. 88.
7 John F. Danby, *Wordsworth: The Prelude and Other Poems*, Edward Arnold 1963, p. 25.
8 ibid., p. 24.
9 Geoffrey H. Hartman, *Wordsworth's Poetry 1787–1814*, Yale University Press 1964, pp. 262–6.
10 Christopher Salvesen, *The Landscape of Memory*, Edward Arnold 1965, p. 150.
11 David Ferry, *The Limits of Mortality*, Wesleyan University Press 1959, p. 64.
12 John Beer, *Wordsworth in Time*, Faber & Faber 1979, p. 184.
13 See *PW* II. 'Notes', pp. 479–84.
14 Jonathan Wordsworth, *The Music of Humanity*, Nelson 1969, pp. 229–30.
15 ibid., p. 109.

CHAPTER 4: THE EYE AMONG THE BLIND

1 Mary Jacobus, *Tradition and Experiment in Wordsworth's Lyrical Ballads (1798)*, Clarendon Press 1976, p. 258. The quotations from the poem here differ from mine since Jacobus takes hers from the 1798 edition – rightly since her book takes a scholarly approach to a very specific moment in literary history. For my less specialized purposes, the 1845 text of *The Idiot Boy*, like that of many Wordsworth poems, seems to me adequate. My readers are still far more likely to possess the later versions of the verse, and I have tried to confine textual debates to the few areas where it seems crucial to all Wordsworth's readers – such as *The Ruined Cottage*.

2 ibid.

3 J. F. Danby, *The Simple Wordsworth*, Routledge & Kegan Paul 1960, pp. 35–7.

4 Paul D. Sheats, *The Making of Wordsworth's Poetry, 1785–1798*, Harvard University Press 1973, p. 193.

5 *To My Sister*, like *The Idiot Boy*, was composed in spring 1798. See Mark Reed's *Wordsworth: The Chronology of the Early Years*, Harvard University Press 1967, pp. 32, 221.

6 Danby, op. cit., pp. 35–57.

7 S. T. Coleridge, *Biographia Literaria*, ed. J. Shawcross, Oxford University Press 1907, vol. II, pp. 5–6.

8 Note dictated to Isabella Fenwick, *PW*, II. 478.

9 *The Letters of William and Dorothy Wordsworth: The Early Years 1787–1805*, ed. Ernest de Selincourt, rev. Chester Shaver, Clarendon Press 1967, p. 375.

10 Ramond's translation of Coxe's *Travels* was acknowledged as a source in Wordsworth's note to *Descriptive Sketches* (see *PW*, II. 325).

11 To Lady Beaumont, 21 May 1807.

CHAPTER 5: THE EYE OF NATURE

1 *Specimens of the Table Talk of the late Samuel Taylor Coleridge*, 2 vols, 1835, I, pp. 61–2.

2 David Perkins, *Wordsworth and the Poetry of Sincerity*, Harvard University Press 1964, p. 116.

3 Geoffrey Hartman, *Wordsworth's Poetry 1787–1814*, Yale University Press 1964, p. 147.

4 See John Colmer's 'Coleridge and politics', in *S. T. Coleridge*, ed. R. L. Brett, London 1971, p. 260.

5 F. W. Bateson. *Wordsworth, A Reinterpretation*, Longman 1954, p. 23.

6 ibid., pp. 22, 24.

7 John Jones, *The Egotistical Sublime*, Chatto & Windus 1964, pp. 63, 66.

8 John Beer, *Wordsworth and the Human Heart*, Macmillan 1978, pp. 70–1.

9 *Table Talk of Coleridge*, op. cit.
10 Christopher Salvesen, *The Landscape of Memory*, Edward Arnold 1965, p. 155.
11 Cleanth Brooks, 'Wordsworth and human suffering: notes on two early poems', in *From Sensibility to Romanticism, Essays Presented to Frederick A. Pottle*, ed. Frederick W. Hilles and Harold Bloom, Oxford University Press 1965, p. 377.
12 Jonathan Wordsworth, *The Music of Humanity*, Nelson 1969, p. 146.
13 Jones, op. cit., pp. 69–70.
14 Helen Darbishire, *The Poet Wordsworth*, Oxford University Press 1950, p. 132.

CHAPTER 6: THE MIND'S EYE

1 See Mark L. Reed, *Wordsworth: The Chronology of the Early Years*, Harvard University Press 1967, pp. 29–30, 342.
2 David Pirie, 'A letter to Asra', in *Bicentenary Wordsworth Studies*, ed. Jonathan Wordsworth, Cornell University Press 1970, pp. 294–339.
3 Dorothy's Journal for 13 September and 3 October 1800.
4 Geoffrey H. Hartman, *Wordsworth's Poetry 1787–1814*, Yale University Press 1964, p. 272.
5 F. W. Bateson, *Wordsworth, A Reinterpretation*, Longman 1954, p. 161.
6 William Heath, *Wordsworth and Coleridge*, Clarendon Press 1970, pp. 128–9.
7 Frederick Garber, *Wordsworth and the Poetry of Encounter*, University of Illinois Press 1971, pp. 181–2.
8 Heath, op. cit., pp. 134–5.
9 A. C. Bradley, *Oxford Lectures on Poetry*, Macmillan 1909.
10 Hartman, op. cit., p. 242, note 33.
11 John Jones, *The Egotistical Sublime*, Chatto & Windus 1964, p. 128.

CHAPTER 7: THE REACH OF WORDS

1 *The Letters of William and Dorothy Wordsworth: The Early Years 1787–1805*, ed. Ernest de Selincourt, rev. Chester Shaver, Clarendon Press 1967, p. 664.
2 ibid., p. 586.
3 *Collected Letters of Samuel Taylor Coleridge* ed. E. L. Griggs, Clarendon Press 1956, vol. II, pp. 1033–4.
4 ibid., p. 349.
5 ibid., p. 1013.
6 I have argued elsewhere that Coleridge himself may not expect us to share the Mariner's view. See *Coleridge's Verse: A Selection*, eds William Empson and David Pirie, Faber & Faber 1972, pp. 222–4, 227–8, 240–2.

7 William Empson, *The Structure of Complex Words*, Chatto & Windus 1951, p. 290.

8 Christopher Ricks, 'Wordsworth: "A pure organic pleasure from the lines"', *Essays in Criticism*, vol. 21, 1971.

9 Jonathan Bishop, 'Wordsworth and the "Spots of Time"', *Journal of English Literary History*, XXVI, 1959.

10 *Collected Letters of Coleridge*, op. cit., p. 817. For an account of the textual history of *Dejection: An Ode*, see my chapter in *Bicentenary Wordsworth Studies*, ed. Jonathan Wordsworth, Cornell University Press 1970, pp. 294–339.

CHAPTER 8: THE BURTHEN OF THE MYSTERY

1 See *PW*, II. 517.

2 A. P. Rossiter, *Angel with Horns*, Longman 1961, pp. 302–3.

3 *The Letters of William and Dorothy Wordsworth: The Early Years 1787–1805*, ed. Ernest de Selincourt, rev. Chester Shaver, Clarendon Press 1967, p. 556.

4 *The Letters of John Keats*, ed. Hyder E. Rollins, Cambridge University Press 1958, vol. I, p. 186.

5 ibid., pp. 193–4.

6 ibid., p. 282.

7 ibid., p. 281.

8 ibid., p. 277.

9 ibid., pp. 277–8.

10 ibid., p. 278.

11 ibid., p. 279.

12 ibid., p. 282.

INDEX OF
WORDSWORTH'S POEMS